Sutton Hoo: Fifty Years After

Edited by Robert Farrell
and Carol Neuman de Vegvar

American Early Medieval
Studies 2
1992

Published by American Early Medieval Studies
Miami University
Department of Art
124 Art Building
Oxford, Ohio 45056

First Published 1992

Printed by American Printing, Hamilton, Ohio

ISBN 1-879836-02-7

Price $27.00 post free throughout the world. Orders, which must be accompanied by payment, may be sent to the publisher at the above address. Payment should be made in U.S. dollars only. Checks should be made payable to American Early Medieval Studies.

Contents

Introduction

The papers in this volume were given at the twenty-fourth conference on Medieval Studies held at Western Michigan University, from 4 to 7 May, 1989. The contributors were asked to write *prospectives*, that is, presentations of their areas of interest and their relation to Sutton Hoo that were not simply reviews of past work. Quite clearly, some of the papers by their very nature had to review the field, most particularly those of David Wilson, Allen Frantzen and Robert Farrell. The purpose of this very brief introduction is to provide prospective readers of the volume with an outline of its contents; we do not believe that an attempt at synthesis is appropriate to a preface, but rather that a book such as this can best be synthesized by those who have found it of sufficient worth and value to read through to the end. We make no case for this collection as either a complete or a fully balanced account of all aspects of Sutton Hoo; difficulties with funding the conference, accident and illness made this impossible.

Sir David Wilson's paper reviews the growth of the Sutton Hoo industry; he praises those few who were bold enough to address the larger questions raised by Mound One and its contents before the massive and long-awaited publication of the site by Dr. Bruce-Mitford, and he addresses the problem of the use and not-infrequent misuse of the evidence of Mound One by scholars in disciplines other than archaeology. Some readers will find his remarks provocative, others perhaps will view them as acerbic, but no dispassionate reader will fail to agree that the initially excavated Sutton Hoo ship burial has often been used with less than a full appreciation of all the inferences it raises. For those unaware of the persons, personalities, and sequence of events leading up to both the publication of Mound One, and the initial responses to the British Museum publication, Wilson provides a useful review and commentary.

Two papers deal specifically with the relationship between the study of Anglo-Saxon literature and archaeology in the broadest sense, both with particular reference to Sutton Hoo. Robert Farrell studies the difficulties and misunderstandings which arose in the course of the preparation of the British Museum publication of Mound One. Farrell attempts to show that Dr. Bruce-Mitford derived a good deal of his information about literature, and most particularly *Beowulf*, from a single philologist, Charles Wrenn. In his turn, Wrenn (and a number of students of Anglo-Saxon literature after him) made overenthusiastic use of the Mound One materials. Farrell holds that the very limited information base of one poem and one archaeological find, no matter how important both may be, is not sufficient to make generalizations about a culture. Archaeologists, literary critics and philologists must communicate more clearly, and have a better comprehension of one another's territory. Basic literacy in the other field is essential for progress in our understanding of culture.

Allen Frantzen approaches the question of Anglo-Saxon literature and archaeology from a theoretical perspective. He briefly reviews the way in which Anglo-Saxon literature is currently studied, and expresses concern that long-held assumptions about methodology are inadequate to handle the information base. He proposes what some would describe as a semiotic approach, as the best way to work with a common mode of understanding and approach to the subject for both archaeologists and literary critics/philologists.

Richard Bailey's brief contribution on "Sutton Hoo and Seventh-Century Art," is useful for a number of reasons. First of all, he proposes a new and convincing interpretation of the Herebericht slab, an important decorated stone from Monkwearmouth. On the evidence of epigraphy and erasure, it appears that the stone was adopted and reused as a memorial stone, but it is clearly of eighth-century date. Bailey proposes that the fragmentary minimal decoration is best interpreted as a pair of confronted eagle's heads. This mode of ornament is therefore a late reflection of the Sutton Hoo style, with its closest parallels in the border panels of the shoulder clasp, or the maplewood bottle mounts. Citing other examples of this backward-looking taste, Bailey further holds that it "co-existed alongside an enthusiasm for the transplanted ornamental motifs of the Mediterranean world..." The late continuance of the taste makes more comprehensible the closeness of important motifs in the Book of Durrow, which are close to elements of decoration from Sutton Hoo. Paleographical evidence makes it unlikely that Durrow can be very close in time to Sutton Hoo, but as there are now other examples of the late survival of elements of the Sutton Hoo style, there is no longer a necessary tension over dates. Bailey provides a number of later parallels from the north of England for Sutton Hoo metalwork. A final point of linkage in metalwork is a 3cm. long fragment from Bamburgh, a piece of animal ornament which shows stylistic affinities with both Sutton Hoo and Durrow.

Kelley Wickham-Crowley considers the bird ornaments from the Sutton Hoo and Taplow instruments in the light of the depiction and context of birds in Germanic art, and the linkage of birds to poetry, song, and the cult of Odin as it concerns death, metamorphosis and intellect. Three examples of Germanic art may represent the linkage of Odin and birds: a stone from Lärbro St. Hammers III, Sweden that probably shows Odin in the form of a bird; two fifth-century gilded fibulas from Anderlingen, Lower Saxony (Niedersächsisches Landesmuseum), which show human faces in birds' bodies; and the Sutton Hoo shield bird, which has a winged human head on its tail. Wickham-Crowley also examines the etymology of *scop* and *wothbora*, both harpists, as respectively dancer poet and prophetic shaman, and concludes that the birds on the Sutton Hoo instrument are emblems of "a close relationship between Odin, a harp player and the king honored at Sutton Hoo."

Carol Neuman de Vegvar examines the Sutton Hoo drinking horns in the broader context of Germanic archaeology and literature. The Sutton Hoo horns are both too large and too richly ornamented to stand simply as part of a larger banqueting assemblage, as they have been considered heretofore. The role of drinking and the shared vessel in bonding warlord and follower is widespread and consistent in both the Germanic and the Celtic world. The appearance of horns and a possible cauldron on the triumphal arch at Carpetras (Vaucluse) suggests that horns were recognized by the Romans as Germanic symbols of authority, analogous to the ritual objects from the Temple of Jerusalem on the Arch of Titus. The horns in Mound One at Sutton Hoo are seen as regalia, with the whetstone and the "standard."

The goal of Leslie Webster's paper is stated clearly in her opening sentence, "to review the range of evidence ... presented by a ... number of Continental, Scandinavian and Anglo-Saxon burials, and thereby see how they might affect the way in which we judge Sutton Hoo as a statement of power." Mrs. Webster traces out the elements of *Germanitas* and *Romanitas* in the graves or accounts of burials of such rulers as Alaric I, Childeric, Clovis and Theodoric. She notes the interesting temporal juxtaposition of the development of ostentatious and well-endowed barrow burials (usually at boundaries and/or headlands) in Scandinavia and England, and the transition to burial within churches (presumably without grave-goods) of newly converted Kentish rulers. Both developments seem to take place *circa* 600, significantly, the date suggested for the Sutton Hoo assemblage on the basis of Dr. Stahl's reconsideration of the coin evidence. Mrs. Webster also joins the growing group of scholars who contend that some of the most significant Sutton Hoo grave-goods must have come to East Anglia via Kent.

Dr. Michael Ryan provides an account of two of the most important object-classes, the scepter and the hanging bowls, of the Mound One burial in his treatment of what might be called "the Celtic connection." His paper is of particular interest because it presents a range of newly-discovered and hitherto unpublished evidence, a good deal of it from underwater contexts in the lakes of central Ireland. The study of "Celtic," or Irish, material from the early Middle Ages is sometimes tinged with nationalism, as the accounts of the hanging bowls in Anglo-Saxon contexts in *Ireland and Insular Art* (ed. M. Ryan 1988) attest. Ryan's paper is useful because he makes his case on all known examples of whetstones and of all metalwork parallels for significant diagnostic details of the Sutton Hoo hanging bowls. His stance is clear. Simply put, he holds that the Sutton Hoo whetstone is not Celtic, and more particularly not Irish, but the hanging bowls are clearly Irish. Both Ryan's evidence, and his interpretation of it, should give rise to extensive debate.

David Whitehouse's "The Mediterranean Perspective," an account of seventh-century England's contact with the culture of ancient and early medieval Rome presents a series of paradoxes. Romanized Britain had become singularly un-Roman, despite having been part of the Empire for four hundred years. After the fifth century, Canterbury, London, Lincoln and York were still occupied, but no longer urban. Contact after this time is most clearly seen in the west, and primarily the southwest. Five types of objects do show up in the east, most spectacularly at Sutton Hoo itself: coins, "Coptic" and other metal vessels, garnets, amethysts, and cowrie shells. All of this evidence comes to no more than a "trickle of more or less prestigious objects." By what route did these objects get to England? With imported glass and its distribution as a starting point, Kent appears to be the primary point of entry with two routes from Europe as points of origin. The first is Ravenna-Alps-Rhine-Northern France; the second, Marseille to the Rhone valley. Whitehouse ends with a consideration of the Sutton Hoo silver assemblage, which he views as most probably "gifts from a Frankish Court -- reinforcements, perhaps, of the kind of alliance created when Aethelbert, King of Kent (*circa* 560-616) married Bertha, a Frankish princess."

Dr. Alan Stahl's study of the Sutton Hoo coins, written with W.M. Oddy of the British Museum, attacks the long-standing date of the coins to *circa* 625, a date which accords nicely with the burial of Rædwald. The technical nature of the evidence presented in this paper, and the nature of the coinage attributed to St. Eligius are hard for nonspecialists to evaluate, but if Stahl and Oddy's interpretation of the entire question of the fineness of the gold in the sixth and seventh centuries is correct (as their studies seem amply to support), the date of the Sutton Hoo Mound One burial is in very close parallel to the horizon Mrs. Webster proposes for what one might perhaps define as the international barrow burial style, with a congruent target-date of *circa* 600. It remains to be seen how strongly other scholars will argue for the connection with Rædwald.

Nancy Wicker considers the Scandinavian connection at Sutton Hoo in light of an investigation of communication between Scandinavia and Anglian England in the preceding (sixth) century. Her focus is on the Scandinavian-type gold bracteates and their silver derivatives found in England, as a demonstration of cultural interaction. Particular parallels in the structure, usage and iconography of bracteates are identified between Anglia and Sweden, especially Gotland, suggesting contact between these areas, possibly in the form of travelling craftsmen. The evidence of Scandinavian elements in the Mound One material from Sutton Hoo is seen as a continuation of long-established contacts.

Martin Carver's paper is an attempt to view *all* of the Sutton Hoo grave systems (as they were known in May 1989) in the broadest geographic and cultural contexts. In his view, the Sutton Hoo mounds, and the lesser but important burials which surround them, provide information about the nature of a culture, one which has chosen to make a dramatic, pointed and extremely costly statement, expressing cultural choice, and intentions of dominance of an area. In this sense, Carver holds that the Sutton Hoo site can be viewed rather like a poem.

ACKNOWLEDGEMENTS

Support for the conference which was the basis of this book came from many sources. Professor Otto Gründler, Director of the Medieval and Renaissance Studies Center at Western Michigan University waived all fees and living expenses for non-North American speakers. He also provided generous support for Sir David Wilson's visit as speaker at a plenary session. Professor Thomas Ohlgren, Director of the Medieval Studies Program at Purdue University provided co-sponsorship for speakers and financial support for the series. Cornell University bore the brunt of covering international travel costs and direct financial support; sources within Cornell were the University Lecture Committee, the Vice President for Research, the College of Arts and Sciences, the Department of English, the Department of the History of Art, and the fields of Archaeology and Medieval Studies.

Robert Farrell
Ithaca, New York, May 1992

Sutton Hoo - Pros and Cons

DAVID WILSON

There are certain items of early medieval origin which are generally used or, more often, misused by scholars of all disciplines, I would cite three such – the Utrecht Psalter, the Bayeux Tapestry and the 1939 Sutton Hoo ship-burial. The latter forms the main subject of this paper, but a brief mention of the other two illustrates my theme as they are and have been used as universal panaceas for historical influenzas. A scholar wishing to illustrate an early medieval town will, as likely as not, turn to an illustration in the Utrecht Psalter, or more probably, because photographs are more easily obtainable from the British Library, will turn to copies of the Utrecht Psalter – Harley 603, for example. A simple example of this occurs in a scene of ploughing from Harley 603 which is illustrated in Hodgkin's *History of the Anglo-Saxons*, over the simple caption "Agriculture."[1] How many people, however, using such pictures in such a general fashion pause to think that the Utrecht Psalter was produced by a number of hands either in Reims of the nearby monastery of Hautvillers, probably between 816 and 823? The scenes portrayed there have nothing to do with England. The Utrecht Psalter was written in France and was copied, in so far as its drawings go, from a Late Antique prototype which may well have been written down as far away as Byzantium. C. R. Dodwell describes it as, "the most significant work of art of the whole Carolingian period."[2] It was in England, at Christ Church, Canterbury, at some time in the tenth century and an exact copy was made of it, one of a number. Stylistically the copies are much less disciplined, breathless, and more lively and were to influence much of the art of English drawing for many years to come. Use either the Utrecht Psalter or its copies at your peril to illustrate daily life in Anglo-Saxon England.

A similarly abused monument is the Bayeux Tapestry. Since it has been carefully researched by historians it is used more critically than the Utrecht Psalter, but all are familiar with its misuse. The tapestry is, however, used to illustrate everything – dress, ships, pots, eating habits, churches, castles and particularly armor. I have discussed some of the uses and misuses of the Tapestry in the latest facsimile, particularly in relation to the formula which serves to illustrate an earthwork, castle, motte or town, and attempted to show the advantages and disadvantages of the process.[3] We are all guilty of glib parallels on these lines, but I am not clear that we are all aware of the dangers which we store up for ourselves and others in our use of such pictures.

Sutton Hoo is the third example of a fascinating physical reminder of the early Middle Ages which is daily used by scholars of all disciplines to illustrate these themes. No one can deny the usefulness and intrinsic worth of Sutton Hoo, nor can one deny the extent to which it has added to our knowledge and understanding of the Anglo-Saxon period. It is one of the most brilliant, most positive archaeological finds ever made in Europe and it was perhaps not too much of an exaggeration to call it, as the press did at the time, the "English Tutankhamen." By its very prestige, however, it is a dangerous animal, and one which must be handled with great care. For that reason I shall examine some elements of the impact of Sutton Hoo on Anglo-Saxon studies.

I have lived with Sutton Hoo for much of my working life, and I have written about it – the first time some thirty years ago – and although I am no real specialist in this particular subject, I, like many other people, have had to make assertive or apologetic statements concerning this great find from time to time. As a university teacher I remember trying to reconcile Sutton Hoo with the normality of Anglo-Saxon pagan or Christian finds and being overwhelmed by its very grandeur. I grew up in Anglo-Saxon studies before the publication of the great third edition of R. W. Chambers' *Beowulf* with its influential supplemental essay on "Sutton Hoo and *Beowulf*" by Professor Wrenn.[4] I thus avoided some of the more baleful exaggerations which arose as a result of the

[1]R. H. Hodgkin, *A History of the Anglo-Saxons*, (Oxford 1952), 3rd ed., fig. 61.

[2]C. R. Dodwell, *Painting in Europe 800-1200* (Harmondsworth 1971), 30.

[3]D. M. Wilson, *The Bayeux Tapestry* (London 1985), 213-27.

[4]R. W. Chambers, *Beowulf: An Introduction to the Study of the Poem with a Discussion of the Stories of Offa and Finn*, 3rd ed. with a supplement by C. L. Wrenn (Cambridge 1959), 508-23.

misunderstandings of Old English specialists concerning Sutton Hoo. Despite much earlier scholarship Wrenn's essay was perhaps the most influential element in bringing Sutton Hoo to the general attention of non-archaeologically literate scholars. The seeds sewn by H. M. Chadwick in his 1940 article on the identity of the Sutton Hoo king; by Rupert Bruce-Mitford's British Museum guide of 1947; by the same author's appendices to the third edition of Hodgkin's *History of the Anglo-Saxons*, and to the second edition of Ritchie Girvan's *Beowulf and the Seventh Century*; and by Rosemary Cramp in her article "*Beowulf* and Archaeology,"[5] all seem to me to have crystallized out in Wrenn's essay and are now the foundation of almost any service teaching of the background to Old English literature. I want to examine the phenomenon of Sutton Hoo and its relation to neighboring disciplines in this paper.

We celebrate this year fifty years of Sutton Hoo studies. There can hardly have been a period since the seventeenth century when there have been so many advances in the Anglo-Saxon field. Although Sutton Hoo was a major influence in this advance, as I shall hope to show, it was not the only one. And just as the period between the publication of William Somner's *Dictionary* in 1659 and the death of Humfrey Wanley in 1762, was not without its harbingers, so 1939 was not without its background of hard labor by other scholars. Henry Spelman, Matthew Parker, William Dugdale, and William Somner working on the newly available records of the monasteries and the public records in the Tower of London and at Westminster, created the atmosphere in which Humfrey Wanley, George Hickes, Henry Wharton, Thomas Hearne, Anthony Wood and others were to revolutionize Anglo-Saxon studies. In the same manner Chambers, Allen Mawer, Sir Frank Stenton, Sir Thomas Kendrick and Edward Thurlow Leeds were building on the work of the great editors and excavators of the last century and on the polymathic learning of such high standing figures as Hector Munro Chadwick, Neil Ripley Kerr, Felix Liebermann and the editors of the *Monumenta Germaniae Historiae*, to produce works of synthesis which are still used today. Particularly interesting were the emergence of the Cambridge school led by Hector Munro Chadwick, with the great editions of wills, writs, laws and letters associated with such names as Dorothy Whitelock, Florence Harmer, Frederick Attenborough, Agnes Robertson and so on, and the growth of place-name studies triggered by Mawer and Chambers at University College London. The world of Anglo-Saxon scholarship was small, integrated and on the whole friendly; German, Scandinavian, American scholars all knew each other and corresponded freely.

The year 1939 was a caesura. As Sutton Hoo was making front page news in England, so was Adolf Hitler. Charles Phillips arrived at Sutton Hoo on July 3; war was declared on September 3. In 1940 three groups of articles were quickly published in *Antiquity*, *The Antiquaries Journal* and *The British Museum Quarterly* and the treasure was then hidden until 1945. For five years academic audiences held their breath, but it gradually became known both in England and on the Continent. The first photographs and articles had reached Denmark and Norway before the German invasion. Haakon Shetelig published an article on Sutton Hoo in *Viking* in 1940, whilst in France Raymond Lantier published an article on the burial in *Révue Archéologique*. Greta Arwidsson in her Uppsala doctoral thesis *Vendelstile, Email und Glas*, published in 1942, referred to it twice.

When Rupert Bruce-Mitford was put in charge of Sutton Hoo after the war he produced, with commendable efficiency, the *Sutton Hoo Guide*, published in 1947. It was technically a high quality production – an impressive feat, as this was one of the periods of greatest austerity in England. At the time I became a student in Cambridge in 1950 this was practically the only source for the subject, although it was referred to in passing in *Beowulf* classes and in more detail by Peter Hunter-Blair, and Tom Lethbridge. Most people of my generation only stumbled on Sutton Hoo in their post-graduate years. In 1948 in Sweden, Sune Lindqvist, professor of archaeology at Uppsala, wrote a crucial paper "Sutton Hoo och *Beowulf*," which, translated by Rupert Bruce-Mitford in the same year,[6] raised the specter of the Swedish influence at Sutton Hoo which still haunts us forty years later. He was almost

[5]H. M. Chadwick, "Who Was He?" *Antiquity* 14.53 (1940), 76-87; R. L. S. Bruce-Mitford, *Sutton Hoo Guide* (London 1947); Hodgkin, *History* (1939); R. Girvan, *Beowulf and the Seventh Century: Language and Content*, 2nd ed. (London 1971); R. Cramp, "*Beowulf* and Archaeology," *MA* 1 (1957), 57-77.

[6]S. Lindqvist, "Sutton Hoo och *Beowulf*," *Fornvännen* 43 (1948), 94-110; R. L. S. Bruce-Mitford, "Sutton Hoo and *Beowulf*," *Antiquity* 12, (1948), 131-40.

beaten to the post by Birger Nerman whose paper in the same issue of *Fornvännen*[7] asked the question whether the Sutton Hoo burial was that of a Swedish king or chieftain.

By 1954 it was possible for Francis Magoun to write a bibliography of Sutton Hoo in *Speculum*, becoming the first American academic to write an article on the subject. About this time I became professionally involved with Sutton Hoo as an Assistant Keeper in the British Museum, where I understudied Bruce-Mitford and worked on practically everything other than Sutton Hoo, although I had quite a lot to do with its day-to-day management. Because Bruce-Mitford had the job of publishing Sutton Hoo, those of us working professionally in Anglo-Saxon archaeology in those days had to keep well away from the subject. When we founded the Society of Medieval Archaeology in 1957 we could move into much wider areas and after Rosemary Cramp published "*Beowulf* and Archaeology," a summary of her graduate thesis, in the first volume of *Medieval Archaeology*, no articles on Sutton Hoo appeared in that journal until 1964, when an historian, J. L. N. O'Loughlin, published a paper called "Sutton Hoo – the Evidence of the Documents."[8] Archaeologists published little about Sutton Hoo as they waited for the publication of Bruce-Mitford's report, which after all only began to appear in 1975.[9] The study of Anglo-Saxon archaeology consequently moved away from grave-goods, which had been its staple diet since the mid-nineteenth century, to a more general examination, through excavation and source criticism, of the social and economic sides of the subject more in tune with the work of our contemporaries in the prehistoric and Roman disciplines. It was left to colleagues in other disciplines – Old English language, literature and history – to start the Sutton Hoo discussion. In fact the teaching of the archaeological background to Old English literature was provided in London University from about 1948 onwards, first by Hugh Smith and later by John Dodgson and Vera Evison, all of whom, save the latter who did a post-graduate diploma in archaeology, were trained as English specialists and all of whom taught in English departments. Durham followed suit in 1956, or thereabouts, when an English don, Rosemary Cramp, was appointed to a similar position. Until I was appointed to a readership in London in 1964, there was no full-time teacher of the archaeology of the Anglo-Saxon period in the United Kingdom, although Brian Hope-Taylor taught it alongside the pre-Roman Iron Age in Cambridge. I was appointed to the University College London English department and it is clear that the only reason this post was created was that Hugh Smith wanted somebody who was qualified to teach the archaeological – that is to say Sutton Hoo – background to *Beowulf*.

I hope it is not too much to say that by a very convoluted route, Sutton Hoo was responsible for the establishment of Anglo-Saxon and, later, medieval archaeology generally, as a major discipline in the arts faculties of British universities. Perhaps this is the greatest "pro" for Sutton Hoo.

The second "pro" is undoubtedly the publication by Rupert Bruce-Mitford and his assistants of the three volume report, *The Sutton Hoo Ship Burial*, between 1975 and 1983. There was originally a plan to produce a final volume of summary, but it was felt that this would have been too one-sided and complicated in view of the vast literature on the subject, and the plan after long debate was aborted. Rupert Bruce-Mitford has had his say, not only in the final publication, but also in his book *Aspects of Anglo-Saxon Archaeology*.[10] The present excavations were initiated in order to answer some of the questions raised by this publication. So much has emerged from Martin Carver's excavations that this decision has been vindicated over and over again. Further, Leslie Webster's re-examination of the Taplow find will undoubtedly throw even more light on the material culture of this stratum of Anglo-Saxon society.

The third "pro" is the gradual acceptance of archaeological evidence by our colleagues in the historical, literary and philological disciplines. I am sure that this would have come much more grudgingly if teachers of Anglo-Saxon literature and history had not had Sutton Hoo thrust upon them. As Sutton Hoo was used as a brilliant example of specific details of sixth/seventh-century life in England, historians came to realize that, inaccurate as many of our ways were, their understanding of texts and primary sources was not always as clear as they had thought. The

---

[7]B. Nerman, "Sutton Hoo, en svensk kung-eller hövdinggrav," *Fornvännen* 43 (1948), 65-93.

[8]*MA* 8 (1964), 1-19.

[9]R. L. S. Bruce-Mitford, *The Sutton-Hoo Ship Burial*, vol. I (London 1975).

[10]London 1974.

philologists also began to realize that their own accuracy was not as real as they had conceived; Raymond Page and Christine Fell, for example, began to examine philological problems against the backgrounds of other disciplines and thus questioned their own.

Whilst the archaeologist kept away from Sutton Hoo problems out of respect for the work being pursued by Bruce-Mitford, the vacuum began to be filled by scholars of other disciplines. I would particularly mention here the work of Robert Kaske on the spoons; of Robert Farrell on the Swedish connections; of J. M. Wallace-Hadrill on the royalty problem; of Sir Frank Stenton on the dynasty of the Wuffingas of East Anglia; of Philip Grierson and Stuart Rigold on numismatic interpretation of the coins found in the grave, and, of course, of innumerable scholars who wrote on *Beowulf*, the kingdom of East Anglia, Anglo-Saxon heroic poetry and so on. An enormous literature grew up, in which more or less imperfectly-understood archaeological theses were quoted, not always altogether critically, by scholars in other disciplines. And it is here that the "cons" begin.

To see what I mean let me examine two statements made by a highly respected Anglo-Saxon historian, James Campbell. In doing so I am merely choosing one example of many to illustrate the use of James Campbell's statement from the book *The Anglo-Saxons*, which he edited in 1982: "If anyone wants to know the true importance of Sutton Hoo, the answer is: read Bede's *Ecclesiastical History* II,12, II,15, and II,18 without having considered the treasure, then read those chapters again having done so."[11]

Apart from the difficulty of an ability to be so detached, particularly as this statement comes at the end of a long discussion of the burial, the statement itself is too ingenious. The Bede chapters deal with Edwin's exile at Rædwald's court and the steps leading up to his conversion; with Eorpwald's conversion and Sigeberht's succession to the throne of East Anglia; and with Fursa's mission to East Anglia. First, I am tempted to quote Campbell's teacher against him. In his notes on Bede's *Ecclesiastical History*, published posthumously, Wallace-Hadrill wrote, "The fact remains that Sutton Hoo was unknown to Bede and had it been known, would have struck him as repellent and irrelevant."[12] Sutton Hoo hardly illuminates Bede at all. Bede – at least the chapters quoted – does not necessarily illuminate Sutton Hoo, unless we believe that it was Rædwald who was buried there, and even then its illumination amounts to very little.

What Sutton Hoo really illuminates is the general culture of the seventh century. It illustrates the technical brilliance and world-class skill of a particular jeweler; it illustrates the wide-ranging contacts of East Anglia with the whole of Christendom and beyond; with Egypt, Byzantium, the Rhineland, France, even with Scandinavia. It represents wealth at a standard not surviving anywhere else in England, nor even in contemporary France or Germany. This is not to say that more wealth did not exist, but here are real riches and exotic materials. Technically, it tells of shipping, of music, of weaponry, and of at least some of the economic and social implications of the East Anglian kingdom. The burial tells possibly of a pagan/Christian syncretism. The art illuminates and explains some of the great problems in the history of Anglo-Saxon style. It redresses many judgements about Anglo-Saxon jewelry made by Leeds, Kendrick and their contemporaries in the 1930s. It helps us to understand an important non-English element in English art of this and later periods, and it enables us to probe towards an idea of conspicuous consumption in Anglo-Saxon society. It perhaps reveals something of royalty and of paganism, and enables us with caution to explain two or three words of *Beowulf.*

But it must not be abused as a source. Let me take a passage written by Campbell in 1971, concerning a chalice from Chelles; he says it was of "gold, a foot high, inlaid, probably with garnets, in a cloisonné style similar to that of some of the Sutton Hoo jewellery; it must have been such a chalice as Aldhelm praises in his poem on Bugge's monastery."[13] This is the sort of statement we all make at moments of heightened excitement. But let us examine it. The Chelles chalice, as Campbell points out, is lost but is depicted in a late seventeenth-century engraving. It was technically nothing like the Sutton Hoo jewelry, it was decorated with garnets and blue, white and green stones and may even have been made by the same hand – Eligius's – which made the St. Denis Cross, of which a

---

[11]J. Campbell, *et al.* (eds.) *The Anglo-Saxons* (London 1982), 33.

[12]J. M. Wallace-Hadrill, *Bede's Ecclesiastical History of the English People, A Historical Commentary* (Oxford 1988), 77.

[13]Reprinted in J. Campbell, *Essays in Anglo-Saxon History* (London and Ronceverte 1986), 62.

fragment apparently survives.[14] I do not really feel that there is any evidence for Eligius making this chalice, but the style of Eligius's workshop is certainly there. Making two assumptions – one, that the engraving is a reasonably correct representation of the chalice, and two, that the workmanship is related to that of the Eligius school – we may say that it is work of an entirely different quality, probably encompassing stones set *en cabochon* (a technique not found at Sutton Hoo) as well as garnets cut in a much simpler form than those at Sutton Hoo. Aldhelm, a late seventh-century abbot of Malmesbury, is praising a chalice that had existed at Winchcombe in Gloucestershire. We do not know what the metalwork of Gloucestershire looked like at the period. Similarly, we do not know what was the normal form of an English chalice of this period, although we certainly know what a chalice looked like in the ninth century[15] and possibly earlier. But if you wish to point to a contemporary European chalice, certainly Chelles is one, but there are others, including such Irish cups as the so-called Ardagh and Derrynaflan "chalices,"[16] which are as near in date, and nearer in geography and possibly in taste, to the western English church of this time. Use Chelles as a comparison by all means, but do not drag Sutton Hoo into the saga.

I have weighed rather heavily on Campbell, because his reputation is unassailable, because he is a great historian. But like many others he has not had the patience to discuss the problems of the Chelles chalice with someone who really knows about it. I am afraid that many scholars make remarks of a general nature concerning the Sutton Hoo ship burial to make a particular point. He is one of many such. It is this need of historians to personalize things that also has us struggling around trying to identify the king, if it indeed is a king, who was buried at Sutton Hoo. Nearly thirty years ago Wallace-Hadrill cast doubt on its identification as a royal burial,[17] although he later alleged that he had not actually gone so far as to deny that it was the burial place of a royal East Anglian potentate.[18]

In a way I wish we were not able to reconstruct the East Anglian royal genealogy at all. The equation that Sutton Hoo equals Rædwald has become an accepted statement. I would draw attention to two such acceptances by English scholars, one an historian, the other an archaeologist.

George Henderson in a book published in 1987 wrote: "When Rædwald died in 624, his funeral was marked by pagan rituals of the greatest splendour. He was laid in a ninety-foot boat, surrounded by treasures."[19] And Sonia Hawkes in 1982 wrote: "Rædwald of East Anglia's known ambivalence after conversion early in the seventh century is well represented by the Christian baptismal spoons and bowls in his otherwise heathen ship burial at Sutton Hoo."[20]

Apart from the minor question as to whether the bowls had any function as Christian objects, could I emphasize that we do not know that Rædwald was buried at Sutton Hoo? We do not know that it was a king buried there as there is no distinct royal attribute. Indeed, we do not know what a distinct royal attribute of the seventh century looks like. The scepter, if it be a scepter, need not be a royal one. It is pushing coin dating to its absolute limit (and, in my opinion, beyond it) to refine the date to 624, the normally accepted date for Rædwald's death. The re-evaluation of the coin evidence by Stahl and Oddy, below, further supports this view. John Kent, who wrote up the coins for the Sutton Hoo publication,[21] was much more cautious, not dismissing the possibility that the date of the latest coin was 635, although the 624 date was not unacceptable. Others have said that it is very much earlier

---

[14]For the most convenient discussion of the Chelles chalice and the Eligius theory see J. Hoops, *Reallexikon*, 2nd edition (Berlin 1971), 4, 147, 425, 427 and cited sources. For illustration of the St. Denis fragment see J. Hubert, *et al.*(eds.) *Europe in the Dark Ages* (New York and London 1969), 266.

[15]D. M. Wilson, *Anglo-Saxon Ornamental Metalwork 700-1100 in the British Museum* (London 1964), pl. 34.

[16]M. Ryan, *Early Irish Communion Vessels* (Dublin 1985).

[17]J. M. Wallice-Hadrill, "The Graves of Kings: an Historical Note on Some Archaeological Evidence," *SM*, 3rd. series, 1 (1960), 177-94.

[18]J. M. Wallace-Hadrill, *Early Germanic Kingship in England and on the Continent* (Oxford 1971), 69-70.

[19]G. Henderson, *From Durrow to Kells* (London 1987), 11.

[20]S. C. Hawkes, in Campbell *The Anglo-Saxons*, 48.

[21]Bruce-Mitford, *The Sutton Hoo Ship Burial*, I, 578-653.

than 624. I, however, find it worrying that the hoard is untypically broad in its chronological span and that there is no bunching at the end of the series. (It may have been deliberately put together, for no other hoard with such a spread of coins has ever been found.) Remember also that all the coins come from France (and from all over France). Suffice it to say that although 624 is a *possible* date for Sutton Hoo, it is by no means certain. The atypicality of the hoard increases the likelihood that this is a very special burial, but if you write or teach on this subject, please, the little word *may* should be brought into any identification of Rædwald. After all it *may* or even *might* be Sigeberht who died in the early 630s, or it *might* be his illegitimate brother if he had one (and most people did), or any other great man of East Anglia from 610 to 650. On balance I think that Sutton Hoo is a royal burial of an East Anglian prince or king, but it need not be Rædwald, although either he or Sigeberht may be good candidates. Leslie Webster jolted me by suggesting that Bede's dates for Rædwald may not be entirely reliable, a very wise caution.

There is, as I have said, a compulsion among historians to personalize everything. Because Rædwald is a great king who happens to appear in Bede, and because Sutton Hoo is a rich grave of about the same time in the right area, the syllogism must be completed by saying that it must be Rædwald who is buried there. This is false logic. It is also perhaps overstating the case, for there is more to the pro-Rædwald argument: the Christian/heathen syncretism for one thing and the Frankish connection for another. But let us have a little more doubt, and a little less laying down of the law.

And so to the Swedish end of the story. Some words from Robert Farrell's 1972 book, *Beowulf, Swedes and Geats* could be taken as a text for this part of my lecture. "*Beowulf*, Sutton Hoo and Scandinavian archaeology and legend all somehow enrich one another, but the relation between all or even any two members of the series is not easy to define"[22] You can say that again!

Beowulf and Sweden have been intimately connected in academic imagination (and I use the word advisedly) for years. Toward the end of the last century Knut Stjerna wrote a series of essays on *Beowulf* which stressed the Swedish contacts.[23] These were gathered together and published posthumously in 1912. It is clear that it was Stjerna's book that influenced those extraordinary illustrations which Klaeber included in his edition of *Beowulf*, that so many of us used as undergraduates. When Sutton Hoo was found with its parallels to the Vendel material illustrated by Klaeber it was open season for declaring Swedish parallels: Beowulf - Sutton Hoo - Sweden, beginning with Lindqvist and Nerman. Lindqvist[24] argued for the Swedish origin of the dynasty of the East Anglian kings, the Wuffingas, a member of which family was said to have been buried at Sutton Hoo. Lindqvist held that the dynasty was of Swedish origin, a branch of the royal house of Uppsala and the descendants of Wiglaf who is mentioned in *Beowulf*. This led to a series of circular arguments. Because there is a Swedish element in Sutton Hoo, therefore there is a Swedish element in the East Anglian genealogies, therefore there is a Swedish element at Sutton Hoo. And so it goes on. Let us examine the Swedish element at Sutton Hoo.

Four elements are said to be Swedish, the sword, the helmet, the shield and the ship burial. The sword can most easily be dismissed. Technical work by Birgit Arrhenius on the cement used behind the garnets of sword pommels shows that the Sutton Hoo pommel was almost certainly made on the Rhine or at least in a Frankish workshop.[25] The helmet has convincing parallels in Sweden, but differs noticeably from its Swedish parallels, particularly because the face-mask, neck guard and ear flaps do not occur in Sweden. In my view, as I have argued elsewhere,[26] the Sutton Hoo helmet and its Swedish counterparts are derived from common sources on the Continent which Bruce-Mitford has identified as late Constantinian (fourth-century) infantry and cavalry helmets.[27] A later example of similar form of undoubtedly Anglo-Saxon manufacture has been found in York, which very much

---

[22] R. Farrell, *Beowulf, Swedes and Geats* (London 1972), 54.

[23] K. Stjerna, *Essays on Questions Connected with the Old English Poem of* Beowulf (Coventry 1912).

[24] Linqvist, "Sutton Hoo and *Beowulf*," 94-100.

[25] B. Arrhenius, *Merovingian Garnet Jewellery* (Stockholm 1985), 147.

[26] J. P. Lamm and H. A. Nordström (eds.) *Vendel Period Studies* (Stockholm 1983), 164.

[27] R. L. S. Bruce-Mitford, *The Sutton Hoo Ship Burial*, II (London 1978), 220-225.

strengthens an argument against a Swedish origin for the Sutton Hoo helmet. The ornament of the helmet and the parallel decoration on the plaques from Torslunda on the Swedish island of Öland[28] are also of common Germanic form. Consider, for example, the Plietzhausen disc[29] which also has parallel ornament to the helmet. The shield is a different matter. The shield-boss particularly is very close in form to shield-bosses from Vendel and Valsgärde.[30] It is close in ornament and scale, but the Sutton Hoo shield is unique, possibly a shield of parade, and may have its origins on the Continent.

The rite of ship-burial provides a close parallel with Sweden: burials of this character appear nowhere else on the Continent outside Scandinavia and East Anglia. Only one other certain example is known from England of this date, at Snape in Suffolk.[31] The boats found at Vendel and Valsgärde in Sweden are much smaller, the earlier Danish examples from Slusegård on Bornholm are perhaps only parts of boats. Other ships' timbers used as coffins or lids may only be a down-market boat burial or the result of economy of material. But the rite is rare, and there is a distinct possibility that the Sutton Hoo and Snape rite is derived from Sweden. And it is here that *Beowulf* is useful – not as a document of Swedish history, but as a document of some centuries after the Sutton Hoo ship was buried. For here, indeed, are two accounts of the disposal of a body in a ship, the one by fire and the other by pushing it out to sea. The "motif" to use literary jargon, is familiar, and we are not too surprised to read an account by a monk of Ruys in Brittany of St Gildas's body being disposed of by being pushed out to sea.

Sutton Hoo has parallels in Sweden – or rather objects from Sutton Hoo have parallels in Sweden – but so Sutton Hoo has parallels in many countries in Europe. What sets Sutton Hoo apart is the richness of the grave and the enormously high quality of the grave goods. We must, of course, produce the parallels but it is clearly senseless to try and derive the whole, bag-and-baggage, from some distant proto-ancestral connection with a handful of jungly chieftains in Uppland more than 1500 miles away.

What sets Sutton Hoo apart is its wealth, and also the many-faceted elements that went into its make-up. Catherine Hills has some wise words to say on the subject:

> The Sutton Hoo treasure springs unexpectedly out of a rural agricultural society, in a part of the region where there is no very obvious density of population, nor immediate source of wealth. In the context of other burials from early Saxon England, it is even more extraordinary. The richest burials elsewhere in England come from Taplow, in Buckinghamshire, and from various cemeteries in Kent. There is nothing comparable in East Anglia ... Even the other burials excavated at Sutton Hoo ... are still no match for the main ship burial. It is difficult to set in its context a phenomenon which has so little in common with its background, and which appears without precedent of successor.[32]

The excavations at Sutton Hoo carried out by Martin Carver over the last five years have only served to emphasize this statement. It is possible that there was more than one rich burial at Sutton Hoo, but the remarkable element of this great research undertaking has been to see the burial in its context amongst other graves of little or no wealth. I am not going to hare down the alleyway most temptingly opened up recently by Martin Carver when he talked of "retainers and sacrificial victims"[33] in the poor graves at the Sutton Hoo site. Rather, I would cautiously ask whether the Sutton Hoo site is not more typical than had previously been thought.

It is interesting that excavations at the nearby site of Snape, where in 1862 a boat burial was excavated which produced hints of wealth, have produced a similar mixed cemetery. These investigations are a spin-off of those at

---

[28] *Ibid.*, fig. 156.

[29] *Ibid.*, fig. 146.

[30] *Ibid.*, 34-35.

[31] R. L. S. Bruce-Mitford, "The Snape Boat-grave," *Proc. of the Suffolk Inst. of Archaeol.* 26 (1952), 1-26.

[32] Lamm and Nortström, *Vendel Period Studies*, 103.

[33] *Bulletin of the Sutton Hoo Research Committee* 5 (1989), 8.

Sutton Hoo,[34] and they appear to tell a similar story. A rich casual find a few hundred yards away from the Sutton Hoo site, but in the next parish, suggests that rich burials are more common than one might have expected in this area of East Anglia.[35] But I may well be proceeding ahead of the evidence.

I am convinced that Martin Carver's work at Sutton Hoo, Filmer-Sankey's excavations at Snape, and the work of the Suffolk Archaeological Unit under Keith Wade in examining the archaeological evidence for settlement in this area of East Anglia are the right way to go about the furtherance of Sutton Hoo studies. I am particularly struck by the rich material coming from Wade's excavation of the seventh- and eighth-century levels in the Anglo-Saxon town of Ipswich. All these studies will add much to our knowledge of Sutton Hoo and the region, but I do not think they will add much to our knowledge of *Beowulf*, although I suppose they may find a grave which is covered by a name stone which says *Hic jacit Redwald, Rex Anglorum*. If it is found, I hope it is a truly Christian burial with no accompanying finery.

I trust that you do not think that I have spoken either with undue levity or with hypocritical archaeological arrogance about the past fifty years of Sutton Hoo studies. I have merely switched on a few hazard lights. What has been achieved through Sutton Hoo over this half century is a great cross-fertilization between all our different disciplines. This has, in some instances, led to miscegenation, but a few by-blows are a small cost to pay in relation to the greater understanding of the Anglo-Saxon period that has come about. New discoveries are made by taking leaps in the dark.

Let us remember and take to heart Edmund Burke's speech on American taxation in 1774 in which he said, "it is the nature of all greatness not to be exact."

---

[34]*Ibid.*, 13-17.

[35]M. M. Mango, *et al.*, "A Sixth-Century Mediterranean Bucket from Bromeswell Parish, Suffolk," *Antiquity* 63 (1989), 295-311.

Anglo-Saxon Literary Studies and Archaeology: A Nuts and Bolts Approach

ROBERT FARRELL

In writing this paper, I am breaking two self-made rules: (1) Never – or never *again* – write on "*Beowulf* and Sutton Hoo"; and (2) Never – or never *again* – give a paper in a conference which I have had a hand in organizing. These are solid rules, for the first prevents one from becoming tiresome, by presenting once again the same ideas on which one has spoken and written before; and the second spares one's having to organize a fairly large-scale event, while trying to pull together coherent thoughts on a scholarly topic. The two are not compatible.

I have failed in my resolve first because Roberta Frank pressed me to speak, and who can refuse so distinguished a colleague, especially when our friendship extends back to an enormous and somewhat bizarre class seminar on *Beowulf*, taught by Kemp Malone, to an exceedingly motley group of students at New York University, in 1964-65? I am also pleased to exchange ideas with Allen Frantzen, a colleague I have long held in esteem, but never yet worked with.

As for my writing on Sutton Hoo and *Beowulf* once again, it should become clear that I do not believe that *Beowulf* and Sutton Hoo are to be "read" in tandem; I *do* believe that there is a much broader case to be made, in favor of close cooperation on all fronts, between archaeologists and philologists whose interests lie in the same period.

The title of this paper arose in discussion with Professor Frantzen; we agreed that I would take up the practical and direct aspect of the reasons for studying, or perhaps more accurately, *attempting* to study Anglo-Saxon literature and archaeology in tandem, while he would take the higher ground on historical, contextual and theoretical approaches. It is impossible to proceed without giving some account of my own move towards practical archaeology, but it is to be hoped that what I say will be more broadly applicable.

From the standpoint of discipline boundaries in most American universities, archaeology is very often part and parcel of an anthropology department. In the European tradition, the classical route is archaeology via literature/philology both in the Latin and Greek and to a lesser extent the Germanic and Romance languages. Americans have followed this route; the career of A. S. Cook at Yale is the clearest example of a Germanic philologist and distinguished Anglo-Saxonist, who played an important role in the study of such monuments as the Bewcastle Cross.[1] It does not matter that his views on the monument are now clearly wrong, for his strong interest in the "archaeology" of the cross, and his collection and republication of important early accounts of it were major impetus to further research. European scholars, in respectful reviews, referred to him as an antiquarian, a term which covers a broad range of interests regarding the past, though what is now called dirt archaeology played almost no part in Cook's work. Cook had a keen interest in the Germanic past, and used this knowledge to explicate Anglo-Saxon texts, even those which drew on Latin exemplars.

Thus literature and archaeology have been studied in tandem early on. As Professor Frantzen will demonstrate, Cook's broad antiquarian interests were part and parcel of the nineteenth-century scholarly tradition and might will be described in a paraphrase of Ezra Cornell's ideal description of the proper extent of university study: *Nihil Anglo-Saxonicum mihi alienum puto*.

When we turn to Sutton Hoo, it is very instructive to review the initial publication of the site and of the finds. Firstly, there is much myth and lore about the excavation of Mound One, in addition to the wealth of written commentary. One of the persistent fallacies is that *Beowulf*, and its account of a treasure intentionally abandoned by being shoved out to sea, played a part in the inquest. There is no doubt that *press* accounts mentioned *Beowulf*,

[1] A. S. Cook, *Some Accounts of the Bewcastle Cross...* re-issued, with a new preface by R. T. Farrell, as *The Anglo-Saxon Cross* (Hamden 1977), 127-282.

notably both the *London Times* and the *East Anglian Daily Times*, for 17 August, 1939. Bruce-Mitford makes it clear that there was *NO* specific mention of *Beowulf* at the inquest.[2] C. W. Phillips stated at the inquiry:

> There is contemporary literary evidence that the burial of chieftains among the northern nations in the Dark Ages was the occasion of celebrations and feasting which lasted several days, and nothing can be more certain than the public character of the Sutton Hoo burial.[3]

This would certainly encompass *Beowulf*, but the connection is not specific.

Sune Lindqvist, in his 1948 article, "*Beowulf* och Sutton Hoo" appears to have been the first scholar to hold that *Beowulf* was quoted at the inquest.[4] In 1957 and 1959 studies were published by two scholars who had their initial training in philology, one of whom, C. L. Wrenn, followed Lindqvist's error. Charles Wrenn presented his case on *Beowulf* and archaeology in two venues; his supplement to Chambers' book on *Beowulf*,[5] and in an essay in the Fernand Mossé *Festschrift*.[6] Rosemary Cramp wrote an article on "*Beowulf* and Archaeology" in the first volume of the now distinguished journal, *Medieval Archaeology*.[7] Cramp's work will be dealt with later, as it is first necessary to follow through with Wrenn's accounts of Sutton Hoo, and their aftermath.

Wrenn enlarged upon Lindqvist's error, firmly claiming that the decision of the jury at the Sutton Hoo inquest was reached after they had read to them not one but *two* extended passages from *Beowulf*. The notion of *Beowulf* at the Sutton Hoo inquest has had a long life since then; as recently as 1981 Eric Stanley seemed inclined towards this view, though he cites with praise Rupert Bruce-Mitford's first Sutton Hoo volume, in which the connection is firmly denied.[8]

There is much in what Charles Wrenn had to say that is over-enthusiastic. First, he accepted without question the interesting but clearly very speculative interpretations Karl Hauck made of the "pagan iconography," of certain objects from Sutton Hoo.[9] Second, there is a heavy use of words like "astonishingly," "exact," and "amazing." Broadly speaking, the closeness of *Beowulf* and Sutton Hoo is astonishing, the parallels between the burial ship and the poem exact, and the potential of the ship burial to throw light on the poem amazing.

Wrenn starts with a quotation from Bruce-Mitford's translation of Sune Lindqvist's 1948 article:

> It is obvious that the *rapprochement* that was at once made between the Sutton Hoo burial and the substance of *Beowulf* was fully warranted, and rich with possibilities. Everything seems to show that these two documents complement one another admirably. Both become the clearer by comparison.[10]

The extreme and uncritical claims of the archaeologist are echoed and perhaps even intensified by Wrenn, who claims that, "the famous description of the ship passing of Scyld Scefing" amazingly seems to remember Sutton Hoo, and that the Sutton Hoo helmet clarifies ll. 1030-31 of *Beowulf*:[11]

---

[2]R. L. S. Bruce-Mitford, *The Sutton Hoo Ship Burial*, vol. I (London 1975), 722.

[3]*Ibid*.

[4]*Fornvännen* 43 (1948), 94-110; trans. R. L. S. Bruce-Mitford, "Sutton Hoo and *Beowulf*," *Antiquity* 22 (1948), 131-40.

[5]C. L. Wrenn, "Sutton Hoo and *Beowulf*," supplement to R. W. Chambers, *Beowulf: an Introduction to the Study of the Poem with a Discussion of the Stories of Offa and Finn*, 3rd ed., (Cambridge 1959).

[6]C. L. Wrenn, "Sutton Hoo and *Beowulf*," *Mélanges de linguistique et de philologie: Fernand Mossé in Memoriam* (Paris 1959), 495-507; reprinted in L. E. Nicholson (ed.) *An Anthology of Beowulf Criticism* (Notre Dame 1963), 311-30.

[7]R. Cramp, "*Beowulf* and Archaeology," *MA* 1 (1957), 57-77.

[8]E. G. Stanley, "The Date of *Beowulf*: Some Doubts and No Conclusions," in C. Chase (ed.) *The Dating of Beowulf* (Toronto 1981), 197-211.

[9]K. Hauck, "Herrschaftszeichen eines wodanistischen Königtums," in *Festgabe Anton Ernstberger herausgegeben vom Institut für fränkische Landesforschung der Universität Erlangen* (Erlangen 1954), 9-65.

[10]Wrenn, Sutton Hoo and *Beowulf*, 314.

[11]*Ibid*.

Ymb þæs helmes hrof heafodbeorge
wirum bewunden walu utan heold.

Most significant of all is Wrenn's hope that the further study of poem and ship burial will yield *complementary clarification*.

In the most significant initial publications of Sutton Hoo, both in the *British Museum Quarterly* and *Antiquity*,[12] more temperate and cautious conclusions were reached. One essay in particular stands out, H. Munro Chadwick's "Who was He?"[13] Chadwick worked on the assumption that the coin evidence rendered improbable any date before 640. This more firmly limited the date than either of the initial numismatic reports, but it also appears that the trend towards a 650-70 date had already set in. Despite this, Chadwick held for *Rædwald* as the likeliest candidate for the ship burial/cenotaph. In his discussion of the Sutton Hoo burial *ordo*, Chadwick is considerably more cautious and correct than either Charles Wrenn was to be in 1959, or Rupert Bruce-Mitford was to be in 1975, for Chambers carefully points out that the ship in Scyld's burial was set adrift, not buried. Where Wrenn saw Scyld's funeral as a *recollection* of the Sutton Hoo ship burial, Chadwick saw interesting analogies.

In the great first volume of the Sutton Hoo report published in 1975, Bruce-Mitford's account of text and archaeological site is strangely structured. He begins by citing a translation of some lines from *The Seafarer* as, "a literary record of the survival of the custom of depositing grave-goods in a Christian context."[14] It is not my purpose here to find fault peevishly or pyrotechnically in the mode of Professor Page of Cambridge, but it is quite clear that this passage is extremely difficult to deal with, for complex problems of syntax and semantics abound.[15] Suffice it to say that Dr. Bruce-Mitford was satisfied to quote the translation cited by Chadwick in 1940 without troubling either to credit the translator, or to update his information. This is a minor flaw, his subsequent use of the text of *Beowulf*, however, is singularly problematic. The lengthy account of a cremation/mound burial at the end - *the climax of the poem* - is dismissed, by Bruce-Mitford who claims: "The mixture of rites in Beowulf's own funeral at the end of the poem is almost certainly the result of confusion of thought or text, or of distance in time from the days when such ceremonies were performed."[16]

Scyld's funeral, however, is seen as of the "same kind and class" as the rite at Sutton Hoo, this despite the publication in 1969 of Angus Cameron's important little study, "St. Gildas and Scyld Scefing," in which Cameron showed that the closest parallel is not Germanic and pagan, but Celtic and Christian.[17] I know that Bruce-Mitford was aware of Cameron's work, because he heard me stress its importance in a 1971 lecture given to the Viking Society in London which he attended.

To sum up the burial question, as it is presented in Wrenn and Bruce-Mitford: (1) Chadwick's 1940 assessment was cautious and suasive; (2) Wrenn, to some extent paralleling Lindqvist, saw astonishing parallels not seen by Chadwick, between Sutton Hoo and *Beowulf*; and (3) Bruce-Mitford in 1975 failed to use scholarly material readily available to him, and simply made what he wished to make of the literary evidence.

It must be stressed that Bruce-Mitford's error is quite understandable. First, Lindqvist was Bruce-Mitford's friend and teacher, and it was to him that the second volume of Sutton Hoo was dedicated. I am not certain of the inversion of an *ad hominem* argument; perhaps *pro hominem* would do. Bruce-Mitford could not but have been swayed by the argument of his teacher, especially as Lindqvist's work became more widely available because Bruce-Mitford himself had translated it. Wrenn, in his turn, seems to have been quite spellbound by Bruce-Mitford, as the somewhat passionate conclusion of his brief paper on Sutton Hoo and *Beowulf* makes clear:

---

[12]*British Musuem Quarterly* 13:4 (December 1939), 111-136; and *Antiquity* 14:53 (March, 1940), 6-87.

[13]H. M. Chadwick, "Who was He?" *Antiquity* 14.53 (March 1940), 76-87.

[14]Bruce-Mitford, *Sutton Hoo*, I, 71.

[15]See I. L. Gordon (ed.) *The Seafarer* (New York 1960).

[16]Bruce-Mitford, *Sutton Hoo Ship Burial*, I, 717.

[17]A. Cameron, "Saint Gildas and Scyld Scefing," *NM* 70.2 (1969), 240-46.

It has been my purpose rather to emphasize the new lines of study suggested by Sutton Hoo than to attempt new results. For guidance throughout I have been especially indebted to the work of Mr Rupert Bruce-Mitford, to whom students of this, the greatest archaeological discovery in Britain of our century, are more indebted than to anyone.[18]

This scenario seems to imply consultation between the archaeologist Bruce-Mitford and the philologist Wrenn. Instead of providing one another with the best detailed information, however, each appears to have used the other to skim the broad outline of what each in fact wanted to hear. The real question is this: have things gotten better?

A more recent pair of publications indicate that, at least in some respects, improvement is still possible. In 1981, the University of Toronto Press published *The Dating of Beowulf*, under the editorship of the late Colin Chase. This is a valuable work, for it presents interesting, vigorous and enthusiastic defenses of a wide spectrum of dates for *Beowulf*. At the segment of this conference open to the scholarly public, I raised an objection to the curious lack of input by any archaeologist. Professor Stanley in discussion of the stance I took made it clear that his opinion of archaeologists was not very high, because they tended to change their minds on dates. Presumably philologists do not. Sutton Hoo *per se* is adverted to by several of the conferees, notably Alexander Callander Murray, who offers as neat a put-down as one could wish: "Archaeology is now invoked as being more likely to illustrate the poem's origins than literary history. Perhaps one day, but certainly not an present."[19] Professor Stanley, in a conclusion, in which a là Samuel Johnson's *Rasselas* he feels nothing is concluded, shows some knowledge and some respect for archaeologists and their stock in trade, but one feels the mordant bite of irony when he says: "It has been proposed to dig over our mound for a third time. A corpse for Charon, that is what we want. A bit of Redwald, *demonstrably* Redwald, would do well."[20]

Of the conferees, Roberta Frank had perhaps the most accurate assessment of the relationship between *Beowulf*, its date, and Sutton Hoo when she wrote: "The *Beowulf* poet pondered his northern heathens and northern heroes, and raised to their memory a monument far more Christian, and at the same time, far more Scandinavian than Sutton Hoo."[21] I am afraid that I am perhaps not exactly unbiased in my endorsement of this view because I expressed similar notions as early as 1971, at least on the "more Scandinavian" evaluation.[22]

On what one might call the archaeological side, Angela Care Evans, in her recent edition of *The Sutton Hoo Ship Burial* (the latest version of what started as the *Handbook*), seems to be unaware of the Toronto volume, though it had been in print and available for at least several years before her handbook came out. She states, as fact, that *Beowulf* was written in Old English in the first half of the eighth century.[23] I do *not* mean to cast aspersions on anyone in these remarks; the point must be made that "crosses" between disciplines take a *very* long time to come about, and that there is a curious lack of swift communication from discipline to discipline, even on so limited a front as *Beowulf* and Sutton Hoo. Despite this difficulty, I am convinced that work must be carried out on a much broader front, that of the ever-increasing base of particularizing information that archaeology can provide to literature, and the valuable commentary that texts can provide on places, things, and perhaps people, the proper ultimate goal of both disciplines. It seems to me that to call on one site, to help the understanding of a single poem, is a misguided effort.

In her conclusion to "*Beowulf* and Archaeology," Rosemary Cramp set the standard for what we perhaps ought better to do. The only expansion or enlargement of what she wrote is the vast increase in the body of archaeological evidence and, to a much lesser extent, the new literary insights on this poem:

---

[18]Wrenn, "Sutton Hoo and *Beowulf*," in Nicholson, *Anthology*, 329-30.

[19]A. C. Murray, "*Beowulf*, the Danish Invasions and the Royal Genealogy," in C. Chase (ed.) *The Dating of Beowulf* (Toronto 1981), 101-11.

[20]E. G. Stanley, "The Date of *Beowulf*: Some Doubts and No Conclusions," in Chase, *The Dating of Beowulf*, 205.

[21]R. Frank, "Skaldic Verse and the Date of *Beowulf*," in Chase, *The Dating of Beowulf*, 139.

[22]R. T. Farrell, *Beowulf, Swedes and Geats* (London 1972).

[23]A. C. Evans, *The Sutton Hoo Ship Burial* (London 1986), 111.

> What archaeology brings to the poem is not yet a solution of its date; there is not a sufficient body of relevant evidence to do this. If enough of such evidence is ever forthcoming to prove that the poet muddled together objects and conditions of widely different dates, then the latest of these might give a clue to the poet's own time. However, even if all the background could be closely fixed to one era, it would still be necessary to refute or support the undoubted historical sense he sometimes shows. The archaeological evidence that is now available, however, can enrich considerably the study of the poem; it can supply relevant illustrations so that simple words such as "hall" or "sword" conjure up a precise picture in the mind of the modern reader. Moreover a knowledge of the excellencies and refinements of Anglo-Saxon craftsmanship enables us to appreciate what governed the poet's choice of epithet in stressing the features that he did stress in more complicated passages of description.[24]

I began to study archaeology for precisely the reason that Professor Cramp set forward here, to give a local habitation and a name, a placement in a material culture, for Anglo-Saxon literature. It has been my experience that a combined approach works very well indeed with students, probably because Old English presents such difficulties as a language, with minimal and confusing morphology, and complex lexical and syntactic problems. In fact, it is probably best to speak of the archaeologies that can be articulated with the poem: first, the *realia* of millenial England; second the several courts and contexts that could have served as patrons and economic bases for the poem during the eighth, ninth and tenth centuries; and lastly the archaeology of the pre-Viking period, most particularly that of early Scandinavia, the age in which the mythical Beowulf flourished.

To sum up: literary critics seem to be dismissing "archaeology" because it will not precisely answer the exact questions in which they are interested. A strong archaeological case for the milieu which could have given rise to *Beowulf* can be made in various kingdoms throughout England in the eighth, ninth, and tenth centuries, and though there are gaps, it is also possible to make a case for the seventh and the eleventh centuries. It is simply not on to ask archaeology to produce a demonstrable hunk of Rædwald, perhaps with a garnet-decorated version of the Alfred jewel around his neck, to return irony for irony, (*pace* Professor Stanley, who sought such a token).[25] It is my belief that archaeology will never precisely date *Beowulf*, and my conviction that to expect it to do so shows a singular lack of understanding of the nature of archaeological evidence.

Archaeological and cultural backgrounding is essential for other texts as well. Advances in our understanding of continuity from the Romano-British period to the Anglo-Saxon make a facile connection of *The Ruin* with Bath reductive. In the case of the *Dream of the Rood* and its cognate text on the Ruthwell Cross, close study of the cross leads to harsh truths: the damage to that monument is massive; only a small portion of the original iconography is recoverable; and the surface of the stone is so hacked back that no recovery of original decoration or inscription is possible on about half the surface area.[26] The major runic inscriptions on the vinescroll panels of the lower stone are most emphatically *not* a transcript of the *Dream of the Rood* from the Vercelli Book. As Éamonn Ó Carragáin has clearly demonstrated in a recent study, what we have on the cross is a cognate but independent poem, a series of *sententiae* on the cross.[27] It is reasonable, I think, to say that it is impossible to study any single aspect of the Ruthwell Cross, its decoration, and the tradition with which aspects of that monument articulate without having as full an understanding as possible of all the appropriate disciplines. Baldly put, to see the major vernacular runic inscriptions on the Ruthwell Cross as a convenient cross-reference for the Vercelli Book text is as myopic and misguided as the efforts of those students of eighteenth- and nineteenth-century English Literature who choose to interpret the bare texts of William Blake's poems without taking heed of the enormously complex mixed media artefacts he left us, in which poetry was part of a complex pattern of drawings, watercolors, and engravings.

---

[24] R. J. Cramp, "*Beowulf* and Archaeology," 77.

[25] Stanley, "The Date of *Beowulf*."

[26] R. T. Farrell, "Reflections on the Ruthwell and Bewcastle Crosses," in P. Szarmach and V. D. Oggins (eds.) *Sources of Anglo-Saxon Culture* (Kalamazoo 1986), 357-76.

[27] É Ó Carragáin, "The Ruthwell Cross and Irish High Crosses: Some Points of Comparison and Contrast," in M. Ryan (ed.) *Ireland and Insular Art AD 500-1200* (Dublin 1987), 118-28.

The gloomy side of all this is daunting. Given the number of scholars engaged in the study of the early Middle Ages, and the consequent copious flow of scholarship, any attempt at the absolute mastery of two fields is foredoomed to failure. *But we must try.*

It is probably safe to say that the archaeologists are doing better at providing us with summaries of where things stand. A case in point is Leslie Webster's chapter, "Anglo-Saxon England AD 400-1100" in *Archaeology in Britain Since 1945*.[28] In a concise, humanistic and amazingly rich account of a field which has expanded beyond recognition since World War II, Webster concludes by stressing two urgent needs:

> The first lies in the field; it is the need to excavate more waterlogged sites, both for the better-preserved organic artefacts which are largely absent from the Anglo-Saxon archaeological record, and more particularly for the microscopic potential of the deposits - those tiny seeds, pips, plant debris and micro-organisms which help to show, among other things, what the climate was, how the land was used, how people ate, lived, fell sick and died.
>
> The other and perhaps even more important need is for more armchair archaeology. Now that Anglo-Saxon archaeology has, as it were, come of age in terms of breadth and sufficiency of data, the need for more overall synthesis becomes more pressing. With it goes a need for a revised philosophy of the subject.[29]

Two interesting concepts, the need for a revised philosophy, and for more overall synthesis. There are clear evidences that the first has already begun. Ian Hodder of Cambridge very recently edited two collections of essays, *The Archaeology of Contextual Meanings*, and *Archaeology as Long-Term History*.[30] In his own essay in the former, Hodder claims all of the following terms are germane to archaeology: "semiotics, sign, index, signal, icon, symbol, metaphor, structure, syntagmatic, paradigmatic, style, culture, tradition, type, norm, content."[31] As my own university is the home of Jonathan Culler and a host of like-minded colleagues, I cannot but recognize the literary progenitors of these terms. Certainly a radical revision is under way here.

Equally interesting is *Pragmatic Archaeology: Theory in Crisis?* The introductory essay, entitled as the collection, starts with a gem of witty – and anti-theoretical – gloom:

> Despite the recent increase in published archaeological works, we have not witnessed a similar increase in innovative archaeological problems. Indeed, archaeology is still dedicated to elucidating some very basic questions about how people lived. Consequently it is very dispiriting to realise to what depths the morale of the discipline appears to have sunk regarding its achievements and potential. The heady, euphoric days of the sixties, and the optimism of the seventies, when we felt that all human behavior was reducible to a series of fundamental statements or laws, has died. The funeral was not well attended but the offspring have been squabbling about the inheritance ever since. The cynic might question whether we can remember what we were arguing about in the first place.[32]

Later in the volume we find a rather militant essay, co-authored by R. Yorstan and the editors, that is interesting for its strong stress on a humanistic approach:

---

[28]L. Webster, "Anglo-Saxon England AD 400-1100," in I. Longworth and J. Cherry (eds.) *Archaeology in Britain Since 1945* (London 1986), 119-59.

[29]*Ibid.*, 157.

[30]I. Hodder (ed.) *The Archaeology of Contextual Meanings* (Cambridge 1987); I. Hodder (ed.), *Archaeology as Long-Term History* (Cambridge 1987).

[31]Hodder, *Contextual Meanings*, 1.

[32]C. F. Gaffney and V. L. Gaffney, "Pragmatic Archaeology: Theory in Crisis," in C. F. Gaffney and V. L. Gaffney (eds.) *Pragmatic Archaeology: Theory in Crisis*, B.A.R. Brit. Ser. 167 (Oxford 1987), 3.

A pragmatic archaeology should have the following characteristics:

> it should be humanistic
> it should accept the context-dependence of knowledge
> it should be free in its use of hypotheses
> it should use theory as a "leading principle."[33]

The most clear call for an interdisciplinary approach, and for the proper use of the written record comes in the 1987 volume of *Medieval Archaeology*. The title of the article is self-explanatory: "Archaeology and the Middle Ages, Recommendation by the Society for Medieval Archaeology to the Historic Buildings and Monuments Concern for England." The primary point of this essay is the proper and appropriate use of the written record. The second – and more general point – is that archaeology should throw light on the society as a whole.

It is interesting and significant that in the year of the fiftieth anniversary of the excavation of Mound One at Sutton Hoo, the Society for Medieval Archaeology should re-stress the importance of texts to archaeology, an issue addressed by Rosemary Cramp on the more limited front of *Beowulf* and archaeology in the first issue of the Society's journal.

For those with primary training in literature and philology, as well as for historians and archivists, the door is open. Some would, I think, greatly prefer to close it firmly, and go about their business of textual analysis and source study. Such research is safe; it can best be done by finding Latin texts which are, in the view of such researchers, *the* sources of Anglo-Saxon literature. The analogy of slogging away at the coal-face, beloved by Professor James Cross, is surprisingly apt. One gets a limited appreciation of the rest of the world, deep in the bowels of the earth, or in the minutiae of Christian hagiography. There is nothing intrinsically wrong in doing source study, and it is certainly useful. I have a good deal of respect for such work, and those who do it. The problem is that some of those who choose this specific task see no validity in attempts to use evidence from another field, and seem to disapprove of others doing so. It is not difficult to recall the discussion after the first series of papers on the sources of Anglo-Saxon culture at Kalamazoo, during which some source-minded participants proposed quite firmly that art historical, cultural, and most particularly archaeological papers be dropped in subsequent years as they were not relevant to Anglo-Saxon studies. This view is not by any means universal, as the heavy attendance at these archaeological sessions in the Congresses on Medieval Studies at Western Michigan University attest. The anti-archaeological stance is, however, pervasive, and deep-rooted. A 1988 graduate from Cornell with high honors, and majors in medieval archaeology and medieval literature went on to graduate study in English, only to be told that archaeology had nothing to do with the study of Old English literature. I would hope that for some of us, and perhaps more importantly, for our students, this is not true.

In an ideal world, we would have medieval archaeologists with full competence in one or more vernacular languages. They would be skilled in Latin, and they would be firmly grounded in literature and paleography, with perhaps even some basic competence in runeology. We would also have literary critics who had spent several seasons in the nasty business of recovering the material evidence of the Anglo-Saxon period from under earth or water, and who would thereafter be capable of interpreting a site report. They would thus have left the coal mine and engaged in other kinds of digging. Failing in this, the second-best solution would be the establishment of a close, long-term, and strong working bond between the fields, so that the time-lags in information exchange could be cut back. It is possible to span two fields, as is most clearly shown in the distinguished work of Richard Bailey, among others. It is, however, interesting to note that in recent times the crossover from literature and philology to archaeology is fairly common, but a cross in the other direction is hard to find. I suggest that this is because the corpus of Old English literature has been virtually unchanged for the past hundred years, while the amount of totally new information recovered in the fifty years since the opening of Mound One at Sutton Hoo has been almost

[33] R. Yorstan, C. F. Gaffney and V. L Gaffney, "A Manifesto for Pragmatic Archaeology," in Gaffney and Gaffney (eds.) *Pragmatic Archaeology*, 109.

overwhelming. Speaking for myself, I find it satisfying to write on praetero-present verbs in *Beowulf*,[34] but exciting to locate some forty hitherto unknown features – some at least of early medieval date – in a small part of an Irish lake in the course of a single season.[35]

On the basis of experience and observation, medieval archaeology (I do not think it appropriate to limit one's perspective by saying Anglo-Saxon) is neither better nor worse, more or less valid, than any other research tool or body of knowledge. Anglo-Saxon studies are in a fortunate position. We are blessed in having the *Concordance*,[36] the great *Dictionary* is forging on at the University of Toronto, and Mitchell's *Syntax*[37] is in hand. I would hold that the new understandings of the Anglo-Saxons and their society provided by archaeology are at least as valuable as those provided by these other research tools. If the broad and yet precise picture archaeology can now give us of many sites and landscapes is used in conjunction with literature, all of us will be the richer for it. A student of mid and late Anglo-Saxon culture, one interested in Winchester, cannot but be aided by the picture and placement of that city Martin Biddle provides for us. In like manner, no one interested in the age of Bede can afford to ignore the magnificent and detailed information available through Professor Cramp's excavations and publications of that one house in two places, Monkwearmouth and Jarrow. In both places, continuity from the Roman tradition, sophisticated Anglo-Saxon architecture, and clear indications of a remarkable standard of material culture are evident. To ignore such useful, precise, and elegant milieux for literature and culture seems foolhardy in the extreme.

[34]C. Karkov with R. T. Farrell, "The Gnomic Passages of *Beowulf*," *NM* 3 XCI (1990), 295-310.

[35]R. T. Farrell, *et al.*, "Reports on the Survey of Artificial Islands in the Irish Midlands," to appear in *IJNA*.

[36]A. diPaolo Healey and R. L. Venezky (eds.) *A Microfiche Concordance to Old English* (Toronto 1980).

[37]B. Mitchell, *Old English Syntax*, 2 vols., (Oxford 1985).

Literature, Archaeology, and Anglo-Saxon Studies: Reconstruction and Deconstruction

ALLEN J. FRANTZEN

Along with hundreds of Anglo-Saxonists, I have admired the treasures of Sutton Hoo in the British Museum, and have also peered dubiously into pits at various sites in England and Ireland as the excavations – and my shoes – filled with water. Most recently, during the visit to Repton that was part of the 1985 meeting of the International Society of Anglo-Saxonists, I observed Martin Biddle with some wonder. He was standing in a downpour in the vicarage garden of St. Wystan's Church, gesturing animatedly at a beautifully situated grave in which some 250 Vikings had once been buried. No heath and harebells there, and certainly no benign sky, but indeed "unquiet slumbers for the sleepers in that quiet earth," the kind of slumber that Emily Brontë's narrator could not imagine as she observed the graves of Edgar Linton and Heathcliff at the end of *Wuthering Heights*.[1] I will return to the nineteenth century in my conclusion; at the moment, I suggest that "unquiet slumbers" for the dead of Anglo-Saxon England are an essential by-product of archaeology, as Biddle reminded us at Repton, for archaeology not only records the importance of what it studies, but also "inevitably removes and destroys" the evidence it awakens to new life.[2] The ravages of literary criticism are different. There are thirty-four sessions in progress at this moment; twenty-one of them can be described as "literary" in focus, and five of those involve Anglo-Saxon or Old Norse. On the grand scale of Kalamazoo, literary criticism may be more likely to put the living to sleep than rob the dead of theirs.

A discussion of literature and Sutton Hoo appears to be an exercise in interdisciplinary learning of the kind supposedly traditional in Anglo-Saxon studies. But interdisciplinary discourse, in more than a nominal sense, will require Anglo-Saxonists – archaeologists, literary critics, source scholars, and historians – to rethink the meaning of the interdisciplinary label of which they are so fond. In the interest of promoting exchange, I will discuss the meaning of interdisciplinary study in general, and will look in particular at the theoretical language shared by contemporary literary criticism and by critiques of the "new archaeology" in their efforts to make interdisciplinary study meaningful. Finally, I will sketch a pilot project of an interdisciplinary kind in which literature, archaeology, and other modes of inquiry could cooperate.[3]

Discussions of the theoretical attitudes that structure disciplinary practices are essential, not secondary, but I understand the impatience with which some scholars regard such discussions; theoretical discourse sometimes only discusses the discussion rather than furthers it. But if we are to do more than reconstruct the past, which is what so much current literary criticism and archaeology seek to do, it is beneficial to deconstruct our reconstructions: to view them oppositionally, to ask how they have been historically produced, and to try to understand how they have been perpetuated. Oppositional analysis is important; as we concentrate on the history of the disciplines we practice, we need to keep our own desires, and our own histories, in focus and in the foreground, rather than tucked discreetly out of sight.

My awareness of the history of interdisciplinary study has expanded considerably thanks to an article by Roberta Frank that traces the application of the word "interdisciplinary" from its apparent beginnings to the present. In the beginning "interdisciplinary" was a vague concept that a few people used tentatively; in the present it is still a vague

---

[1] "I lingered round them, under that benign sky; watched the moths fluttering among the heath and harebells, listened to the soft wind breathing through the grass, and wondered how any one could ever imagine unquiet slumbers for the sleepers in that quiet earth." Emily Brontë, *Wuthering Heights* (New York 1947), 352.

[2] M. Biddle and B. Kjølbye-Biddle, "Repton 1984," pamphlet distributed on tour of Repton Church, August 1985, p.3.

[3] The argument made here is presented in expanded form as "Documents and Monuments: Difference and Interdisciplinarity in the Study of Medieval Culture," the first chapter of *Speaking Two Languages: Traditional Disciplines and Contemporary Theory in Medieval Studies*, ed. by A. J. Frantzen (Albany 1991), 1-33. The shorter version appears in this collection at the request of the editors. I thank Roberta Frank for inviting me to join the session and Robert Farrell and John Ruffing for helpful comments on this paper.

concept, but it is now used by everybody, and used resolutely. The term "interdisciplinary" was coined in the 1920s to describe the lofty ideal of cooperation in intellectual ventures; by the mid-1980s, it had become far more basic. A writer in a Canadian journal declared that "life" itself was interdisciplinary, while the Association of American Colleges, not to be outdone, announced that "real life" had achieved the same status.[4] Thus, a term created to promote the *cooperation* of various scholarly specializations was reduced to the pious asseveration that specializations should work together in the *academy* because they worked together in *life*. Michel Foucault would have smiled at this self-congratulatory folly; it offers stunning confirmation of his thesis that scholars use the signifying practices of theory and method to create what they study, and then try to justify those practices by insisting that they have a reality outside and independent of that which has just been created for them.

Interdisciplinary studies have a short history for the simple reason that their cause, the increasing, and now extreme, specialization of scholarly disciplines, is a new phenomenon. This specialization, as Gerald Graff has demonstrated in the case of English studies in America, was an effort to increase the demand for new Ph.D.s to meet the increased supply of trained academics looking for jobs.[5] Jess Bessinger recently told me that Francis Magoun's introductory Old English classes enrolled up to one hundred students in 1947 and for several years thereafter (private correspondence). To cope with this overflow of budding specialists in the next decade, the humanities had to accelerate their growth. In the main that was a process of enlargement by subdivision, a process already underway to ensure that new Ph.D.s could not only find jobs, and then keep them, but, having kept them, enlarge their petty estates into independent disciplinary kingdoms (English literature was divided into periods, major authors, and so forth). The next step, now apparent everywhere in North American universities, is to invent *inter*disciplinary programs and find foundations to support them so that, without undoing our specialization, we can paper over it with another layer of institutions, programs, and employment.

Frank concludes her essay with some thoughts about the historical preference for "discipline" over "field." A "discipline" sounds precise and scientific, while a "field," with its "mud, cows, and corn," she says, is messy.[6] We talk about fields and border lands, rather than disciplines, because fields and borders not only define the territorial divisions in what we do, but also convey the risk of permeable barriers. As we step into a new field, we routinely note that, "this is not my field." The next word, invariably, is "but." That is, we observe the boundary even as we recognize that professional discourse cannot take place if we stay within it; it is in the nature of interdisciplinary work to take chances and to speak about other disciplines in ways likely to offend those who specialize in them. What impresses me about the durability of these barriers is the level at which they have been formed; not a level of theoretical discourse, but of practical, even empirical knowledge. Interdisciplinary study is thwarted not so much by the sheer mass of material that various disciplines organize – although this is surely intimidating enough – but by the failure to reconceptualize disciplinary goals at the theoretical level, a level, I believe, at which the barriers exist in quite different and much less rigid form. The difficulty with bringing theoretical levels into the discussion is, obviously, that many scholars in all disciplines conceive of new work in the discipline as "theory" itself, and, as such, a kind of labor far removed from, and derived from, traditional practice, which is always imagined as theory-free. To take only the most glaring example of this folly in literary criticism, I will take the massive projects of "source" study that dominate work in Anglo-Saxon at the International Congresses on Medieval Studies at Kalamazoo; these projects can be traced directly to the patristic criticism of D. W. Robertson, Jr., and Robert E. Kaske, work that created a revolution of its own when it took hold in the 1950s. Then it was an innovation; today it is a tradition. What is there to reassure any of us that today's innovations – deconstruction, Foucauldian archaeological analysis, or third-world feminism – will not, in time, form orthodoxies of their own?

The difficulty of interdisciplinary work is not solved by a shift in terminology from "discipline" to "field," from abstract to concrete. The "field" image illustrates the basic misconception at the heart of interdisciplinary claims,

---

[4]R. Frank, "'Interdisciplinary': The First Half-Century," in E. G. Stanley and T.F. Hoad, *Words: For Robert Burchfield's Sixty-Fifth Birthday* (Cambridge and Wolfeboro, NH 1988), 91-101.

[5]G. Graff, *Professing Literature: An Institutional History* (Chicago 1987).

[6]Frank, "Interdisciplinary," 100.

and that is the principle of "coverage." Adjacent fields cover related, but different, territory. This image is especially inappropriate to Anglo-Saxon studies, since the various fields within Anglo-Saxon studies do not cover, or concern themselves, with different evidence. Instead, Anglo-Saxon studies is a stack of "fields" covering the same territory and concerned with the same evidence, and that is why we usually find ourselves working in or through two fields. We are slow to see this point because the disciplines look different: the evidence of Anglo-Saxon England has been divided up and parceled out, over the last century and a half, according to what we now recognize as disciplines – objects to archaeology, illustrations to art history, some texts (artistic) to literature, others (utilitarian) to history, behavior to sociology, and so forth.

We tend to forget that this dividing up has taken place over a long period, and in very different circumstances, in both England and America; sociology is a more recent discipline than literary criticism, which, in the belletristic sense, is more recent the philology. A century ago, scholars began their careers in Anglo-Saxon studies as "antiquarians" interested in archaeology. Archaeology was not regarded as scientific; instead, it was defined as the analysis of ancient monuments in their artistic aspect – an aesthetic evaluation, in other words, that followed on geology, paleontology, and anthropology.[7] Archaeology was a place to begin and a focus for first impressions of material culture that inspired later work with language and texts. This paradigm of amateurism and professionalism, which also juxtaposes analysis of physical remains and literary records, speaks to us most pointedly in terms of a figure who reversed it: he is John Mitchell Kemble, who began as a philologist and ended as an archaeologist and antiquarian.[8] Today, Anglo-Saxonists are either archaeologists or textual scholars. There are significant exceptions – Robert Farrell, Rosemary Cramp, Richard Bailey – but the chasm between literary work and archaeology seems to be growing.

Interdisciplinary work is supposed to reintegrate, but that cannot happen until we theorize about the disciplines. *Inter*disciplinary work means that you bring evidence from another field into your own – as I am supposedly doing here as a literary historian talking about Sutton Hoo – and view it through your own disciplinary spectacles. We assume that data viewed in a new context will reveal new insight, and in some measure this is true. Data seen differently from one discipline to the next are not different data; what is different is the vocabulary used to conceptualize, and to value, objects or texts. Although the vocabularies of various disciplines are different, they belong to systems of organization of data and detail that, from discipline to discipline, vary little if at all. The limitations of the "field" image are of concern to some archaeologists taking revisionary perspectives: they include J. C. Barrett[9] and Michael Shanks and Christopher Tilley. With the help of a striking pair of books on archaeology by Shanks and Tilley, *Re-Constructing Archaeology: Theory and Practice* and *Social Theory and Archaeology*, I would like to examine the relation of disciplines to identity and difference.[10]

To distinguish a discipline from interdiscipline, let us consider the relationship of identity to difference. Disciplines focus on identity – the identity of objects and texts within their own catagories: literary genres, in my case, or other intra-disciplinary distinctions, such as that between artistic and utilitarian writing; oral versus written tradition, and so forth. Like archaeologists, as they shift and classify data, scholars in all disciplines fit their materials into abstract catagories, which Shanks and Tilley call typologies (not to be confused with typology in the sense usual in medieval literary criticism). In this operation, the identity of a specific typological category will require that some data be left to one side as contingent. "Such a typological framework systematically excludes *difference* and instead asserts *identity*," they write. The identity of all members of one class allows them to be

---

[7]See P. Levine, *The Amateur and the Professional: Antiquarians, Historians and Archaeologists in Victorian England, 1838-1886* (Cambridge 1986).

[8]See R. A. Wiley (ed.) *John Mitchell Kemble and Jakob Grimm: A Correspondence* (Leiden 1971); and G. P. Ackerman, "J. M. Kemble and Sir Frederick Madden: 'Conceit and too much Germanism?'" in C. T. Berkhout and M. McC. Gatch (eds.) *Anglo-Saxon Scholarship: The First Three Centuries* (Boston 1982), 167-81.

[9]J. C. Barrett, "Fields of Discourse: Reconstituting a Social Archaeology," *Critique of Archaeology* 7.3 (1987-88), 5-16. See also S. M. Foster, "Analysis of Spacial Patterns in Buildings (Access Analysis) as an Insight into Social Structure: Examples from the Scottish Atlantic Iron Age," *Antiquity* 63 (1989), 40-50.

[10]M. Shanks and C. Tilley, *Reconstructing Archaeology: Theory and Practice* (Cambridge 1987); *Social Theory and Archaeology* (Albuquerque 1988).

differentiated from other classes. They continue, "However, difference is not to be derived from the supposed identity of differential social forms – it makes these abstract catagories possible in the first place."[11] They conclude that difference therefore deconstructs the possibility of rigid catagories. I would like to extend this concept of typologies to describe the methods by which all disciplines sort and classify evidence, and would like to suggest that difference for disciplines also deconstructs the possibility of rigid intellectual categories, not only difference within a given discipline, but difference between two disciplines, the difference that *defines* them. The construction of disciplinary identity is only possible in the presence of recognized differences. Difference is not derived from the identity it makes possible.

Intradisciplinary identities are constructed by all disciplines as ways of organizing data. Intradisciplinary identities seem to establish interdisciplinary differences, but how does an individual discipline know what is proper to it, and what is not? How does the discipline decide what belongs to it and what does not. Disciplines could not maintain their individual identities without interdisciplinary differences; but interdisciplinary differences are created by the identifying procedures of the disciplines themselves. The answer is that no one knew, but that someone somewhere began to take action, to classify and label, and that his (I am pretty sure of "his") decisions were institutionalized (first repeated once, then many times, finally constituting a norm). We have forgotten this point, I think. We regard disciplines as antiques when they are modern reproductions. The conditions in which they were produced (thought up, invented) in the last century in particular ensured that the disciplines themselves could not be too dissimilar. It was 1936 before Tolkien declared that *Beowulf* had been too much a poem for history and not enough a poem for art;[12] the controversy about Kevin Kiernan's book on the dating of the poem (and not an attack on its artistic integrity) shows that the historicity of *Beowulf* still matters more than anything else about it.[13]

The vocabularies of various disciplines may be distinct, but the disciplines themselves, in large part because of the circumstances of their historical formation (which I do not want to oversimplify), reflect and reinforce similar classification systems, and similar class attitudes. They may be seen as homologous systems; they are matching in structure, position, character. Rather than several disciplines that do different things, we have a vast homology that does the same thing in several ways. No wonder literary historians, archaeologists, and others agree and find it relatively easy to speak to each other. At a fundamental level, they speak the same language, they reconstruct the same culture.

Let me illustrate this idea of typologies, with reference to Sutton Hoo and *Beowulf*. The most famous and influential example of relating archaeology to literature is C.L. Wrenn's essay on *Beowulf* scholarship up to 1958 in his revision of Chambers' introduction to *Beowulf*. Wrenn regarded the discovery of Sutton Hoo as "the most important happening" since Thorkelin made a transcript of the *Beowulf* manuscript and first published the poem. This is a significant equation of textual and material evidence to which I will return. Wrenn reads *Beowulf* in the light of Sutton Hoo and reads Sutton Hoo in the light of *Beowulf*, a classic version of the hermeneutic circle, but not the first in Anglo-Saxon studies. The 1910 discovery of the burial mound of Ottar Vendel-Crow prompted Birger Nerman, and then Chambers himself, to use archaeological evidence to explain the struggles between the Geatas and the Swedes in *Beowulf*, and then use the chronology of *Beowulf* (none too certain!) to establish the position of Sweden as "the oldest of all European kingdoms."[14] It was not Wrenn in 1958, but Sune Lindqvist in 1948, who established the most important relationship between the poem and the find; Lindqvist enthusiastically remarked of *Beowulf* and Sutton Hoo that "both become the clearer by the comparison."[15]

It is not easy to see how either of two things can become clearer by comparison only to the other; there must be a third term in this equation, a place where they are brought together, compared, and found compatible. The

---

[11]Shanks and Tilley, *Social Theory and Archaeology*, 149.

[12]J. R. R. Tolkien, "Beowulf: the Monsters and the Critics," *PBA* 22 (1936), 245-95; reprinted in L. E. Nicholson (ed.) *An Anthology of Beowulf Criticism* (Notre Dame 1963), 51-103.

[13]K. Kiernan, *"Beowulf" and the Beowulf Manuscript* (New Brunswick 1981).

[14]R. W. Chambers, *Beowulf: an Introduction to the Study of the Poem with a Discussion of the Stories of Offa and Finn*, 3rd ed., with a Supplement by C. L. Wrenn (Cambridge 1959), 417-18.

[15]Quoted in Chambers, *Beowulf*, 510.

"third term," as I call it, is a typological concept created and made traditional, inflected by ideology, and quite independent of the vocabulary of any single discipline. Wrenn, Lindqvist, and others found the evidence of the poem and of the burial compatible because the poem and the archaeological evidence both already conformed to overriding ideas of Anglo-Saxon England and its culture that these scholars accepted. Such ideas govern classification systems. We can call them "ideologies" or "desires" or, so far as I am concerned, anything so long as the term does not imply neutrality, as, for example, "commonplace" or "tradition" or "paradigm" may do. Typologies explain things before they are recognized as problems; they create the expectation of patterns of change and continuity; and they assist scholars in establishing the relationships of pieces of evidence to one another and to a larger social schema. Typologies in the disciplines that comprise Anglo-Saxon studies serve a normative function as they create ordering concepts: the categories are not value-neutral, but actually help determine what will be remembered by means of them. Without such concepts we could not have disciplines of knowledge; with them, however, and only with them, we cannot have interdisciplines of knowledge.

The typology of Anglo-Saxon culture most familiar to us is that preferred by many of the culture's historians and archaeologists. It is the world of the epic, of aristocracy, of Germanic antiquity sauced with monastic learning, with pagan and Christian mixed just right. The Sutton Hoo artefacts point to aristocratic culture; *Beowulf* points the same way. That is why so many of these comparisons focus on armor and decoration and gold, with the splendor that these objects imparted to the words in the poem. Sutton Hoo furnished "the lavish world of the poem," as Patrick Wormald calls it, with "the material deposits of seventh-century Britain."[16] The treasures of Sutton Hoo are a powerful temptation to furnish Anglo-Saxon kingship with splendors described rather generically in *Beowulf*. The ideological force of a magnificent material culture, even incompletely represented, is difficult to resist. Ferdinand Braudel is one of the few to write about its allure – what he calls the world of wealth and riches to which the scholars are "secretly drawn."[17]

Attention to aristocratic levels of culture is almost automatic, even among some theorists who think in both archaeological and literary terms. Paul Zumthor, in *Speaking in the Middle Ages*, writes that we are archaeologists, not tourists, "in the city of the medieval culture" and that it is our job to fit together and to speculate on the relationship of pieces "with enough sensitivity to discern where that now broken line was leading, to see which way was pointed that sculpted arrow you just picked up among the thorns."[18] In this example, a literary critic speculates helpfully about contact with material culture, but does so in the context of an urban reference for medieval culture and with visual focus on a weapon. Anglo-Saxon archaeology is not particularly urban in emphasis, but it is aristocratic. The city and the court are much more impressive than the barbarism that surrounded them.

Eager to save Anglo-Saxon England from its reputation for barbarism, we glory in the brooches and regalia that testify to sophisticated taste and craftsmanship. We trace treasures to the aristocratic milieu of *Beowulf*, whether or not they illustrated it, as Wrenn thought them to do, and use them to reinforce the gaze of the poem itself on the highest levels of the culture. Swords, helmets, royal standards, drinking bowls, and the little harp are the objects on which Wrenn lavishes attention, all because they are also important in *Beowulf*. Best of all, the artefacts are abundantly multicultural: silver spoons with inscriptions in Greek majuscule attesting to Christian belief, Merovingian coins, Swedish work on the sword, and so forth; thus Sutton Hoo supplies evidence for nearly every cultural perspective on Anglo-Saxon England that has been taken, and so fuels contradictory arguments about the poem's genesis (not to mention the culture's) without forcing awkward retractions. Sutton Hoo was a treasure indeed.

---

[16]P. Wormald, "Bede, 'Beowulf' and the Conversion of the Anglo-Saxon Aristocracy," in R. T. Farrell (ed.) *Bede and Anglo-Saxon England* (Oxford 1978), 32-95; quotation from p. 36.

[17]F. Braudel, *On History*, trans. S. Matthews (Chicago 1980), 125; L. Patterson quotes Braudel and comments on the reaction to emphasis on the aristocratic in Renaissance New Historicism; see *Negotiating the Past: The Historical Understanding of Medieval Literature* (Madison 1987), 70.

[18]P. Zumthor, *Speaking of the Middle Ages*, trans. S. White (Lincoln and London 1986), 27.

I propose that we consider an interdisciplinary investigation into some aspect of Sutton Hoo, or any other archaeological discovery that links the literary and the material, by divesting ourselves of the disciplinary apparatus that turns such conferences as this one into the unassimilable circuses that they are. For example, we could take a concept central to Sutton Hoo, "aristocracy" and take up its inconspicuous counterpart, "slavery" or perhaps better, "labor," and build our seminar around these two words and the third that they make necessary and that Sutton Hoo makes obvious: "power." "Aristocracy" and "labor" are typological concepts that subsume concrete data (objects or texts) into systems of organization. They posit social systems around objects and texts, but often with little reference to the constructedness – the unexamined historical character – of the system. Our notion of an "Anglo-Saxon king" is such a notion; so is our idea of the "Anglo-Saxon hero," and the Old English elegy is another.

The kind of interdisciplinary venture I imagine could begin with a material object – a crown, a pin – and grow to include every known reference to its manufacture, importation or exportation, restoration, and discovery; the textuality of the object – writing on it and about it – would be assembled. With enough planning and funding, participants could visit the site of its discovery or manufacture and become familiar with the circumstances of the site and its history. We could assemble evidence and interpretations of evidence from as many perspectives as possible, not because we would want these views to reinforce each other, but because we could then begin to undo the homologies and deconstruct the categories, the systems of organizing data and texts that are themselves part of larger concepts.

Undoing those homologies is an essential first step. Each disciplinary typology has an attitude towards history and culture, but on one important point our disciplines conform. Discussing the typology used to explain evolutionary theory, Shanks and Tilley write that it casts history as "an overall intelligible unity and continuum,"[19] or what I would call a unified concept conforming to the paradigm of progress. This notion of progress, the idea that human history moves forward without significant disruption from age to age, changing inevitably as new discoveries are made, posits the very harmony and logic to the study of the past that study of the past is supposed to investigate. The disciplines of Anglo-Saxon studies cooperate so well because they share the same underlying assumptions about history and culture. The most important of those assumptions is that Anglo-Saxon England was a culture on its way to becoming our culture. That is why it made progress from pagan to Christian, from oral to lettered, from illiterate to literate, from chaos to order. Those transitions were made first and surest at the aristocratic level; hence that is the level that holds our gaze.

The seminar I propose would begin by challenging the assumptions of the paradigm of progress (not that this is a new idea, I know), and the role such assumptions play in validating our work. We would then be identifying the points in the history of scholarship at which these assumptions began to take hold. A seminar in "aristocracy," as the concept is constituted by history, archaeology, literary criticism, and political science, would include more than kings and queens. In the evidence of Anglo-Saxon culture, it would direct our attention to non-aristocratic levels assumed to be unimportant, even though without them the aristocracy could not have survived; outside Anglo-Saxon culture, it would direct our attention to the history of our disciplines and the power disciplines have over the evidence they study. We would have to examine the political theory of kingship; we would have to examine the narratives of royal force, including chronicle, genealogy, history, and epic; we would have to discuss the objects of the aristocracy, as well as their religion, laws, and recreation.

The point of the seminar would be to emphasize how the assumptions of a given discipline control the way it structures evidence, and why a different discipline structures that evidence – and, therefore, sees it as "true" – in another way. We would have a genuinely "interdisciplinary" or (better) "historically contextual" discussion: not a contest to see who was right, but a comparison of the relation of truth claims to fundamental disciplinary theory and method. We would not be arguing that one discipline had more truth at its disposal than another, or that the signifying practices of one were better than those of the other. Instead we would look for what all the disciplines leave out; and we would find ourselves discussing the relationship of truth claims to those who have constructed them. The seminar would force us to look not so much at the boundaries of our "fields" but at the points at which

---

[19]Shanks and Tilley, *Social Theory*, 148.

the discursive regularities of our disciplines – habits of thought, traditions of regarding evidence, modes of classification – intersect. The model for the seminar would be a web rather than a series of parallel and regularly spaced lines; the seminar would negate the discursive definitions that distinguish literature from history, archaeology from art history, philology from literary criticism, and would replace them with new concepts that acknowledge the obvious condition of the evidence: that "Anglo-Saxon England" was once an undifferentiated mass of artefacts and texts that have been organized into the shapes of the modern curriculum. However neat that organization is, every Anglo-Saxonist, I believe, acknowledges not only that it is artificial but also that it is inadequate.[20]

My emphasis on "labor" and "slavery" as a counterpoint to "aristocracy" has an unmistakably political and revisionist ring to it. I do not wish to imply that interdisciplinary learning requires us to adopt only oppositional or deconstructionist perspectives, but I do believe that analysis that challenges received ideas and typologies is precisely what we should undertake. The concept of a discipline of knowledge implies limitations that create the necessity for interdisciplinary approaches. Disciplines are inadequate, but not because none of them can include all evidence relevant to certain issues; indeed, such limitation – that is, difference – is the very reason disciplines are perpetuated. Rather, the disciplines that together study Anglo-Saxon culture are inadequate because they all do the same thing, and all likewise fail to do other things. Women's and black studies programs, among other interdisciplinary undertakings, succeed for an important reason: not to proliferate academic positions, but to address cultural problems that traditional disciplines have ignored. The *in*adequacy of these disciplines, not their adequacy, undergirds, and gives great strength to, the theses of these cultural studies programs. A seminar such as that I propose would be an attempt to address cultural issues in Anglo-Saxon studies that are largely neglected by all its disciplines. The treasures of Sutton Hoo, like the material splendors of *Beowulf*, offer vivid reminders of what it is that scholarship of Anglo-Saxon culture so often seems to slight.

The impact of Sutton Hoo on Anglo-Saxon literary criticism cannot be observed only by reading what Wrenn and others wrote after the find. Equally interesting is what was thought about Anglo-Saxon civilization before the treasure was discovered, uncovered, and recovered. E. T. Leeds's 1936 publication on the primitive Anglo-Saxon village at Sutton Courtenay supplies an interesting view of Anglo-Saxon culture as far from the material splendor that Wrenn describes as one could hope. Leeds writes of small huts, ten by twelve feet, with little headroom, sometimes with postholes for looms that took up even more of the scant room available. (These looms were sites for weaving – for story-telling and for making fabric; they were places in the middle of the huts, not apart from the domestic dwelling in weaving sheds. Their importance for narrative theory awaits attention; I wish that as much had been written about looms in Anglo-Saxon England as about harps.) Leeds writes:

> In such cabins, with bare head-room, amid a filthy litter of broken bones, of food and shattered pottery, with logs or planks raised on stones for their seats or couches, lived the Anglo-Saxons. The fact that the house described above represents the most pretentious effort among thirty hardly leaves hope that at first even the chieftains could provide themselves with much greater comfort or luxury...[21]

Of course, *Beowulf* is not about a primitive culture; and Leeds did find a "more pleasing picture" in Kent.[22] Leeds's remark reminds me of John Ruskin's comment about the lovely sixth-century church on Torcello, the inconspicuous island near Venice, with a single church, modest enough after the splendors of Venice, but very beautiful. Ruskin notes that the pillars and arches seen on the approach to the church of Santa Fosca lift it only "to the height of a cattle shed" – not very promising – and adds that:

---

[20]For a clear and helpful discussion of some of these concepts, see F. Lentricchia's analysis of Foucault in *After the New Criticism* (Chicago 1980), 199-210.

[21]E. T. Leeds, *Early Anglo-Saxon Art and Archaeology* (Oxford 1936; repr. Westport, CN 1970), 26.

[22]*Ibid.*

> The first strong impression which the spectator receives from the whole scene is, that whatever sin it may have been which has on this spot been visited with so utter a desolation, it could not at least have been ambition.[23]

We should not imitate Ruskin's deprecating glance at a simple material culture because it fails to rise to the image of what we want it to look like. For Ruskin, an enormously influential art and architecture critic, and a philosopher of labor (after a fashion), to look on Venice was to look on the sad emptiness of his own failed sexuality. The tragedy of Venice, its fall to the East, was the corruption of the medieval virgin into the Renaissance whore. Venice and Torcello were stages for the play of his psyche. "Mother and daughter," he wrote, "you behold them both in their widow-hood."[24] But it was not only his mother's sexuality, or his own, that obsessed him. The Middle Ages were corrupted by commerce, Ruskin believed, in much the same way that industrialization had destroyed English life. In "The Nature of Gothic," another essay from *The Stones of Venice*, Ruskin wrote, "And now, reader, look around this English room of yours, of which you have been proud so often, because the work of it was so good and strong, and the ornaments of it so finished." He continued, "Alas! if read rightly, these perfectnesses are signs of slavery in our England a thousand times more bitter and more degrading than that of the scourged African, or helot Greek."[25] Ruskin linked the mechanization of labor in his time with the idealization of labor in the Middle Ages; this medieval ideal was, he believed, destroyed by commerce, just as modern life was degraded by it.

I have chosen to conclude with a view of medieval material culture through the eyes of a Victorian critic for several reasons. Ruskin was fully conscious of his role as a cultural mediator; he was unrestrained by the academic and disciplinary boundaries already clearly formed around him (he had other constraints, obviously); his reading of the Italian Renaissance shows how material culture becomes textualized as it is "read"; and he expected his readers to reverse the process and move from text to material culture as they held Ruskin's text and looked up from it to regard the surrounding modern space.

Not every visitor to Torcello accepts Ruskin's criticism of Santa Fosca, and not every reader of *Beowulf* has been dazzled by the aristocratic artefacts referred to in the text, or even by the culture's most revered figure, King Alfred. Stuart P. Sherman, taught by George Lyman Kittredge and thereafter a virulent anti-medievalist, compared the atmosphere of Kittredge's seminar after "the analysis and destruction of a great piece of German interpretation" to "a glow of satisfaction as must have thrilled the blood of a red-handed Saxon churl when he assisted good King Alfred in flaying off a Dane skin and nailing it up on a church door."[26] Also concerned about the Anglo-Saxon churl, but rather less sarcastic, was Vida Dutton Scudder, an American medievalist writing about *Beowulf* in 1898, who commented that the poem never so much as took notice of the peasants whose lives framed those of the poem's heroic figures. She wrote:

> In this precious ancient poem, through which the Teutonic race sees dimly its heroic past, a village, slightly mentioned, lies to be sure somewhere in the background, but eyes are fixed on noble Heorot Hall, gold-timbered, fiend-ravaged, where the heroes feast and brag. In battle, the common people hardly exist, even to be slain; in revel the queen herself is cup bearer, for no vulgar hand may minister to the princely warriors. Into this society, fiercely respectful toward the fighter with a pedigree, contemptuous toward the nameless churl, the chanting monks of Augustine, and earlier the Celtic missionaries with a Christianity of more childlike type, introduced a new ideal.[27]

---

[23] J. Ruskin, "Torcello," in *The Stones of Venice*, vol. 2, quoted from E. T. Cook and A. Wedderburn (eds.) *The Works of John Ruskin*, 39 vols. (London 1904), 10:20.

[24] Ruskin, "Torcello," 18.

[25] Ruskin, "The Nature of Gothic," in *The Stones of Venice*, vol. 2 in Cook and Wedderburn (eds.) *Works*, 10:193.

[26] S. P. Sherman, "Professor Kittredge and the Teaching of English," published in *The Nation* in 1913 and reprinted in G. Graff and M. Warner (eds.) *The Origins of Literary Studies in America: A Documentary Anthology* (New York 1989), 147-55; see p. 151.

[27] V. D. Scudder, *Social Ideals in English Letters* (New York 1898), 7. I thank Matt Matcuk for bringing this quote to my attention.

Scudder, of course, was commenting on the world-view of Anglo-Saxons, and I have been commenting on the world-view of Anglo-Saxonists; the similarities in the points of view are, I believe, unfortunate. Speaking of the view of medieval culture she strove for in survey courses she taught, Scudder, some forty years later, observed that the "phenomena of the collective life determined by economic conditions are always implicit as a shaping force, they are the background even when the foreground is occupied by private reaction." She added, "One need be no Marxist to recognize this, though as Marx helps us increasingly in our understanding of life and its movements, I hope and expect that such courses as I feebly sought to initiate are likely to multiply."[28] No Marxist, I must say that Scudder's attention to material culture and economic conditions would still be productive for Anglo-Saxon studies, and, today, no less revolutionary.

It is, no doubt, predictable that thoughts about Anglo-Saxon outsiders should come from a scholar who saw herself as an outsider in American academic life and who entertained no delusions about her place in the Anglo-Saxon scholarship of her time. Ruskin's view of Venice and Torcello is, ostensibly, merely a sentimental correlation of commerce and sexual experience with an idealized desire for a simpler past. His critical paradigm, self-consciously economic and at least subconsciously sexual, demonstrates how his study of medieval texts and artefacts was heavily invested – layered over with – the class preferences, sexual history, and social ambition. Prejudices and preferences of a different kind emerge in the views of medieval studies and Anglo-Saxon England taken by Sherman and Scudder, and both of them offer a real tonic to the attitudes of Ruskin and others whose attitudes shaped the history of our disciplines. Scholarly disciplines embody more than their mental operations. Digging into and under those attitudes and statements, and linking them to the scholarly discourse that constitutes disciplines is what archaeological analysis and interdisciplinary studies demand. Such studies bring us into contact with personal histories and identities, and it is in the intersection of those histories and public, scholarly discourse that we will find the connections we desire when we turn ourselves to interdisciplinary work. Those connections are constructions; they depend on deconstructions that enable others to know not just the past but also ourselves and our image of Anglo-Saxon England.

[28]V. D. Scudder, *On Journey* (New York 1937); quoted in Graff and Warner, *The Origins of Literary Studies in America*, 176-77.

Sutton Hoo and Seventh-Century Art

RICHARD N. BAILEY

T. D. Kendrick's classic study of *Anglo-Saxon Art* was published in 1938.[1] Within a year however much of the thesis which he had advanced in the early chapters of his book had been undermined by the discoveries at Sutton Hoo. Suddenly, as he saw it, "the principal problems of the Pagan Period in England now seem to be simplified, if not indeed resolved."[2] Fifty years later, of course, simplification and resolution still elude us, but Kendrick was clearly correct when he recognized that Sutton Hoo, poised on "the threshold of Christian England," would have a profound effect on our understanding of sixth and seventh-century art in Britain. It has provided crucial evidence for identifying Celtic, Scandinavian and Frankish contributions to early Anglo-Saxon culture as well as enhancing our appreciation of what Leeds described as the "final phase" of pagan art in the seventh century.[3] Chronologically it has been the (somewhat shifting) buoy to which art historical arguments have persistently been moored.[4] Above all, as Kendrick foresaw, it is now impossible "to debate the origins of our Christian art without paying respectful attention to this new evidence from Suffolk;"[5] and that new evidence has subsequently been deployed in every battle which has raged over the disputed territory of early Insular illumination.[6]

In a sense my paper is peripheral to the main concern of this collection of studies. But it follows Kendrick's lead in looking forward from Sutton Hoo, and is only peripheral in a temporal and geographical sense. I propose to examine some aspects of the art of Sutton Hoo from the other end of the century and from the other end of the country, by looking at material emerging from Benedict Biscop's Northumbrian foundations at Monkwearmouth (A.D. 674) and Jarrow (A.D. 685) together with Wilfrid's monastery at Hexham (c. A.D. 673/4). From these relatively safe environs I will then move to the Bernician fortress at Bamburgh before straying into the tangled undergrowth of the Book of Durrow.

II

One of the motifs employed on the silver from Sutton Hoo Mound One reappears briefly among the architectural sculptures of Northumbrian churches in the late seventh and early eighth centuries. Significantly however there has been a change in its function and meaning over the period which separates its occurrence in East Anglia and its use in northern England.

The motif is one which is familiar in Late Antique art. In multiple form it occurs on the edge of the Anastasius dish whilst a disguised linear version makes up the crosses on the ten silver bowls (fig. 1 a-b).[7] The basic design is deliberately ambiguous. When it covers a large surface, as on the Anastasius dish, then it can be read as a series

---

[1]T. D. Kendrick, *Anglo-Saxon Art to A.D. 900* (London 1938).

[2]T. D. Kendrick, "Sutton Hoo and Saxon Archaeology," *British Museum Quarterly* 13 (1939), 136.

[3]E. T. Leeds, *Early Anglo-Saxon Art and Archaeology* (Oxford 1936), 96-114; A. Ozanne, "The Peak Dwellers," *MA* 6-7 (1963), 15-52; A. Meaney and S. C. Hawkes, *Two Anglo-Saxon Cemeteries at Winnall, Winchester, Hampshire*, Medieval Archaeology Monographs IV (London 1970).

[4]See, for example, G. Haseloff, "Fragments of a Hanging Bowl from Bekesbourne, Kent, and some Ornamental Problems," *MA* 2 (1958), 82-83, 88.

[5]Kendrick, "Sutton Hoo," 136.

[6]C. Nordenfalk, "Before the Book of Durrow," *Acta Archaeologica* 18 (1947), 141-74; R. L. S. Bruce-Mitford, "Decoration and Miniatures," in T. D. Kendrick, *et al.* (eds.) *Evangeliorum Quattuor Codex Lindisfarnensis*, II (Olten and Lausanne 1960), 109-260; F. Henry, "Les débuts de la miniature Irlandaise," *Gazette des Beaux-Arts*, 6e pér., 37 (1950), 5-34; F. Henry, *Irish Art in the Early Christian Period to 800 A.D.* (London 1965); D. M. Wilson, *Anglo-Saxon Art from the Seventh Century to the Norman Conquest* (London 1984); G. Henderson, *From Durrow to Kells: The Insular Gospel Books 650-800* (London 1987); D. Ó Cróinín, "Merovingian Politics and Insular Calligraphy: the Historical Background to the Book of Durrow and Related Manuscripts," in M. Ryan (ed.) *Ireland and Insular Art A.D. 500-1200* (Dublin 1987), 40-43.

[7]R. L. S. Bruce-Mitford, *The Sutton Hoo Ship Burial*, III (London 1983), figs. 20C and 61-62, 66.

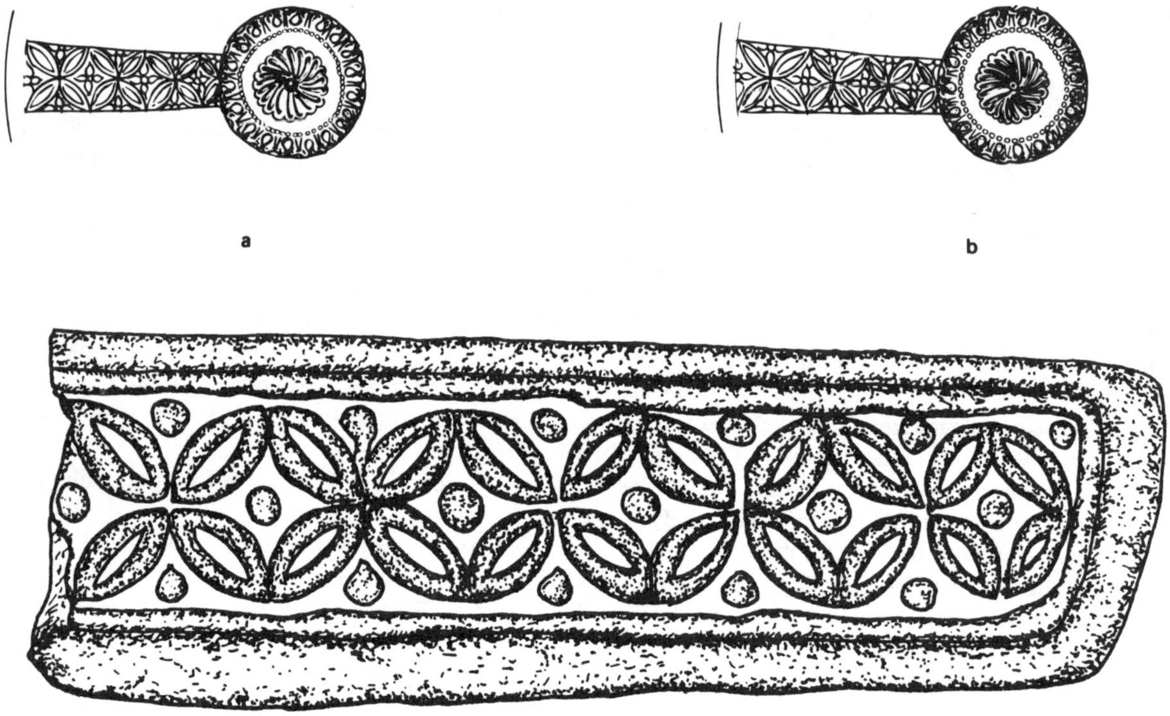

a

b

c

Fig. 1. (a) and (b) Sutton Hoo hanging bowls (after Bruce-Mitford 1983); (c) Ledsham chancel arch frieze.

of interlocking circles; in a simple linear form it can be interpreted as a row of contiguous four-leaved flowers; it can also be seen as a set of circles which each contain a diamond formed with arcuated sides. Rupert Bruce-Mitford has discussed the parallels for the Sutton Hoo pieces[8] but for present purposes it is sufficient to note that this ornament is merely an incidental part of the display of exotic foreign wealth in the burial. The motif itself, apart from its cruciform suggestiveness, is empty of meaning.

Sculptured versions of the same ambiguous decoration are found in Northumbria at Jarrow, at Hexham (and at Simonburn nearby), as well as at Ledsham in North Yorkshire (fig. 1c).[9] Unlike the makers of the Sutton Hoo silver bowls the artists who produced this carved motif were Anglo-Saxons and in choosing it they were making a conscious cultural statement. They were deliberately echoing an ornamental scheme which was familiar in the art and architecture of contemporary churches in Italy, north Africa, Gaul and the Iberian peninsula;[10] a frieze in the church of San Juan de Baños, inscription dated to A.D. 661, provides an excellent parallel from within two

[8] *Ibid.*, 32-45, 114-22.

[9] R. Cramp, *Corpus of Anglo-Saxon Stone Sculpture*, I, *County Durham and Northumberland*, 2 vols. (Oxford 1984), pls. 185 (1015), 218 (1238); R. N. Bailey, "Ledsham," *Bulletin of the C.B.A. Churches Committee* 18 (1983), 6-8.

[10] J. Hubert, *et al.*, *Europe in the Dark Ages* (New York and London 1969), pls. 90, 241, 248, 266; J. B. Ward Perkins and R. G. Goodchild, "The Christian Antiquities of Tripolitania," *Archaeologia* 95 (1953), pls. XVII-XIX; T. Ulbert, "Skulptur in Spanien," in V. H. Elbern and V. Milojčić (eds.) *Kolloquium über spätantike und frühmittelalterliche Skulptur* (Mainz 1971), *passim*; J. Fontaine, *L'art préroman hispanique* (Paris 1973); A. de Lacerda, *História da Arte em Portugal*, I (Porto 1942); G. Panazza and A. Tagliaferri, *Corpus della scultura altomedievale*, III, *La Diocesi di Brescia* (Spoleto 1966), pl. xxvii.

decades of the foundation of both Jarrow and Hexham.[11] The motif represents a transplantation of contemporary Mediterranean *romanitas* to Northumbria. It is an ornamental expression of the unity of a faith which embraced the Mediterranean world *and* Anglo-Saxon England.

This first point of comparison between East Anglia and later Northumbria is not therefore one which involves any direct connection. Indeed, what it emphasizes is a break in tradition during the seventh century which resulted from the conversion. Other carvings from the north however tell a rather different story of continuity and to these I now turn.

III

Four of the sculptures from Monkwearmouth are particularly instructive here because they illustrate a deeply conservative element in the taste of late seventh and early eighth-century Northumbria, a conservatism which emerges when they are compared with material from Sutton Hoo. Two of these carvings are on the west portal of the porch at Monkwearmouth. They are now heavily worn but it is still possible to distinguish two confronting beasts' heads, their sling jaws interlocked, whose snake-like bodies form the arris moulding of the jamb stones on which they are carved. The bodies link together into a simple twist at the bottom of the stone, terminating beneath the beasts' jaws in fish-like tails (fig. 2b).[12] The tau-cross shape of the animals' twisted bodies is probably significant.[13] Since the porch clearly post-dates the west wall of the church (and thus presumably the A.D. 674 foundation date) and since the portal itself may even be a replacement of a less elaborate opening, we are clearly dealing with carvings which date, at earliest, to the end of the century.[14] Yet the beasts' heads, with their prehensile jaws locked together, belong to a menagerie which can be seen much earlier in the century at Sutton Hoo on the border panels of the shoulder clasps or the maplewood bottle mounts;[15] an even more striking parallel is offered by the Bacton mount which has been described as, "perhaps an apprentice product of the Sutton Hoo workshop" (fig. 2a).[16] Whatever Christian and apotropaic significance has been invested in these Northumbrian carvings, therefore, they clearly depend upon an ornamental tradition which extends back to at least the early years of the seventh century.

Another Monkwearmouth beast, on what Rosemary Cramp suggests was part of a closure slab, betrays a similar conservatism (Pl. 1).[17] Its backward-biting prehensile jaws, arched ribbon body and coherent back leg all associate it with the beasts on the border panels of the Sutton Hoo shoulder clasps or the various animals decorating such well-known examples of style II animal art as the Allington Hill disc, the Faversham brooch backplate or the Crundale buckle backplate.[18] None of these parallels can post-date the middle of the century – and some are clearly much earlier – yet the earliest possible context for the Monkwearmouth slab is Benedict Biscop's A.D. 674 church.

---

[11]P. de Palol, *Arte hispanico de la época visigoda* (Barcelona 1968), pl. 53.

[12]Cramp, *Corpus*, I, pls. 112 (612), 113 (613), 115 (616-17).

[13]See R. B. K. Stevenson, "Aspects of Ambiguity in Crosses and Interlace," *UJA* 44-45 (1981-82), 1-27.

[14]H. M. Taylor and J. Taylor, *Anglo-Saxon Architecture*, 3 vols. (Cambridge 1965-78), I, 443; R. Cramp, "Monkwearmouth Church," *ArchJ* 133 (1976), 230-37.

[15]Bruce-Mitford, *Sutton Hoo Ship Burial*, III, fig. 261.

[16]G. Speake, *Anglo-Saxon Animal Art and its Germanic Background* (Oxford 1980), 34. For the entire composition Cramp (*Corpus*, I, 125-26) has pointed to a Merovingian parallel (N. Åberg, *The Occident and the Orient in the Art of the Seventh Century*, III, *The Merovingian Empire* (Stockholm 1947), fig. 22(1)), but equally relevant is the clasp ornament from Desborough, Northants. (Speake, *Anglo-Saxon Animal Art*, pl. 8f).

[17]Cramp, *Corpus*, I, 126, pl. 121 (656).

[18]Speake, *Anglo-Saxon Animal Art*, fig. 8 a, b, c, g. (This fig. also illustrates other relevant examples.)

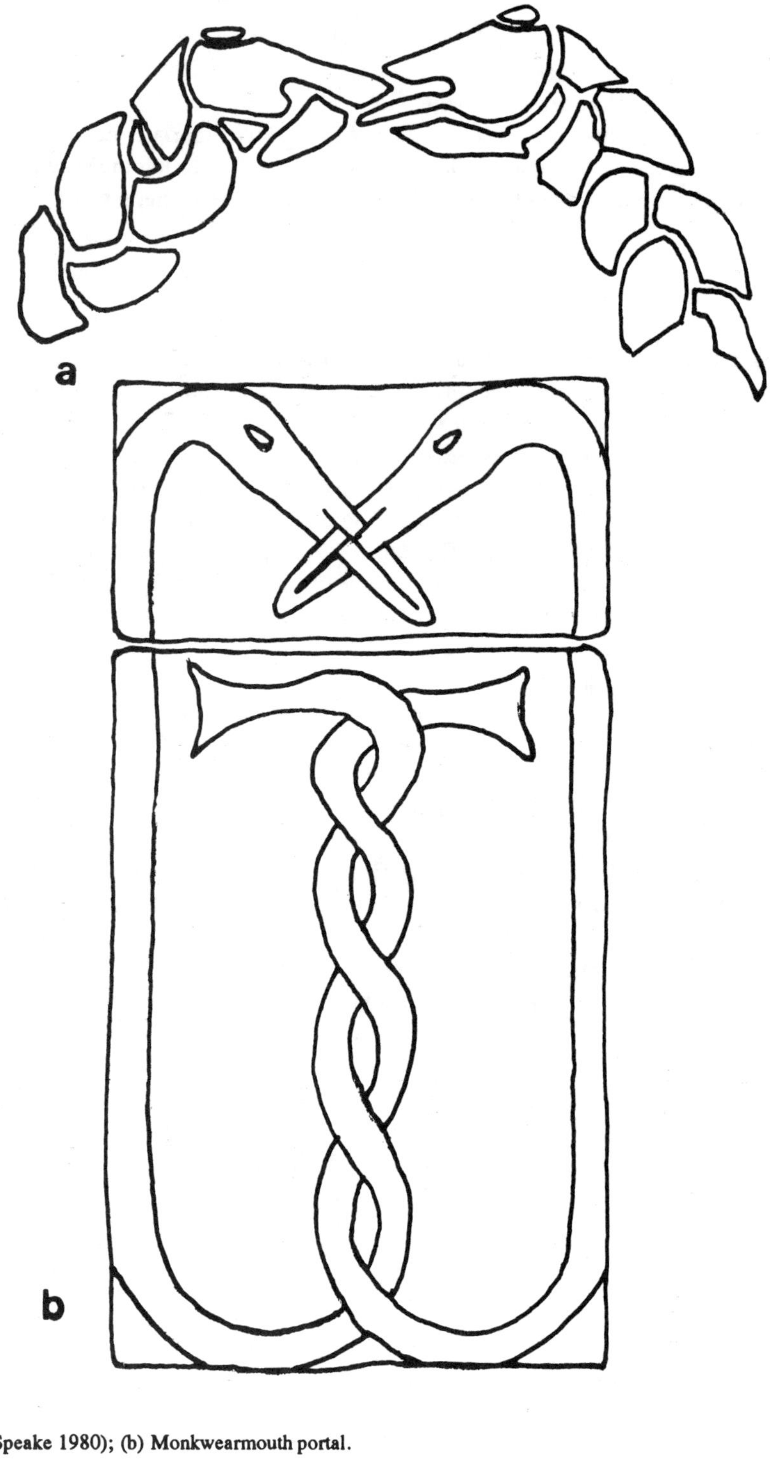

Fig. 2. (a) Bacton (after Speake 1980); (b) Monkwearmouth portal.

A fourth Monkwearmouth carving deserves some reconsideration in this pursuit of the archaic in Northumbria. The Herebericht slab has frequently been described.[19] Its inscription shows that its use as a memorial to Herebericht the priest was secondary; the profile of the stone and the variation in letter forms point to an earlier erasure. John Higgitt has suggested contexts in which the stone might have become available for re-use at an early date after its original carving but for our purposes it is sufficient to note that the sculpture probably belongs to the early years of the eighth century.[20]

The top of the slab has been broken off but above the upper arm of the cross are two features which Cramp has described as "wing-like" (Pl. 2).[21] Close examination shows that these are not wings, but eagles' beaks. If we now combine this identification with the observable fact that the sinister arris moulding thickens and turns inward at the break point on the stone, then it is possible to produce a restoration of the ornamental scheme along the lines illustrated in figure 3.

Fig. 3. Conjectural restoration of the Herebericht slab.

Two side issues require comment. Firstly, this restored version of the Herebericht slab seems to provide another example of that iconographical phenomenon which R. B. K. Stevenson noted in his discussions of the Hunterston

[19]Cramp, *Corpus*, I, pl. 110 (604); J. Higgitt, "The Dedication Inscription at Jarrow and its Context," *AntJ* 59 (1979), 360-61, 364-65.

[20]Higgitt, "Dedication Inscription," 364-65.

[21]Cramp, *Corpus*, I, 124.

brooch and the Monymusk reliquary where eagles' heads are set in close proximity to a cruciform shape.[22] Secondly, these zoomorphic terminals further strengthen the case long advocated by Isabel Henderson that the development of Pictish cross-slabs is dependent on Northumbrian models.[23] Not only does this Monkwearmouth stone offer a prototype for Pictish slabs carrying high relief crosses, it also presents a potential source for the zoomorphic-topped frames seen on such classic carvings as the Aberlemno churchyard stone.[24]

These Herebericht eagles now take their place alongside the portal beasts and the closure-slab animal in sharing a long ancestry in Anglo-Saxon art, reaching back to such Sutton Hoo objects as the gold buckle and the hanging bowl patch.[25] Since none of these Monkwearmouth carvings can pre-date A.D. 674, some fifty years after the last likely date of the Sutton Hoo ship burial, it follows that the Northumbrian artistic repertoire had within it a strongly conservative impulse. Paradoxically this backward-looking taste seems to have co-existed with an enthusiasm for transplanted Mediterranean motifs such as the circle ornament of Jarrow, Hexham and Ledsham – or the modeled animals which adorned the frieze set only four meters above the Monkwearmouth portal beasts.[26]

IV

All of this has a bearing on the vexed question of the relationship between Sutton Hoo and the Book of Durrow. Analogies between the art of the burial and of the manuscript have long been recognized. Bruce-Mitford, for example, emphasized the "closeness of Durrow to the metalwork of the late pagan period,"[27] whilst the wide-ranging links between Sutton Hoo and motifs employed in the Book of Durrow have recently been perceptively summarized in the text and plates of George Henderson's study.[28] The validity of the parallels is not in doubt, but they pose a difficult chronological problem.

It is a problem which was slow to emerge. As long as Sutton Hoo was assumed to belong to the middle years of the seventh century there was no temporal dislocation with the cognate art of the Book of Durrow, which was conventionally assigned to dates in the 650-680 period. But as the date of the burial began to retreat, an obvious difficulty arose. Wilson, writing in 1984, was one of the few scholars to face the issue squarely: "it has frequently been pointed out that the animals in the side panels of the page [f. 192v] are almost exactly the same as the butt end of the Sutton Hoo buckle. The design is so close that one wonders how as much as fifty years may separate them (perhaps it does not!)."[29] One radical solution to Wilson's dilemma was adopted by Uta Roth, who cut the Book of Durrow free from any evolutionary relationship with Durham A.II.10, the Lindisfarne Gospels or Durham A.II.17 and argued that it fits most happily at the beginning of the seventh century.[30] This dating is hardly likely to commend itself to paleographers nor even to those who recognize, with Henry,[31] that scholars should not too easily assume a single evolutionary line for Insular Gospel Books.

A more convincing response to the apparent chronological problem has recently come from Günther Haseloff, whose sensitive analysis has pointed to important differences between the animal art of Durrow and Sutton Hoo.[32]

---

[22]R. B. K. Stevenson, "The Hunterston Brooch and its Significance," *MA* 18 (1974), 38-40; R. B. K. Stevenson, "Further Notes on the Hunterston and 'Tara' Brooches, Monymusk Reliquary and Blackness Bracelet," *PSAS* 113 (1983), 474.

[23]I. Henderson, "Pictish Art and the Book of Kells," in D. Whitelock, *et al.* (eds.) *Ireland in Early Medieval Europe* (Cambridge 1982), 83-84.

[24]I. Henderson, *The Picts* (London 1967), pl.41.

[25]Bruce-Mitford, *Sutton Hoo Ship Burial*, III, fig. 179.

[26]Cramp, *Corpus*, I, pl. 117 (624-25).

[27]Bruce-Mitford, "Decoration and Miniatures," 256.

[28]Henderson, *From Durrow to Kells*, 32.

[29]Wilson, *Anglo-Saxon Art*, 34.

[30]U. Roth, "Early Insular Manuscripts: Ornament and Archaeology with Special Reference to the Dating of the Book of Durrow," in M. Ryan (ed.) *Ireland and Insular Art*, 23-29.

[31]F. Henry, "The Lindisfarne Gospels," *Antiquity* 37 (1963), 100-10.

[32]G. Haseloff, "Insular Animal Styles with Special Reference to Irish Art in the Early Medieval Period," in M. Ryan (ed.) *Ireland and Insular*

Yet another, complementary, approach to the same issue has of course been implicit in the previous section of this essay. If the Book of Durrow is a Northumbrian work (a point to which I will return below) then the evidence of late seventh and early eighth-century sculpture shows that some elements of the taste of Sutton Hoo were still alive north of the Humber some fifty years after the burial. Locating the manuscript in the second half of the seventh century is not therefore as difficult as might first appear.

V

I assumed in the last section that the Book of Durrow was a Northumbrian book. This is a presumption which is widely shared but I am well aware that it is not universally accepted.[33] My concern here is to add another element to the debate about its provenance by taking up a statement in Dáibhí Ó Cróinín's recent paper.[34] He first quotes an unpublished lecture in which D. H. Wright claimed that, "in some way not yet explained the artist of the Book of Durrow must have known a living tradition of the style and technique we find in the Sutton Hoo jewellery." Ó Cróinín then goes on to say that "there is no evidence (as far as I am aware) for metalwork in Northumbria in this period that compares with the material from Sutton Hoo ..." The thrust of his argument is that, even if there were such evidence, it would be irrelevant to the problem of locating the Durrow scriptorium. I do not wish to follow up that part of his article but rather to claim that there *is* evidence, unrecognized because it is so scattered, for the existence of Northumbrian (strictly Bernician) metalwork of the type he seeks. Once we acknowledge this fact, then we can combine it with the testimony of the Monkwearmouth sculptures discussed in section III to argue that there was still a "living tradition" of "Sutton Hoo" type art in late seventh-century Northumbria which could provide an appropriate context for the Book of Durrow.

The metalwork exists in three forms. Two of the three can be ignored since one of them depends upon documentary sources and the other on inference. The documentation comes from Bede who records the treasures of the mid-seventh-century Northumbrian court but since he gives no helpful descriptions his evidence cannot be exploited.[35] The inferential contribution comes from the relics of St. Cuthbert for, whatever deductions we draw from the silver casing of the portable altar, there can be little doubt that the pectoral cross belonged to the saint who died in A.D. 687. It is difficult to believe that its existence does not imply some local tradition of garnet and filigree working which stretches back earlier into the century.

Much more solid, however, is the evidence of surviving material.[36] In the British Museum is a gold and garnet sword hilt from Cumberland together with escutcheons from a hanging bowl which apparently came from Northumberland and are decorated with millefiori glass. From Dalmeny in West Lothian comes a garnet and gold pyramid. From Barrasford in the north Tyne Valley we know of a splendid shield with discs of silver which is now in the Alnwick collection of the Duke of Northumberland, whilst in the Joint Museum of Newcastle there is both a buckle set with garnets *en cabochon* from Boldon in County Durham and a hanging bowl from Capheaton.

This is metalwork which can justifiably be compared with Sutton Hoo. But more relevant to Durrow is a small gold foil fragment, decorated with zoomorphic ornament, which is now in the collection at Bamburgh Castle, where it was excavated by Brian Hope-Taylor.[37] The excavations have not been fully published but this "Bamburgh

---

Art, 45-47.

[33]See, for example, D. Ó Cróinín, "Rath Melsigi, Willibrord and the Earliest Echternach Manuscripts," *Peritia* 3 (1984), 17-49; Ó Cróinín, "Merovingian Politics."

[34]Ó Cróinín, "Merovingian Politics," 42.

[35]B. Colgrave and R. Mynors (eds.) *Bede's Ecclesiastical History of the English People* (Oxford 1969), 230, 290, 328.

[36]For this material see R. Miket, "A Restatement of Evidence for Bernician Anglo-Saxon Burials," in P. Rahtz, *et al.* (eds.) *Anglo-Saxon Cemeteries, 1979* (Oxford 1980), 289-305; L. Alcock, "Quantity or Quality: the Anglian Graves of Bernicia," in V. I. Evison (ed.) *Angles, Saxons and Jutes* (Oxford 1981), 168-83.

[37]B. Hope-Taylor, Report on Bamburgh Excavations, *University of Durham Gazette* (December 1960), 11-12; B. Hope-Taylor, Report on Bamburgh Excavations, *University of Durham Gazette* (March 1962), 5-6; B. Hope-Taylor, *Yeavering: An Anglo-British Centre of Early Northumbria* (London 1977), 370.

Fig. 4. (a) Sutton Hoo buckle; (b) "Bamburgh beast"; (c) and (d) Book of Durrow f.192v.

beast" has long been disseminated in replica form in guidebooks and souvenirs. The fragment shows an animal which fits neatly between the beast on the great gold buckle from Sutton Hoo and the more coherent menagerie of the Durrow procession (fig. 4). Its long jaws, closed in slings like those of the Monkwearmouth animals and the animals on the Caenby disc, can be compared with the extended jaws of the Sutton Hoo beasts, the animals of the Crundale sword pommel and the Allington Hill disc.[38] The eye set close to the back and top of the head reflects a persistent Style II theme which is present, *inter alia*, on the shoulder clasps, hanging bowl repair and shield boss from Sutton Hoo, on the Allington Hill disc, on a brooch from Faversham, on the sword pommel from Crundale and on a clasp from Tongres in Belgium.[39] The Bamburgh beast's foot-biting is, of course, a habit shared with his counterparts on the Sutton Hoo buckle and in the Book of Durrow whilst the three-toed foot set over the back is also a feature shared with the Durrow beasts. Noteworthy too is the looped back leg which is an affliction common to both the Bamburgh animal and the final beast in the Durrow procession.

Until the full report on Bamburgh is published we cannot know the context in which this fragment was found, but it forms a vital part of the evidence for arguing that seventh-century Northumbria, whilst lacking the known splendors of the Wuffinga treasury, nevertheless had its equivalent art which *could* have contributed to a locally-made Book of Durrow. A Northumbrian context might further be argued from Coatsworth's comparison between the manuscript's interlace and the conservatism of the closure slab at Monkwearmouth.[40] And the conservatism of the sculpture from Benedict Biscop's foundation shows that a *late* seventh-century date for Durrow would fit well with Northumbrian taste of that period; the "living tradition" of Sutton Hoo style which Wright sought still existed in the Anglian north at the end of the century.

VI

Having set out parts of a case for a late seventh-century Northumbrian Book of Durrow it is only prudent to acknowledge that there is a sense in which this evidence proves nothing. Whilst Irish-Northumbrian links before the Synod of Whitby have long been recognized, it is now fully apparent that those ties persisted throughout the seventh century and beyond both in ecclesiastical and secular circles.[41] James Campbell has recently suggested that it might be helpful to "think of Northumbria not so much as simply 'influenced' by Ireland but rather as being part of a continuum with it."[42] What sources were available in Northumbria were equally accessible to Ireland and *vice versa*. All that this essay claims therefore is that, in the debates about the origins of early Insular art, Northumbrian metalwork and the conservatism of its sculptural traditions should not be ignored.

ACKNOWLEDGEMENTS

I am grateful to the Bamburgh estate and Dr. Brian Hope-Taylor for permission to reproduce a drawing of the Bamburgh beast.

[38]Speake, *Anglo-Saxon Animal Art*, fig. 8 a, i, j.

[39]*Ibid.*, fig. 8a, c, f, j.

[40]In C. D. Verey, *et al.* (eds.) *The Durham Gospels (Durham, Cathedral Library MS A.II.17)*, EEMF XX (Copenhagen 1980), 57.

[41]K. Hughes, "Evidence for Contacts Between the Churches of the Irish and the English from the Synod of Whitby to the Viking Age," in P. Clemoes and K. Hughes (eds.) *England Before the Conquest* (Cambridge 1971), 49-67; H. Moisl, "The Bernician Royal Dynasty and the Irish in the Seventh Century," *Peritia* 2 (1983), 103-26; D. Ó Cróinín, "Is the Augsburg Gospel Codex a Northumbrian Manuscript?" in G. Bonner, *et al.* (eds.) *St. Cuthbert, His Cult and Community to A.D. 1200* (Woodbridge 1989), 189-201.

[42]J. Campbell, "Elements in the Background to the Life of St. Cuthbert and His Early Cult," in G. Bonner, *et al* (eds.) *St Cuthbert*, 4.

Pl. 1. Monkwearmouth: the closure slab (Photo: T. Middlemass; Copyright: University of Durham).

Pl. 2. Monkwearmouth: upper section of the Hereberícht slab (Photo: T. Middlemass; Copyright: University of Durham).

The Birds on the Sutton Hoo Instrument

KELLEY WICKHAM-CROWLEY

"Some scholars seem to think that science is mainly – even merely – a mechanized technique for collecting and analyzing objective facts. If this were true, no knowledge would be arrived at through insight."[1]

When the Sutton Hoo instrument was found, it was incomplete and broken in pieces, with its two bird ornaments scattered in among the contents of the great hanging bowl. It had apparently fallen from the burial chamber's west wall where it had hung in a beaver-skin bag; in its fall, it broke across the bowl. As first reconstructed, the ornaments were placed vertically along the side of an instrument resembling what we term a harp. After further fragments were pulled from those initially thought part of the burial chamber's roof, the instrument was reconstructed to resemble more closely both Anglo-Saxon manuscript depictions and the Continental analogs known to exist.[2] The ornaments are now correctly placed at the top of the instrument, below the curve of the yoke and across the joint that occurs on each side (Pls. 1-2).

---

[1]Einer Pálsson, "Hypothesis as a Tool in Mythology," in G. Steinsland (ed.) *Words and Objects: Towards a Dialogue Between Archaeology and History of Religion*, Institute for Comparative Research in Human Culture Series 70, (Oslo 1986), 165.

[2]Continental analogs include examples from St. Severin's Church in Cologne, beneath which a so-called "minstrel's grave" was found; a lyre, probably of sixth-century date, from Oberflacht, the replica of which was destroyed in the Berlin Museum für Völkerkunde in World War II; and a second example from Oberflacht, from grave 31, the remains of which are now in the Württembergisches Landesmuseum, Stuttgart. None was of the rounded form shown in Anglo-Saxon manuscripts, though the Oberflacht grave 31 lyre comes closest, and none had decorative or functional metal pieces just below the yoke. Further, while no physical evidence for a bridge survives at Sutton Hoo, the reconstruction possesses one modeled on that found at Broa, Gotland; no Anglo-Saxon manuscript illustration, however, actually depicts a bridge on the front of the instrument.

Two English manuscripts of the eighth century depict musical instruments that have been called lyres in recent times but that are surely the harps described in Anglo-Saxon texts (see note 3 below). The Durham Cassiodorus (Durham, Dean and Chapter Library, MS B.II.30 ff.81v and 172v) contains two full portraits of David, one of which shows him seated and playing an oval harp such as that found at Sutton Hoo. The harp is shown complete with a strap that braces the playing hand (here the left hand), while the right fingers delicately balance the body of the harp. This strap arrangement received archaeological confirmation from Graeme Lawson's discovery of a harp at Bergh Apton, Norfolk, on which metal fittings show where the strap had been attached (G. Lawson, "The Lyre from Grave 22," in B. Green and A. Rogerson, *The Anglo-Saxon Cemetery at Bergh Apton, Norfolk*, East Anglian Archaeology Report No. 7 [Gressenhall 1978], 87-97). Taplow itself may also provide evidence, through surviving pieces of leather strap with polygonal metal fittings (R. L. S. Bruce Mitford, *The Sutton Hoo Ship Burial*, III [London: 1983], 715). The second manuscript depiction in the Vespasian or Canterbury Psalter (London, BL Cotton Vespasian MS A.I, f.30v), again shows David, this time playing with his right hand without a wrist strap.

No other clear depictions of such harps exist. The Utrecht Psalter shows many types of stringed musical instruments, but they are all derived from classical models. Suzy Dufrenne has conveniently collected these illustrations on plate 100 of her work, *Les illustrations du Psautier D'Utrecht: Sources et apport carolingien* (Paris 1978). R. L. S. Bruce-Mitford noted a Gotlandic stone of the sixth century which seems to depict a harp or lyre similar to ours, but he does not show the context or give a complete reference to it (R. L. S. Bruce-Mitford and M. Bruce-Mitford, "The Sutton Hoo Lyre, *Beowulf*, and the Origins of the Frame Harp," *Antiquity* 44 [1970], pl. Vb.). This article also includes a sketch of a now lost patch from a bronze bowl showing a stringed instrument carried by a dancing or walking man. The use of such a patch calls to mind the bird-headed patch on the Sutton Hoo hanging bowl.

I have found one other depiction in sculpture on an Anglo-Saxon piece, but despite its description as a "lyre-like instrument" the slant of the strings and their length relative to the size of the instrument seem to indicate a harp more like the type we now associate with the term. The piece, part of a cross-shaft from Sockburn in County Durham, is illustrated in Professor Cramp's *Corpus of Anglo-Saxon Stone Sculpture in England* (vol. I, *County Durham and Northumberland* [Oxford 1984], pl. 720). My objections to the description "lyre" may, of course, be countered by the damage done to the piece and the difficulty of depicting this instrument, which could cause it to look out of proportion. However, the date assigned to the fragment (first half of the tenth century) would put it at least one-hundred years later than any other depiction of the oval type. While it may indeed be David who appears here, by the tenth century manuscripts show him playing the triangular instrument that we now call a harp, rather than the oval harp we know from Sutton Hoo.

These ornaments are clearly birds, given their beaks, and just as clearly, so are those at Taplow, on mounts of a similar musical instrument. The mounts in both cases are functional since they act as metal guards and reinforcements for the joint occurring on either side, just below the curved yoke section.[3] Of the possibly four Anglo-Saxon harps (or lyres) known, only those from Sutton Hoo and Taplow have individual metal images of figures on these mounts,[4] and these two burials are notably rich. The Bergh Apton, Norfolk, lyre was identified by its small, undecorated metal plates, and the lack of ornament matched the poor furnishings of the burial in general. In contrast, the Abingdon lyre, the possible fourth example, had no metal plates. Bruce-Mitford ascribed this lack to its early date, perhaps c. A.D. 450,[5] suggesting that it was a Continental piece brought over by an immigrant, though we cannot eliminate the possibility that a reinforcement of perishable material might have existed.

Given the notable coincidence of bird ornament in the two richest of the four burials, I would like to propose a context for these birds as deliberate and meaningful depictions. I should say at the outset that I can create sets of information here that need not intersect, using evidence from artefacts and from literary and historical references. I can briefly review evidence in three sets: (1) birds and their depictions and settings in Germanic contexts; (2) the spiritual concepts tying Odin, birds, poetry and song, especially the concept of metamorphosis; (3) and finally, the role of the musician (*scop* and/or *woðbora*) and its possible relationship both to birds and to Odin's worship.

There is no proof which can then unite all these groups of information: they are not perforce proved to interrelate. I can only demonstrate, by sheer weight of information and evidence, and by the apparent overlap of these three areas, that the sets have to do with one another, and that their context deepens our understanding of non-Christian Anglo-Saxon spiritual outlooks.[6]

DEPICTIONS OF BIRDS

Given that the appearance of bird pairs on both instruments is at least a surprising coincidence, I would like to point out several aspects of the birds' heads to fix the details clearly in mind. The main characteristics of the Sutton Hoo set are: (1) the beak, which is formed of a lower, slightly curved half and a longer, more curved upper half; (2) the large eye, formed of a central garnet surrounded by cuttlefish bone or shell, and a brow or crest line which oversails it and then follows down beside it, forming an angle; and (3) the throat, which has a pronounced point or projection to it, a characteristic of Style II. The mouths form a distinctive, Y-shaped indentation, that appears

---

[3]Bruce-Mitford, *Sutton Hoo Ship Burial*, III, 716.

[4]Archaeologists and commentators have used both "harp" and "lyre" to describe the instrument used by the Anglo-Saxons. Bruce-Mitford and his daughter, a professional musician who worked on the Sutton Hoo instrument, consider it a lyre. I use "harp" here purely because the term was that used by the Anglo-Saxons (*hearp*). I see no reason to change their terminology in light of our later understanding of the term as a triangular instrument enclosed on all sides, but I do not intend the use as dismissive of those who have used the term "lyre" in the past.

[5]Bruce-Mitford, *Sutton Hoo Ship Burial*, III, 718.

[6]I am not arguing for a completely non-Christian context for Sutton Hoo, though I certainly believe that the weight of tradition and observed ritual suggest that it was the dominant context. By this I mean that the burial itself, with ship and elaborate wealthy deposits, was not a Christian form, nor was Christianity sufficiently established in Kent at the time to merit terming it the dominant influence. Birds, indeed, have Christian meaning, though perhaps the more important Christian bird is the dove symbolizing the Holy Spirit. As such, it cannot be confused with a predatory bird such as that frequently depicted at Sutton Hoo. The eagle, however, also occurs in Christian contexts as the symbol of the evangelist John; however, no reason exists to connect eagles and John with Sutton Hoo. Similarly, there is a Christian context for the association of David and birds, as shown in many Irish carvings and manuscripts from later periods (see H. Steger, *David Rex et Propheta* [Nürnberg 1961], especially 59-60), namely, inspiration from God via the Holy Spirit and birdsong as emblematic of psalm singing. Other connections suggest ties to the Orpheus myth (Steger, *David Rex*, 59-60). Even later, medieval bestiaries describe various birds as the companions of kings. The caldarius bird, for example, is gifted with prophetic powers and an ability to take on the illnesses of others in order to cure them, an evocation of Christ's death for sinners. None of these contexts, however, fits the Sutton Hoo depictions. I am considering a pre-Christian instrument with royal connections and ties to pre-Christian ritual, buried no more that thirty years after Augustine's arrival in England and quite possibly constructed before he arrived. In such a context, Germanic tradition provides reasonable background for the depictions of predatory birds. Even if we accept the eagle as partly due to Roman influence, combining the temporal power of the empire with the professed religion of what was left of that empire, we might argue that the clarity of the eagle as a Christian religious symbol is, at best, obscured.

on two other Sutton Hoo pieces, notably both including images of birds' heads: the famous gold buckle and the silver patch of the hanging bowl.

On the Taplow birds (Pl. 3), the crest line differs but the beaks and eyes are the same. The two bird pairs, both have the ornament below the head filled with Style II animal interlace consisting of creatures we may term serpents simply because they have heads and no limbs. Both bird pairs were fitted to their harps in specially cut rebates, indicating that the ornament was planned from the first as an integral part of construction. Placement here is not a meaningful parallel, as we know that placement was determined by the joints in the underlying wooden body of the harps. Again, given the noted similarities as well as the marked differences in execution (crest line, throat, neck), the choice of birds seems deliberate, as does their form, which omits the lower body and talons.

Having noted these details, we can now look at parallel forms. On the lid of the Franks Casket (see fig. 1c, Pl. 4), a bird-headed image above the mysterious figure within the arch parallels that on the silver patch of the Sutton Hoo bowl (Pl. 5) and is perhaps itself paralleled on the famous Niederdollendorf stone (fig. 1b). Why would a two-headed bird image appear on a hanging bowl? We know that ritual cauldrons cooked meals of sacrificed animals at occasions such as funeral feasts. Perhaps it was merely further elaboration of a precious piece, but the image chosen suggests that the repair was for a special object, and, quite possibly, for a final special use.

The casket scene here has had many interpretations, but we know that the runes indicate that this is Ægili, possibly Egil of Norse legend; he stands within a crenelated, presumably fortified building, while behind him a strange, hooded figure, sometimes described as Odin, a woman, or a priest, stands with staff or spear in hand. Below the figure is another two-headed image, with a mane and an upper lip that curls back and thus is akin to the type that occurs beneath the Durham Cassiodorus David (who also, incidentally, holds a spear). The figure with a spear is paralleled in the Oseberg tapestry (fig. 1a), where three possibly hooded figures stand at the top right of center. Again the figures may represent women given the trailing of their robes and the parallel in Scandinavian female images we know that carry drinking horns (see for example, fig. 2a). The central figure holds a spear and several important and recurring images appear here that I will return to later: the horned man in the upper left corner who holds weapons and possibly leads the procession; spears (on their own, standing or apparently cast, as well as held by male and female figures); various knots including those in the horses' tails; and notably, birds, several of which seem to be falcons or hawks returning to owners with their feet extended, as in the bird on the Sutton Hoo shield and purse lid.

On the casket lid, in the lower right corner and possibly the upper right as well, a small knotted piece is carved, resembling the *valknut*, a knot often associated with Odin because of his power to loose and bind.[7] Perhaps most significantly, the knot also appears just over the roof of the arched doorway where the mysterious figure stands. No such design occurs in the parallel spaces behind the attacking enemy.

SPIRITUALITY AND METAMORPHOSIS

The Franks Casket provides the first visual clue that birds may embody a spiritual or religious symbolism. Images of birds as sacred go back at least to Indo-European roots and occur in many cultures: the world tree with its cosmic birds survives even in Christian art, with the Tree of Life and its attendant peacocks. George Speake briefly discusses the motif of birds in Germanic and Anglo-Saxon art,[8] connecting them with Odin, whether raven or eagle or some other predatory bird, but we should not be surprised that creatures which apparently live in environments impossible for us should be a source of reverence and wonder. Birds, especially, seem adaptable to a symbolism of spiritual flight. Perhaps the connection with Odin was initially due to his role as god of the dead, since the flight of the soul, once such a concept exists, readily connects with the flight of birds. We have examples from Anglo-Saxon cemeteries of cremations accompanied by feathers or birds' feet, and a now lost cremation pot from Newark pictured in Gelling and Davidson[9] shows two three-dimensional birds on its lid.

---

[7]*Hávámal*, str. 149.

[8]G. Speake, *Anglo-Saxon Animal Art and its Germanic Background* (Oxford 1980).

[9]P. Gelling and H. E. Davidson, *The Chariot of the Sun* (London 1969), fig. 82.

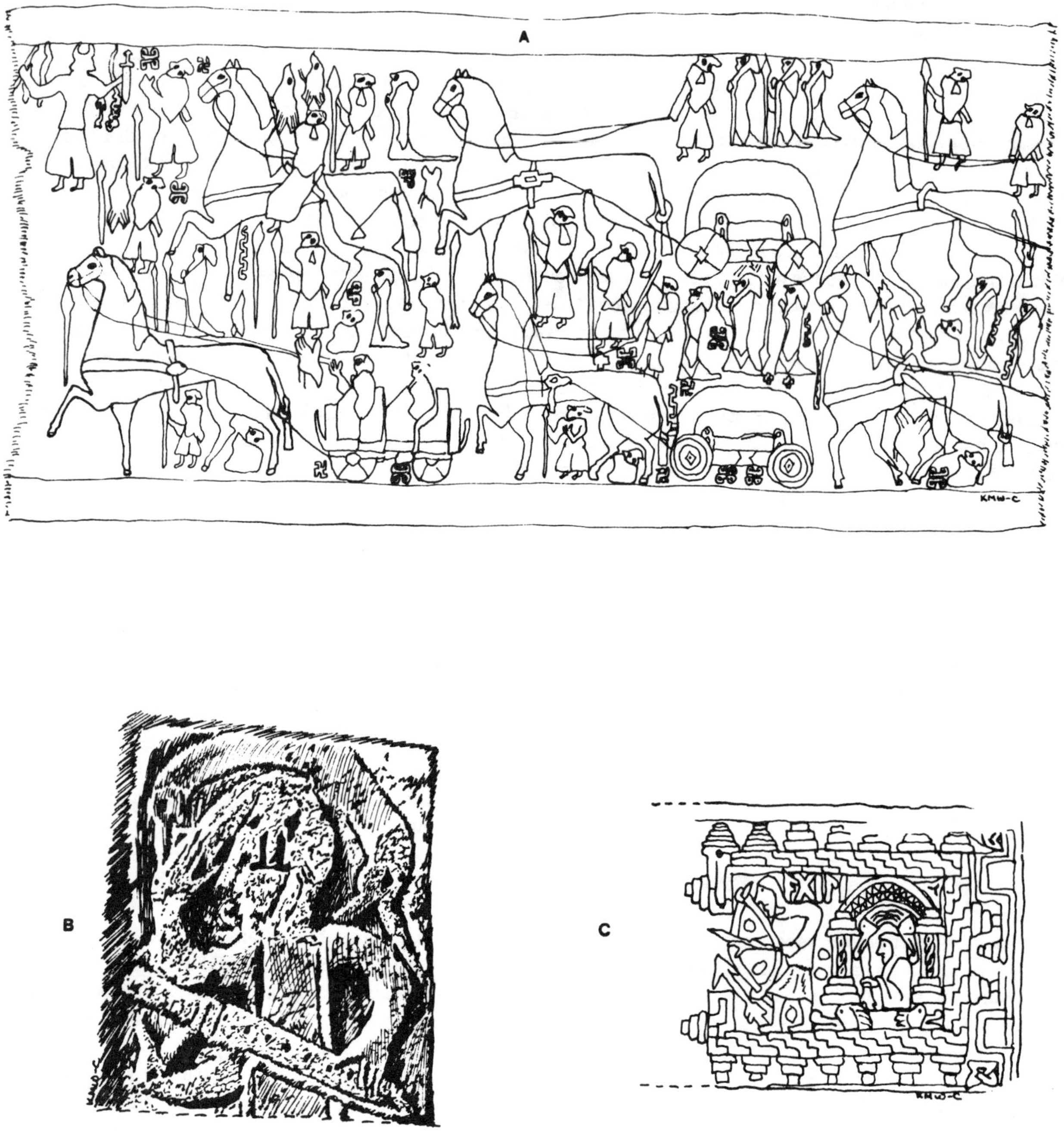

Fig. 1. (a) Oseberg tapestry (after Mary Storm's version); (b) Niederdollendorf stone (fifth- or sixth-century); (c) Ægili, detail from the lid of the Franks Casket.

The specific birds associated with Odin are eagles and ravens. In stealing poetry from the giants, Odin became first, a serpent and, then, an eagle.[10] The latter transformation is probably depicted on a stone from Lärbro St. Hammers III, Sweden[11] which shows a bird with human feet (fig. 2a). An unusual loop or knot appears over the bird's beak, a possibly significant detail to which I shall return later in another context. Note, also, the tear-shaped opening within the bird's body. The imperial eagle of the Romans doubtless reinforced the connection of power with this bird.[12] Ravens too were Odin's, harbingers of death and signs of good omen to those about to fight an enemy in battle. Two ravens in particular represent Odin's knowledge, described in *Grímnismál* and *Odins Korpsmáler*.[13] The names of Huginn and Muninn usually translate as Thought and Memory, presumably aspects of Odin's own mind sent out to retrieve knowledge. The meanings indicate both intellectual and creative powers of the mind as well as the wisdom memory would make possible (the accumulation and retrieval of thought and knowledge by memory allow wisdom to exist). In the context of a kingly burial, birds found on harps in pairs immediately suggest Huginn and Muninn, given their association with poetry and with Odin as god of poetry and warriors. Is so specific a connection necessary if birds are sacred to Odin, whether eagle or raven? The physical depictions on the harp favor an eagle, since ravens have long, straight beaks, but a plaque from a Vendel helmet shows one of each bird flying over a mounted warrior frequently described as Odin.[14]

The connection between birds and Odin is not merely association but at times identity. Metamorphosis was one of Odin's main attributes. He frequently disguised himself or took on other forms in the accounts we have, becoming Grímnir the wanderer (literally hooded or disguised, something to recall in the context of the Franks Casket), or a serpent, or the eagle. He is often connected with verbal metamorphosis also, delighting in obscure or complicated riddling, of a type involving aspects of mind and something taking on another form. In these riddles, a familiar object, the answer, is described from an alien perspective to mislead and then to enlighten – a verbal metamorphosis. Finally, Odin is associated with emotional or spiritual metamorphosis, a change of

---

[10]The story of Odin and the mead of poetry has come down to us in Snorri Sturluson's version. Snorri (1179-1241) collected older stories to preserve them and to promote an appreciation for the stories themselves. His work is called *The Prose Edda*. Roberta Frank has detailed how Snorri dealt with the mead of poetry and myth and its attendant kennings. Relevant to concerns here about reliability and date, she notes that the kennings in question come from the *Vellekla*, a poem written c. 990 for a devout pagan, Earl Håkon of Lade. Snorri may have over-interpreted names, confusing simple metaphors and full kennings, but the action of the story, the focus on how poetry came to Odin and what its effects are, is valid. She states:

> Snorri was consistent in his preference for interpretations that could yield mythological names and allusions; my readings rest on an equally personal view of how skaldic verse works, one that stresses internal coherence. Snorri had access to more information about Old Norse paganism than we have, and knew what he was doing when he placed Odin's mead squarely in the center of his myth; the readings adopted here reinforce this centrality... It seems to me that poetry-kennings of the early skalds had as their base a single concept – that of verse as an intoxicating drink – and as their definer a single concept – that of divine chthonic existence. Inebriation was the goal. The idea of poetry as an offering of strong drink from poet to patron is not restricted to skaldic art, but nowhere else is it so pervasive... The sudden unaccountable surge of power, of exhilaration, that came with comprehension would wash over household troops like the frenzied rage of a berserk after his release from self-imposed psychological stress. Both poet and champion, as Professor Turville-Petre more than once observed, worshipped the lawless, creative god Odin (R. Frank, "Snorri and the Mead of Poetry," in U. Dronke, *et al.* (eds.) *Speculum Norrœnum: Norse Studies in Memory of Gabriel Turville-Petre* [Odense 1981], 169).

[11]H. R. E. Davidson, *The Battle God of the Vikings* (York 1972), 18.

[12]*Ibid.*, 13.

[13]These works are part of the collection we term the *Elder Edda* to distinguish it from Snorri Sturluson's work. Dating individual pieces is impossible, though most are accepted as having been composed in their present forms between 900 and 1050, prior to their collection in the twelfth century. E. V. Gordon notes that these poems preserve traditional Germanic meters and alliterative technique, closely matching Anglo-Saxon poetic tradition. Norse and Old English poetry also share poetic synonyms, though they differ in style. Gordan states that the oldest Norse poems: "... were transmitted from one nation to another, and from one generation to another, but they were preserved almost entirely by oral tradition... and those that are frankly heathen are not likely to be much later than 1000, when all West Norse peoples had been Christianized (E. V. Gordon, *An Introduction to Old Norse*, 2nd ed. [Oxford 1957], xxxvi-xxxviii).

[14]See H. Shetelig, *Kunst*, vol. 27 in *Nordisk Kultur* (Stockholm 1931), fig. 8, p. 209, for the reconstructed panel from the grave I helmet. Note that the bird on the left matches the bird on the rider's helmet, having a curved beak while the right hand bird has a straight beak. The full helmet is illustrated in color in D. M. Wilson, *The Vikings and Their Origins* (New York 1989), ill. 27.

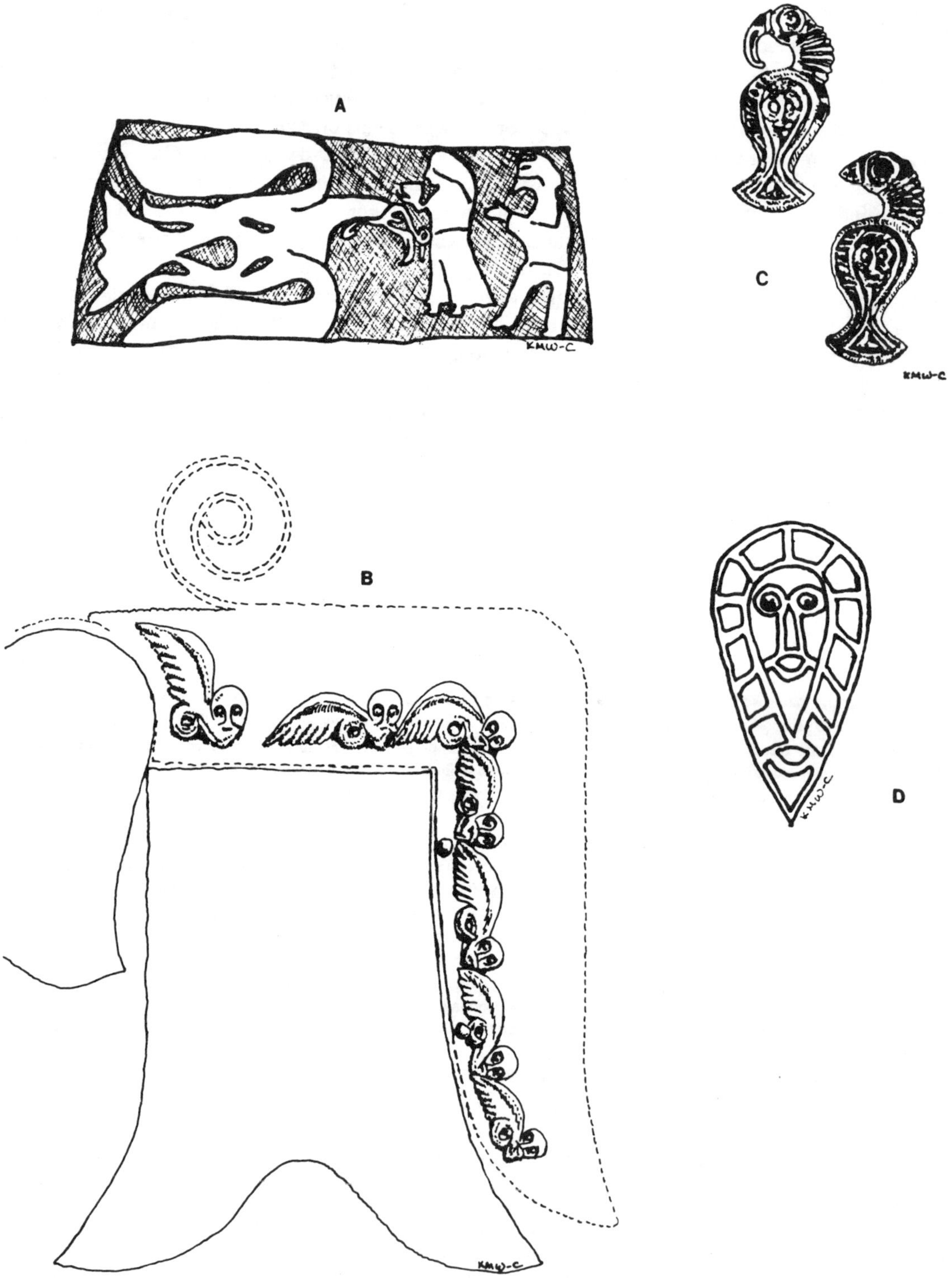

Fig. 2. (a) Lärbro St. Hammers III, Sweden; (b) design on Sutton Hoo shield bird (winged heads only, serpents omitted); (c) Fibulas, Anderlingen, Lower Saxony; (d) inset with human face from the Sutton Hoo shield bird's leg.

consciousness, signified in his hanging on a tree to acquire runes and, in battle settings, in a type of madness and possession that characterized his followers. The berserkers carry a name that designates a symbolic shape change as well as a possible mundane reality of fighting clothed in bear skins. Such possession was identified closely enough with Odin (Wodan) for Adam of Bremen to write "Wodan: id est furor."[15] The key here is metamorphosis: physical, as in becoming animal; verbal, in shifting words and their meaning; and spiritual or emotional.

That Anglo-Saxons may have believed that Odin himself could be a raven or eagle in their own world is not beyond possibility. The two ravens Huginn and Muninn may be seen as aspects of the god, sent forth from himself to gather knowledge and acquire wisdom. The metamorphosis of Odin seems to me the key to understanding bird imagery. A striking image that relates to this assertion appears on two gilded fibulas of the fifth century, from Anderlingen, Lower Saxony (Niedersächsisches Landesmuseum) (fig. 2c).[16] On these examples, the body of the bird contains a human face, and it seems difficult to believe that this image could be other than the depiction of Odin literally contained in another form, that of the bird. The tear-shaped head parallels the shape previously noted on the Lärbro St. Hammers III stone, although the beaks on the birds differ, unless one has been damaged. Are they eagle, with curved beak, and raven, with straight?

The ornamentation of the shield's bird shows that such a dual image has reference to the birds at Sutton Hoo (Pl. 6). Not only is its leg infilled with a human head, again tear-shaped (Pl. 7 and fig. 2d), but the same bird has on its tail a repeated pattern of a winged, tear-shaped head with a small loop or knot (fig. 2b, simplified to emphasize relevant design elements) similar to the one noted on Odin as eagle earlier (fig. 2a). This loop may be an iconographic indication that we are to understand the image as Odin. (The same loop occurs just under the jaws of the serpents which accompany the winged heads, here omitted from the sketch but visible in Speake.[17] I would like to think that depiction of loops, serpents and winged heads on an eagle's body clinches the identification.) Should we doubt that the idea of bird as soul survived to Anglo-Saxon England, we have only to recall Bede's story about human and eternal existence: the sparrow flying through the hall has consistently been understood as representing human life. Notably, this story was told by one of the king's chief men and is part of the occasion which convinced the priest Coifi to convert to Christianity. Perhaps we should not underestimate the apt choice of a bird image here.

We should perhaps inject here the possibility of lesser significance for the bird; or to paraphrase Freud, sometimes a bird is just a bird. Birds such as eagles and the various types of falcons have early connections with nobility and royalty in Germanic contexts, a connection which holds true through the later Middle Ages where specific hunting birds are associated with specific levels of nobility. The *lex salica* of c. A.D. 500 had regulations concerning the catching and theft of birds of prey, while at the same time church councils were trying to prohibit the clergy from keeping falcons. Boniface corresponded with at least two Anglo-Saxon kings about falcons and hawks – Æthelbald of Mercia and Æthelberht of Kent – sending them birds in England since few were available

---

[15]Adam of Bremen was an eleventh-century chronicler who described the temple at Uppsala in a famous passage from his *Gesta Hammaburgensis* (Book IV, xxvi-xxvii). The accepted editions are: *Gesta Hammaburgensis Ecclesiae Pontificum*, ed. B Schmeidler, Scriptores Rerum Germanicarum (Hanover 1917); and a translation by F. J. Tschan, *History of the Archbishops of Hamburg-Bremen* (New York 1959). The following excerpts are from Gwyn Jones's slightly altered version of Tschan's translation, which appears in *A History of the Vikings* (Oxford 1973), 326-27:

> That folk [the Swedes] has a very famous temple called Uppsala. In this temple,... the people worship the statues of three gods... The significance of these gods is as follows... Wodan [Odinn] – that is, the Furious – carries on war and imparts to man strength against his enemies... It is customary also to solemnize in Uppsala, at nine-year intervals, a general feast of all the provinces of Sweden. From attendance at this festival no one is exempted. Kings and people all and singly send their gifts to Uppsala, and what is more distressing than any kind of punishment, those who have already adopted Christianity redeem themselves through these ceremonies. The sacrifice is of this nature: of every living thing that is male, they offer nine heads, with the blood of which it is customary to placate the gods of this sort... Furthermore the incantations [songs] customarily chanted in the ritual of a sacrifice of this kind are manifold and unseemly; therefore, it is better to keep silence about them.

[16]They are illustrated in R. Hachmann, *The Germanic Peoples*, trans. J. Hogarth (Geneva 1971), 131.

[17]Speake, *Anglo-Saxon Animal Art*, pl. 5b.

to them locally.[18] It is likely, however, that the combination of associations, that is, nobility, royalty and the divine, had common origins. If nobility were connected with the gods, either as divinely favored or as descendants of a god, then the connections of a holy bird with that rank would be a natural one. As for whether we should consider the birds on the harp merely as indications of a connection between singing and birdsong, I would note that birds of prey are not noted for their melodious tunes. We know nothing of Anglo-Saxon music, but it does seem likely that if only a reference to song were intended, a more appropriate bird could have been chosen.

SCOP AND *WOÐBORA*

If the bird ornament is symbolic of some spiritual reality, what is the significance of its placement on the harp? The obvious initial correlation unites the story of Odin as eagle and god of poetry with the ravens who personify aspects necessary to a poet, namely thought, both intellectual and creative, and memory, preserving and acquiring knowledge perhaps in imitation of the god of wisdom. It would help if we knew why a harp was buried with a king or high ranking person. Was he himself the player, or the sponsor? Are the birds meant in part almost as a badge of office, designating a particular role for the player of the instrument? Are they signs of a particular devotion to Odin? We cannot recover the answers to most of these questions. We can, however, pull together evidence for those we think used the harp.

Scholars have generally considered the terms *scop* and *woðbora* interchangeable. Egon Werlich, after an etymological examination that traces *scop* back to Gmc **skopon*, meaning "dance, jump, gambol," concludes that the evidence for both terms indicates a poet descended from an earlier priest-poet whose role included dancing.[19] Ida Masters Hollowell, while convinced of the etymological derivation, argues that the two terms, *scop* and *woðbora*, designate two separate roles.[20] The *scop* was mainly an entertainer, while the *woðbora* had a specially skilled role, that of teacher, wanderer and wise man, whose wisdom had a mystical aspect, almost a wizardly knowledge. The first element in the term *woð-*, derives from IE *uat* or *vat*, "to inspire." Latin *vates*, "seer," "wise-sayer" and OIr *faith*, "seer," "prophet," "poet," are two related terms which give credence to her argument. Even more relevant here, the element *woð-* appears in the god Wodan's name. Thus, the *woðbora* is a bearer of prophecy, wisdom, poetry and madness, the kind deemed inspired by a god, a type of possession.

Whether the *scop* and the *woðbora* were two people with different roles or two aspects of a person who could serve both roles, however, is less important here than whether both roles used instruments. We know *scops* played harps, and, based on references in OE and Norse texts, it is likely that *woðboras* did also. Riddle 80 of the Exeter Book may refer to a performance: *Oft ic woðboran wordleana sum / agyfe æfter giedde.* (Often I give to the *woðbora* reward for words after the *gied.*)[21] The riddle is spoken by either a drinking horn, a falcon, a hawk or a spear, depending on your solution. The *gied* referred to can be a song, as shown in *Beowulf* lines 2446-47, "*þonne he gyd wrece, / sarigne sang.*" The passage refers to Hreðel mourning his son Herebeald, a potentially ritual performance by the king himself that is worth noting in the context of the Sutton Hoo find – also both royal and a burial.

Another aspect of the *woðbora* involved what Hollowell terms shamanistic ecstasy, which relates to the etymological derivation from *woð-* and, in the North, involving *seiðr* ("spell", "enchantment"). Hollowell speaks of a ritual as:

> ... being carried out from a platform where, through the intoning of magic chants, a trance state was induced in the practitioner playing the shaman's role. Such a state was one in which Odinn or a human seer was

[18] C. Hicks, "The Birds on the Sutton Hoo Purse," *ASE* 15 (1986), 162.

[19] E. Werlich, "Der westgermanische Skop: der Ursprung des Sängerstandes in semasiologischer und etymologischer Sicht," *Zeitschrift für Deutsche Philologie* 86 (1967), 352-75.

[20] I. M. Hollowell, "*Scop* and *Woðbora* in OE Poetry," *JEGP* 77 (1978), 317-29.

[21] G. P. Krapp and E. V. K. Dobbie (eds.) *The Exeter Book*, vol III, ASPR (New York 1936), 235, ll. 9-10.

> thought to leave his body behind and proceed to a far point in this world or the world beyond to accomplish beneficial acts for his devotees, or inflict evil on enemies.[22]

It is significant that the term *woðbora* is used in *Christ*[23] to describe Isaiah (a mistake for Ezekiel), who travelled up to the eternal city and then prophesied about it. Given the name of "*woð*-bearer" we might even conclude that the shaman became the god for the duration of his trance, much as the bird fibula bore the human face. In any case, this flight to another reality to acquire knowledge was apparently a central aspect of the *woðbora*'s role, and his chanting may well have involved the harp. Adam of Bremen wrote of incantations which believers sang at the temple in Uppsala, Sweden; the *Hávámal* speaks of charms which are sung (e.g. str. 111, 162 and 164); and in this context, Höfler discusses the recitation of gnomic poetry at cult places and, in particular, the connection between chant and the sound of a bird.[24] In Anglo-Saxon contexts, in the Life of St. Gregory episode concerning Edwin's conversion (ch. 16), Paulinus has a raven shot after it sang as if proclaiming an omen in contradiction to Christianity's "new song." He later explains this as a sign that the bird unknowingly sang of its own death and therefore could not "foretell the future to men,"[25] again emphasizing birds and a connection with seers and prophets.

While we can see that Odin's birds could easily function as emblems of the far-seeing shaman, what about a connection between birds and the supposedly older role of the *scop* as dancer poet? I know of nothing in the literary record that supports this association, but the physical record may fill in the gaps. The horns worn by the figure on the Sutton Hoo helmet called the dancing god or the dancer end in beaked heads (fig, 3d, Pls. 8 and 9), as do the horns on the Finglesham, Kent buckle (fig. 3c) and Torslunda die D (fig. 3b).[26] For example, the buckle shows a man dressed only in a belt and buckle, carrying two spears (the weapon of Odin) and wearing a horned headpiece ending in the heads described. It is tempting to suggest that, given the dress or lack of it for the figure, such a buckle is connected with ritual. I should point out here that the birds we noted on the Sutton Hoo buckle are not unique to it; pairs of birds' heads adorn brooch backings and many of the buckles found that parallel the great gold buckle.[27] They may be from a puberty ritual that makes boys men and warriors or perhaps even dedicates them to the warrior god. In this connection, the great gold buckle of Sutton Hoo has a further enticing aspect: it was constructed with a hinged back and closed with clasps, creating a chamber inside. In a Christian context we might wonder if it functioned as a reliquary, and a parallel use, to hold sacred or protective materials, could apply here in Germanic contexts as well.

Horned images also occur on the Oseberg tapestry (fig. 1a) and on the Valsgärde grave 8 helmet (fig. 3a) in somewhat different contexts. On the tapestry, the figure holds weapons in his hands and may perhaps be leading the procession, possibly a funeral cortege.[28] On the helmet plaque from Valsgärde, however, the horned figure is diminutive and perched behind a warrior on his horse. Davidson interprets this figure as one of Odin's *einherjar*,

---

[22] Hollowell, "*Scop* and *Woðbora*," 327. Hollowell relies on the work of Stefán Einarsson (S. Einarsson, "Alternate Recital by Twos," *ARV: Tidskrift för Nordisk Folkminnesforskrung* 7 [1951], 59-83), as well as on Peter Buchholz's dissertation, *Schamanistische Züge in der altisländischen Überlieferung* (Munster 1968). The older, original texts relevant in this context include the *Hávámal* (The Sayings of the High One) and the *Voluspá* (The Song of the Sibyl). The latter can be read as an account of a trance journey such as Hollowell describes.

[23] Krapp and Dobbie, *The Exeter Book*, 11, ll. 301ff.

[24] O. Höfler, "Spervogel – Herger – *Harugwari," in U. Hennig and H. Kolb (eds.) *Mediaevalia litteraria: Festschrift für Helmut de Boor zum 80. Geburtstag* (Munich 1981), 211-17.

[25] B. Colgrave, *The Earliest Life of Gregory the Great* (Lawrence, Kansas 1968), 98-101.

[26] The latter two are illustrated in R. L. S. Bruce-Mitford, *Aspects of Anglo-Saxon Archaeology: Sutton Hoo and Other Discoveries* (London 1974), pls. 57b and 59a.

[27] See Speake, *Anglo-Saxon Animal Art*, pls. 2 and 6 for examples.

[28] Davidson (*The Battle God*, 13) notes Paulsen's work on ritual dance by warriors at funerals, involving the bringing of the weapons of the dead to the place of burial. See, P. Paulsen, *Alamannische Adelsgräber von Niederstotzingen (Kreis Heidenheim)*, Veröffentlichungen des Staatlichen Amtes für Denkmalpflege, Stuttgart, Reihe A, Vor- und Frühgeschichte Heft 12/1 (Stuttgart 1967).

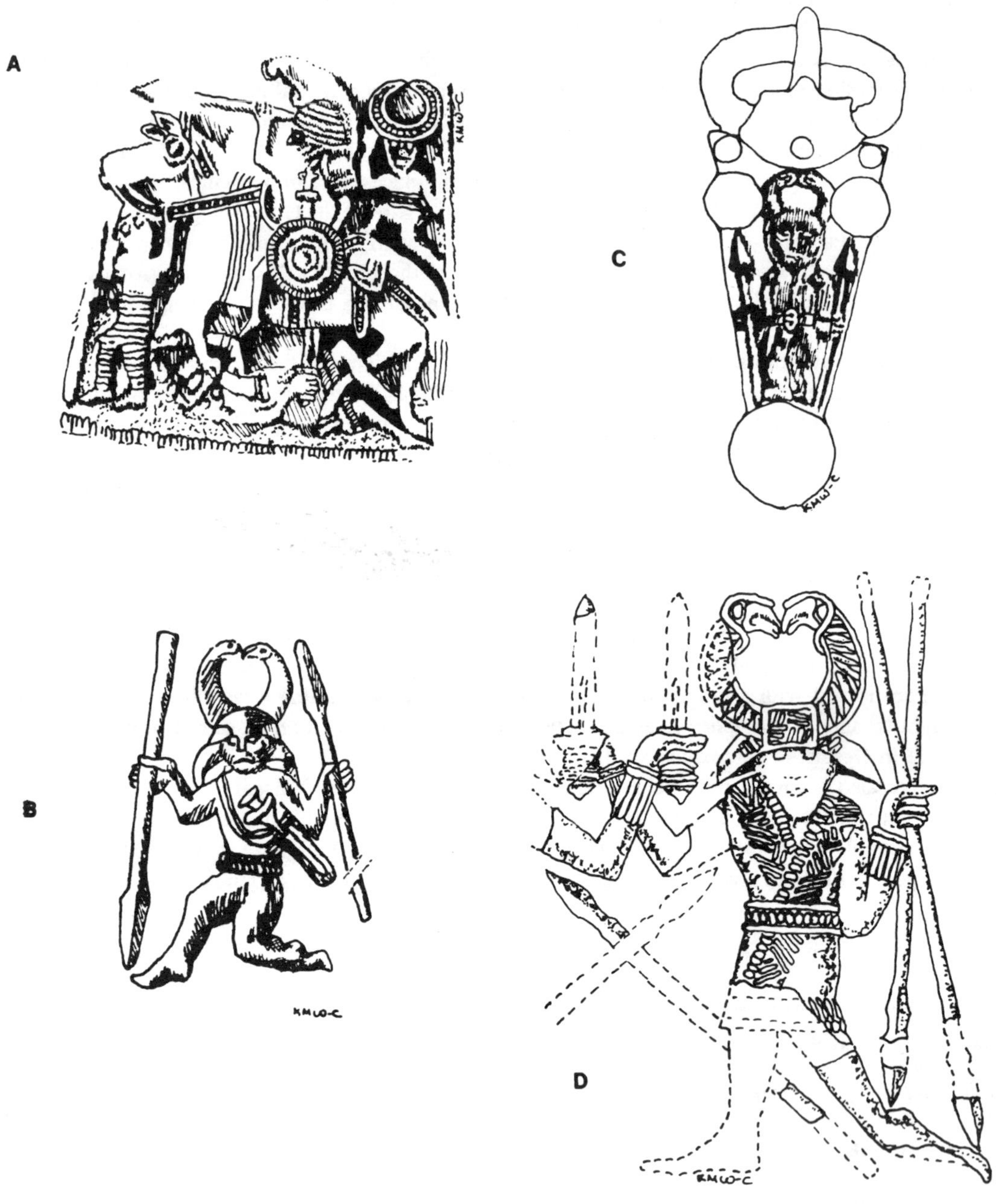

Fig. 3. (a) Valsgärde grave 8 helmet plaque; (b) dancing or running figure, Torslunda die D (figure of bear/man with spear not included); (c) buckle from Finglesham cemetery, Kent; (d) dancing figure (one of a pair), Sutton Hoo helmet plaque.

his champions of the Edda poems who choose the slain and lead his forces at Ragnarök.[29] The small figure has a belt as well as horns (reminiscent of the Finglesham figure), and apparently has appeared just as the rider's horse is stabbed from beneath, condemning the rider. Presumably both Odin's messenger and the rider are now off to Valhalla, and, given the dress of the figure, it is tempting to assert again that it is associated with a warrior spiritualism, some rite that dedicates a man to a god and holds even after death. The Sutton Hoo helmet has a similar scene (Pl. 8), but unfortunately, the section showing the back of the head of the small figure is incomplete, so we do not know if a horned headpiece was shown or flowing hair paralleling that of the rider, as in Bruce-Mitford's reconstruction.[30] In any case, the connection of Odin with horned figures seems to hold, and these figures are too small to display birds' heads clearly.

I am hesitant to propose something which has lurked around the edges of my speculations; namely, whether we should consider this kingly burial as the burial of someone who also performed a priestly function. We know very little about such people in Anglo-Saxon culture. When Bede mentions Coifi, he gives us no information about a specific religion or affiliation, just curious details: Coifi must ride a mare and carry no weapons, attributes which certainly jar if, say, he were the priest of a virile battle god. In fact, they sound as if he may have belonged to a goddess' following, but we have no way of verifying such an idea. Certainly his casting of a spear as an act of desecration would not seem to hold for a temple to Wodan, as we know such castings ("Odin has you all") could be done to call on the god's power.[31] Rædwald may have served as a priest, for his setting up of an altar to the Germanic deities as well as to the Christian god may have made him responsible for the temple. Turville-Petre comments that: "In general, professional priests probably played little part in the religion of the English and Continental Germans," and "in Scandinavia it was chiefly the prince or the king who presided over sacrifice."[32] Certainly Bede gives several instances of kings deciding to convert and the consequent conversion of their subjects as well. The connection between temporal and spiritual power may have been a given; after all, the Easter question was ultimately decided by one king and his councillors.

But Rædwald as priest is perhaps not necessary to our understanding that a close relationship existed between Odin, a harp player and the king honored at Sutton Hoo, and that the birds of Sutton Hoo are emblems pointing to that special relationship. They symbolize power and spiritual metamorphosis, an interpretation of the natural and supernatural worlds. And while a priest or *woðbora* may have been able to mediate between men and deities, the East Anglian house had a further claim. Their genealogies link them with the god Wodan himself, making them his physical heirs and so tying them to his power and authority as well. While we need not naively believe that this genealogy is solely the product of spiritual piety, we can understand that even if we admit political aims, the power of Wodan is nevertheless real, capable of lending credibility and authority to a descendent in this world. In this context, the birds speak to temporal nobility, with their connotation of status and fierceness, but they also speak of life after death, a way of seeing through new eyes to another reality. Change and metamorphosis become the basis of spiritual growth and wisdom gained, where the birds of this world are those of the next as well. The truth of being Odin's follower was that in war, poetry, song and looking to (or into) the future, this king was already participating in the afterlife.

---

[29]Davidson, *The Battle God*, 13.

[30]R. L. S. Bruce-Mitford, *The Sutton Hoo Ship Burial: A Handbook* (London 1979), fig. 35.

[31]For a full discussion of the spear as religious object and its connection with Odin, see Davidson, *The Battle God* (2-6; 30, note 13). She notes that the "dedication of an enemy host to Odin by flinging a spear over them with the words 'Odin has you all' was long remembered in Old Norse literature" (as in *Flateyjarbók*), and she also connects the act with the winning of new territory. She also notes that an early Danish chronicle derives the placename Oddaesund from Otto I's casting his lance into the sea there "to perpetuate the memory of his victory over Harald Bluetooth," while in *Eyrbyggja Saga*, the cast is seen as a custom for good luck before battle.

[32]E. O. G. Turville-Petre, *Myth and Religion of the North: The Religion of Ancient Scandinavia* (New York 1964), 261.

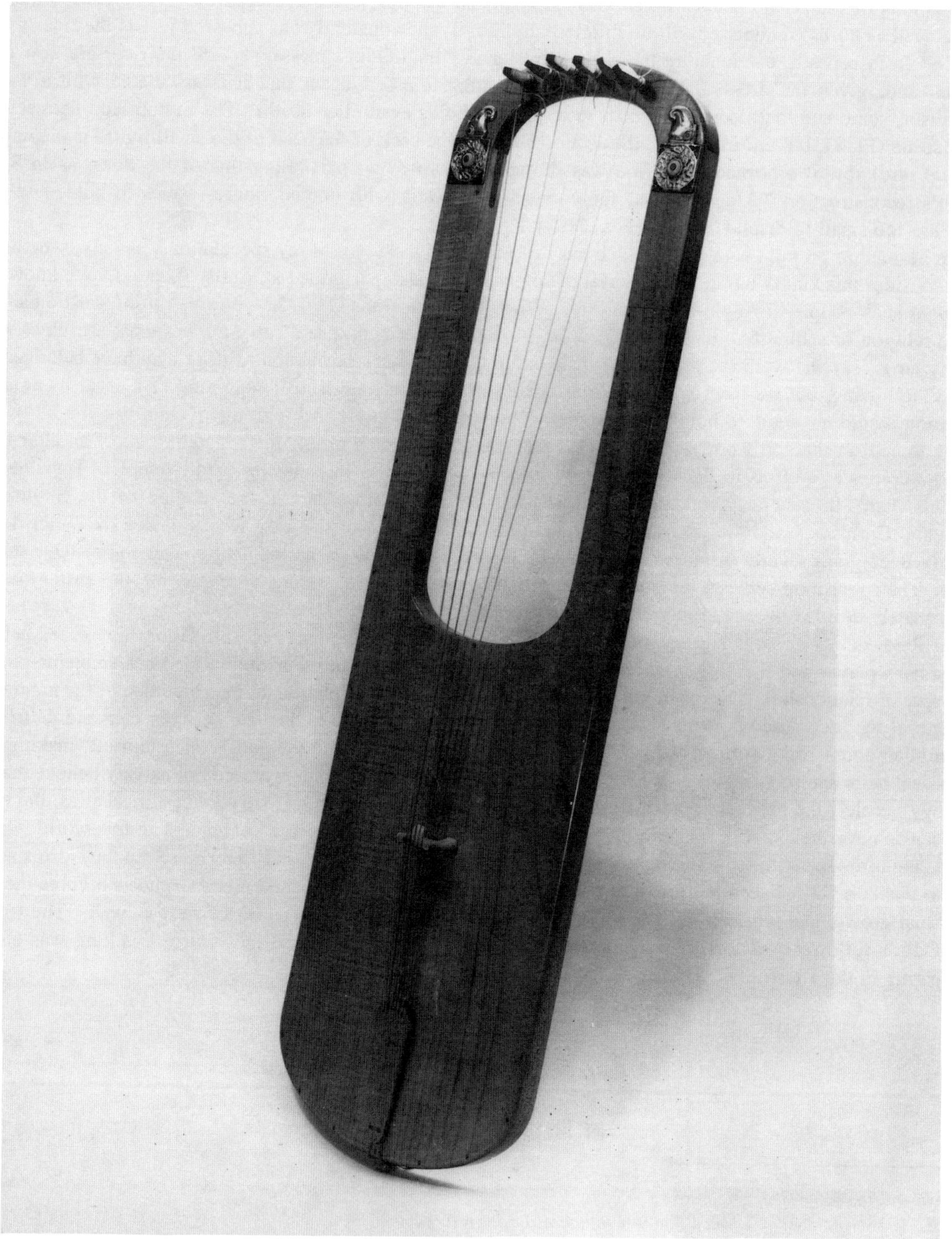

Pl. 1. Sutton Hoo, Mound One: harp; reconstruction. London, The British Museum. (Photo: By permission of the Trustees of the British Museum).

Pl. 2. Sutton Hoo, Mound One: harp; bird mounts. London, The British Museum. (Photo: By permission of the Trustees of the British Museum.

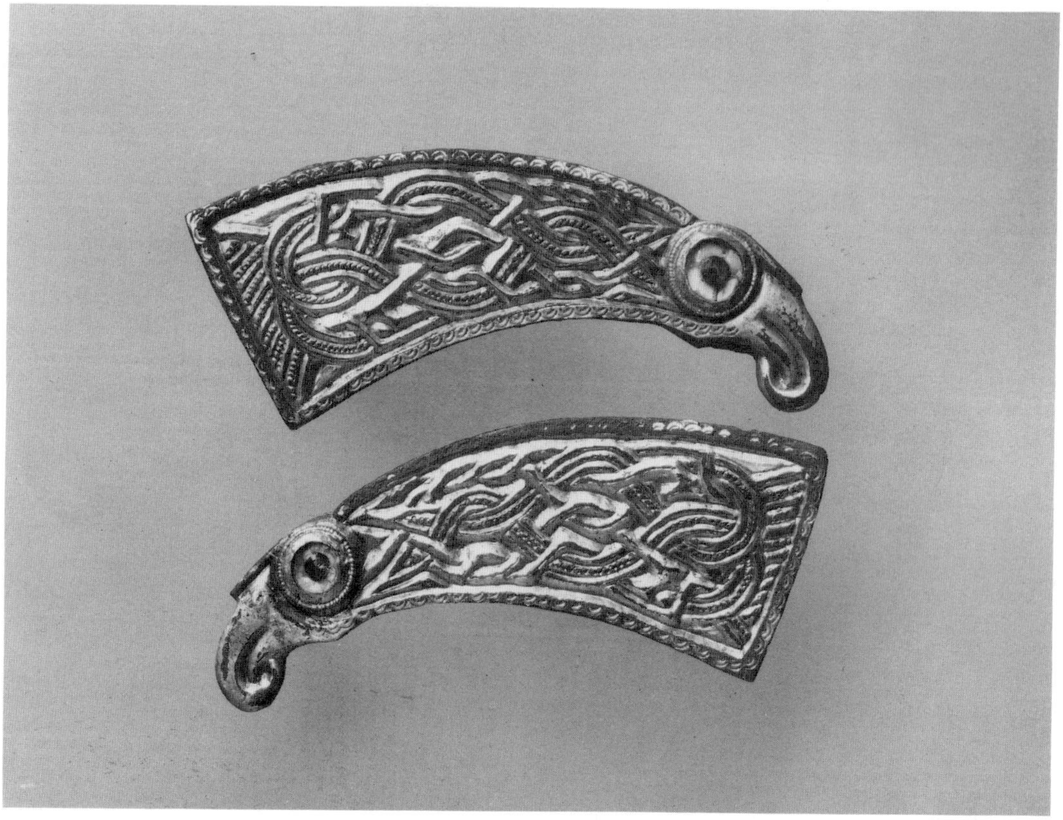

Pl. 3. Taplow: harp; bird mounts. London, The British Museum. (Photo: By permission of the Trustees, British Museum).

Pl. 4. Sutton Hoo, Mound One: large hanging bowl; silver patch with two birds' heads. London, The British Museum. (Photo: By permission of the Trustees, British Museum).

Pl. 5. The Franks Casket: lid; central panel. London, The British Museum. (Photo: By permission of the Trustees, British Museum).

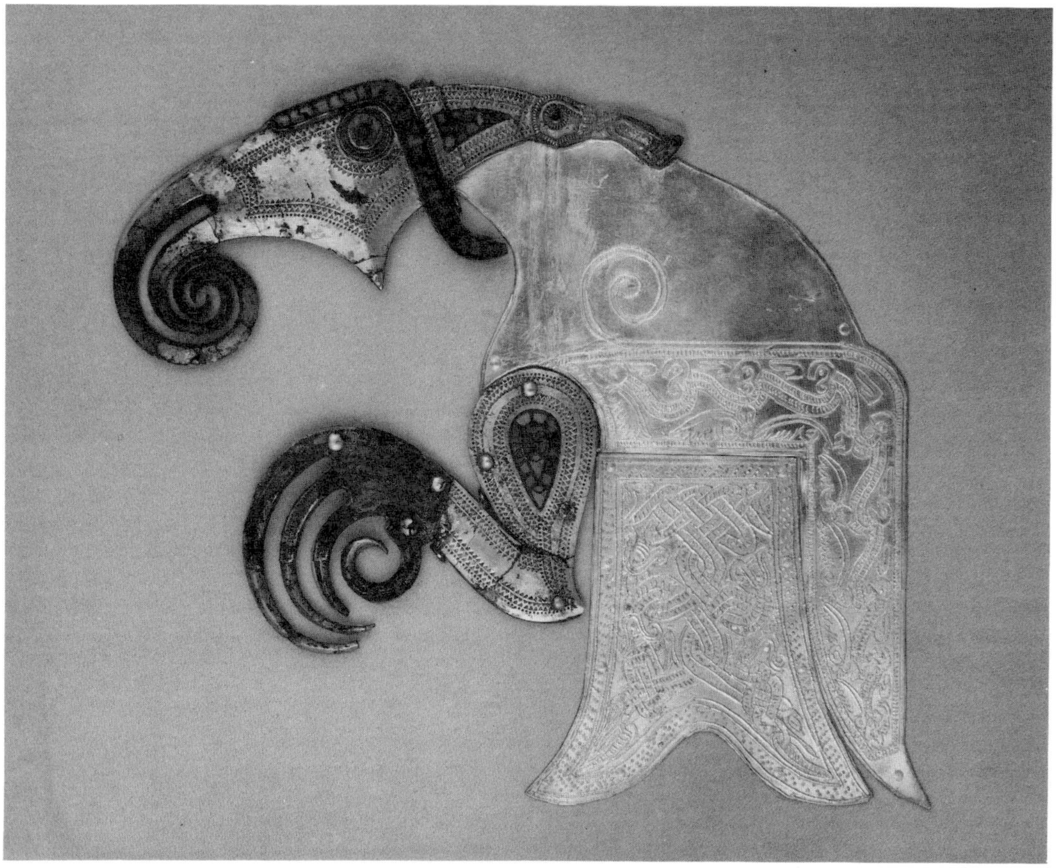

Pl. 6. Sutton Hoo, Mound One: shield; eagle mount. London, The British Museum. (Photo: By permission of the Trustees, British Museum).

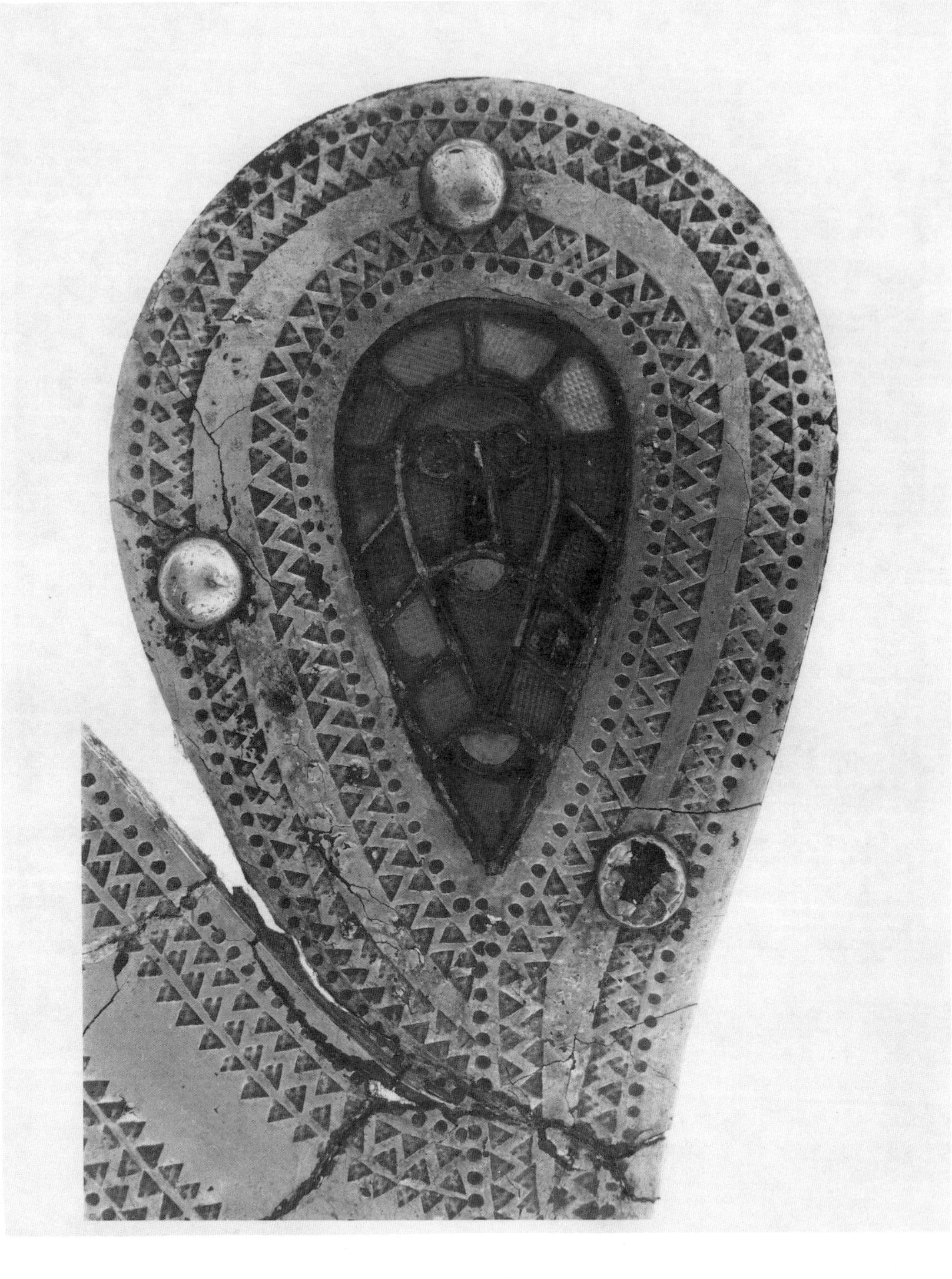

Pl. 7. Sutton Hoo, Mound One: shield; eagle mount; detail. London, The British Museum. (Photo: By permission of the Trustees, British Museum).

Pl. 8. Sutton Hoo, Mound One: helmet; reconstruction, detail. London, The British Museum. (Photo: By permission of the Trustees, British Museum.

Pl. 9. Sutton Hoo, Mound One: helmet plaques; plaster casts based on/taken from original fragments. London, The British Museum. (Photo: By permission of the Trustees, British Museum).

The Sutton Hoo Horns as Regalia

CAROL NEUMAN DE VEGVAR

In 1989 we celebrated the fiftieth anniversary of the excavation of the great ship burial in Mound One at Sutton Hoo.[1] The past decade has been particularly important in the study of the Sutton Hoo material; the site, its contents and its context. Dr. Rupert Bruce-Mitford, in collaboration with twelve contributing specialists, has recently published the third and final volume of what will undoubtedly be the definitive report on the 1939 excavation of the ship barrow, along with all available data on three of the other mounds on the site excavated in the previous year.[2] Along with the long-awaited appearance of this volume has come a renewal of interest in the site as a whole, with the re-examination of a number of the lesser mounds and of the context of Sutton Hoo within the wider spectrum of East Anglian and Anglo-Saxon sites. The current excavations at the site and the new analyses of the 1939 evidence published by Bruce-Mitford and his colleagues, have stimulated challenges to long-standing interpretations of the site and its contents.

The opening of Mound One in 1939 was one of the legendary moments in the history of western archaeology. Here was a great ship laden with a phenomenally valuable and well-preserved treasure: gold, garnet and enamelwork personal ornaments; armor and weaponry; imported silver from distant places; and banqueting equipment. There were also several mysterious objects, including a great whetstone, dubbed a "scepter," and a metal device, which has often been called a "standard" (Pl. 1), albeit the exact purpose and symbolic value of these objects are still hotly contested.[3] One factor debated widely in the early years after the excavation has, nonetheless, reached a state of scholarly consensus. It is now broadly accepted that the burial was royal, and that the ship mound was raised for one of the kings of East Anglia. Which East Anglian ruler he was is still subject to argument, although Bruce-Mitford and many others agree that the most likely candidate is Rædwald, whose reign falls on the cusp of the conversion of the East Angles to Christianity, and whose role as warrior chieftain and high king, with some form of hegemony over lands extending beyond his borders, is documented in Bede's *Ecclesiastical History*.[4]

In recent analyses of the symbolic implications of the contents of the Sutton Hoo ship burial, much attention has been paid to the scepter and the standard in particular (as noted above), to the ornament of the belt pouch and the number and origin of the coins in it,[5] and to the potential ancestral associations and possibly symbolic ornament of the helmet, sword and shield.[6] However, certain objects have been left out of this discussion, on the basis of the assumption that their role was clearly understood. This has been the case with the pair of drinking horns (Pl. 2) and the six associated burrwood drinking bottles, which have been collectively regarded as part of a "banqueting assemblage," without further consideration of what such vessels or such an assemblage might mean in this cultural context.[7] It is my purpose here to explore this question further, and to suggest that the Sutton Hoo drinking horns

---

[1]My thanks are owed to Robert Farrell for the opportunity to present this paper as part of "Sutton Hoo: Past, Present and Future." I also wish to thank Malcolm Thurlby and John Osborne for the opportunity to present a preliminary version of this paper at the Ninth Annual Canadian Conference of Medieval Art Historians at the University of Victoria in March, 1989; and Richard Schneider and Barbara Abou-El-Haj, whose commentaries on the preliminary thesis of the paper and on related projects have been instrumental in helping me formulate and clarify issues and methods in evidence here.

[2]R. L. S. Bruce-Mitford, *The Sutton Hoo Ship Burial*, vol. III (London 1983).

[3]J. Simpson, "The King's Whetstone," *Antiquity* 53 (1979), 96-101; N. Reynolds, "The King's Whetstone: a Footnote," *Antiquity* 54 (1980), 232-37; M. J. Enright, "The Sutton Hoo Whetstone Sceptre: a Study in Iconography and Cultural Milieu," *ASE* 11 (1983), 119-34; S. A. Mitchell, "The Whetstone as Symbol of Authority in Old English and Old Norse," *Scandinavian Studies* 57 (1985), 1-31; L. E. Nicholson, "*Beowulf* and the Pagan Cult of the Stag," *SM* 27 (1986), 637-69; C. Neuman de Vegvar, "The Iconography of Kingship in Anglo-Saxon Archaeological Finds," in J. Rosenthal (ed.), *Kings and Kingship*, *Acta* 11, (Binghamton 1984), 1-15.

[4]B. Colgrave and R. A. B. Mynors (eds.) *Bede's Ecclesiastical History of the English People* (Oxford 1969), ii:5, 148-51.

[5]P. Grierson, "The Purpose of the Sutton Hoo Coins," *Antiquity* 44 (1970), 14-18; P. Grierson, "The Sutton Hoo Coins Again," *Antiquity* 48 (1974), 139-40; C. Hicks, "The Birds on the Sutton Hoo Purse," *ASE* 15 (1986), 153-65.

[6]G. Speake, *Anglo-Saxon Animal Art and its Germanic Background* (Oxford 1980), 77-92.

[7]Bruce-Mitford, *The Sutton Hoo Ship Burial*, III, 380-95; J. Graham-Campbell, "The High-King's Viaticum," *TLS* (June 1, 1984), 608.

are as much a part of the symbolism of kingship at Sutton Hoo as the great "scepter," and that they are intended with the rest of the burial as a specific statement of the power and status of the king buried in Mound One.

The horns and the bottles were found together at the center of the chamber, on the central keel line of the burial ship, in the vicinity of ship rib 13, between the majority of personal ornaments (between ribs 13 and 15) and the Byzantine silver salver with the stamps of the Emperor Anastasius, which rests across the line of rib 12 (Pl. 3). Whether or not there was an inhumation or a cremation burial here or whether Mound One was a cenotaph may never be decided conclusively, so analysis of the placement of the horns relative to the putative location and arrangement of a body is inappropriate. Yet, it is interesting to note that the horns are placed neither with the appurtenances of war and power, including the scepter, the standard, the shield, and the spears and angons, at the west end of the chamber, nor with the more broadly domestically-functional cauldron at the east end.

The drinking horns were the paired horns of a smallish post-glacial aurochs, a species extinct in Britain since the Bronze Age but surviving into the Anglo-Saxon period and even into the seventh century in parts of Continental Europe.[8] The horns themselves no longer survive, but the diameters and find spacing of the silver-gilt fittings at their mouths and tips (Pls. 4-5) indicate that the capacity of each horn was approximately two liters, and that they probably had an outer curve of roughly 90 centimeters and differing mouth diameters of 9.5 and 10.5 centimeters.

The horns were both ornamented with a U-shaped silver-gilt lip around the mouth, held in place by four broad silver-gilt clips developing on the outer face of the horn into four cast pilasters with two human faces on each (Pl. 4).[9] The rim and clips held in place the tops and sides of four rectangular silver-gilt foil sheets. At the base of each pilaster the point developed into a flat disc with a central rivet hole through which it was fastened to the horn. The lower edges of the four rectangular panels were held in place by a thinner more delicate strip of silver-gilt foil attached to the horn with the rivets of the clip pilasters. It also fixed in place the upper ends of twelve triangular pendant pieces of foil, the "van dykes," which were in turn rivetted to the horn at their lower ends. Each horn also had an elaborate end mount extending a full nineteen centimeters down the horn to the point. This consisted of five van dykes, three raised ring collars with flat panels of foil between them, and a large bird-head finial, resembling a raptor.

All the flat foil panels and van dykes were stamped with dies showing animal ornament. The motifs on the dies have been linked by Bruce-Mitford primarily with material from eastern Scandinavia, notably Valsgärde 6, and with bronze mounts from sites in Gotland and Sodermanland.[10] Remnants of the ornament of another horn or possibly a pair of horns were found in the ransacked boat grave in Mound Two at Sutton Hoo, showing the use of the same die that was used to ornament the large van dykes of the Mound One horns. Bruce-Mitford has correctly pointed out that these two pieces of evidence may be interpreted in one of three ways: the horns were all ornamented in Eastern Scandinavia and imported to East Anglia; the die was imported and used by local East Anglian craftsmen; or a mould was made from the large van dykes of an imported Scandinavian horn, and used to make ornaments for another horn or horns. In any case the aurochs horn itself must be imported, and it seems to me unlikely that both horns and dies would be independently imported. Given the sheer quantity of the Sutton Hoo material now assigned a Scandinavian provenance it seems likely that completed ornamented drinking horns might have arrived by the same channels and for the same reasons, possibly due to ancestral connections of the East Anglian royal house.[11]

---

[8] Bruce-Mitford, *The Sutton Hoo Ship Burial*, III, 327.

[9] *Ibid.*, 327-47, fig. 235.

[10] *Ibid.*, 374-79, figs. 275-76; R. L. S. Bruce-Mitford, "The Sutton Hoo Ship Burial: Some Foreign Connections," *Angli e Sassoni al di qua e al di là del mare, Settimane di studio del Centro italiano di studio sull'alto medioevo* 32 (Spoleto 1986), 175-76, fig. 16.

[11] I thank Martin Carver for telling me of the discovery, in the looted and much disturbed ship burial in Mound Two at Sutton Hoo, of a van dyke and a bird-head terminal for a drinking horn virtually identical with those found in the Mound One ship burial. The discovery of these fragments influences the question of the site of manufacture of the Mound One horns, but it does remain possible that more than one pair of ceremonial horns belonged to the royal house of East Anglia and that several pairs may have been imported from the same source at the same time; thus the identity of form does not mandate local manufacture. Also the burial of single or paired horns in Mound Two at Sutton Hoo does not necessarily impinge on the interpretation of the Mound One horns as part of a larger symbolic context of the Mound One assemblage as a separate unity. It is not possible to demonstrate whether the looted ship burial in Mound Two, despite its scale and the

Although drinking horns of various media and sizes are not uncommon in Germanic graves both in England and on the Continent, large-scale horns ornamented with gold or silver gilt are the exception rather than the rule. Horns entirely of gold are limited to two known finds, the now-destroyed pair of horns found at Gallehus in Denmark in the seventeenth and eighteenth century,[12] and the late Avar eighth- or ninth-century single horn found at Nagy-Szent Miklós in Hungary.[13] Aurochs horns trimmed with silver-gilt are almost equally rare, the known examples from the Anglo-Saxon period being limited at present to the Sutton Hoo examples and the horns from Taplow (Pl. 6) in Buckinghamshire, which were also found with an assemblage of drinking bottles.[14] The balance of evidence of early Anglo-Saxon drinking horns with metal mounts is in the form of fragments from very rich graves.[15]

The Gallehus horns had both repoussé and punched animal motifs in a more naturalistic style than the later Germanic animal ornament on the Sutton Hoo and Taplow examples, but as the details of the Gallehus horns are preserved only in early engravings, the accuracy of which is questionable, our chances of being able to reconstruct their iconography and on this basis reconstruct the identity and possible meaning of the ornamental creatures on the Sutton Hoo horns are dubious at best. We do, however, have information useful in interpreting the Sutton Hoo horns: they are very possibly imported objects, drinking horns of unusual intrinsic value and grandeur. Also, they were too large, and when filled, too heavy, for one person to use comfortably as a personal cup for drinking, regardless of physical strength or bibulous capacity. We must seek their function and their meaning in ritual and collective use.

In order to consider the possible meaning the horns may have had for the East Anglian king with whom they were buried, we need to consider the documentary record as well. Caesar (*De bello Gallico* vi:28) narrates that the Germanic tribes hunted the aurochs as a test of courage, and ornamented their horns with silver for use as drinking vessels.[16] Tacitus (*Germania* 22) relates that the Germans indulged in great feasts or *convivia*, at which they drank throughout the entire day and night.[17] Given this, we immediately envision the Germanic ancestors of the East Angles as the equivalent of a pack of modern fraternity rowdies running the bulls at Pamplona when not testing the limits of alcohol toxicity. However, the Romans were foreigners among the Germanic groups they observed, and were not trained anthropologists; they may not have understood what they were observing. The indigenous linguistic and literary evidence suggests that the ale feast had an entirely different role in Germanic society than that envisioned by the Roman chroniclers.

Maurice Cahen was the first to examine the structure of ritual drinking, which he termed "libation," within the Germanic linguistic tradition.[18] His analyses of specific terms have been called into question in the past decade,[19] but the fundamental hypothesis still stands.[20] The central concept is *symbel*, a term denoting a solemn ritual ale-

---

evidence of the single horn, was or was not as rich a burial as Mound One, and whether the intended message of its lost contents was identical or different.

[12]J. Brøndsted, *Guldhornene, en Oversigt* (Copenhagen 1954).

[13]J. Hampel, *Der Goldfund von Nagy-Szent Miklós* (Budapest 1885); G. László, *The Art of the Migration Period* (Coral Gables 1974), 130-35.

[14]J. Stevens, "On the Remains found in an Anglo-Saxon Tumulus at Taplow, Bucks.," *JBAA* 40 (1884), 61-71; E. T. Leeds, *Early Anglo-Saxon Art and Archaeology* (Oxford 1936), 75-76; Bruce-Mitford, *The Sutton Hoo Ship Burial*, III, 383.

[15]D. H. Kennett, "Graves with Swords at Little Wilbraham and Linton Heath," *Proc. of the Cambridge Soc. of Ant.* 63 (1971), 15-17; K. East in Bruce-Mitford, *The Sutton Hoo Ship Burial*, III, 385-95.

[16] Cited in Bruce-Mitford, *The Sutton Hoo Ship Burial*, III, 380-81.

[17]H. Mattingly (ed.) *Tacitus: Germania* (Harmondsworth 1970), 120.

[18]M. Cahen, *La Libation: Études sur le vocabulaire religieux du vieux-Scandinave*, (Paris 1921); see also R. Doht, *Der Rauschtrank im Germanischen Mythos*, Wiener Arbeiten zur germanischen Altertumskunde und Philologie 3 (Vienna 1974).

[19]M. S. Neff, *Germanic Sacrifice: An Analytic Study using Linguistic, Archaeological and Literary Data*, Ph.D. thesis, University of Texas at Austin, 1980; K. Düwel, *Das Opferfest von Lade: Quellenkritische Untersuchungen zur germanische Religionsgeschichte*, Wiener Arbeiten zur germanischen Altertumskunde und Philologie 27 (Vienna 1985).

[20]P. C. Bauschatz, "The Germanic Ritual Feast," in J. Weinstock (ed.) *The Nordic Languages and Modern Linguistics: Proceedings of the Third International Conference of Nordic and General Linguistics* 3 (Austin 1978), 289-95; P. C. Bauschatz, *The Well and the Tree: World and Time in Early Germanic Culture* (Amherst 1982), 72-78.

feast at which the participants sat together, probably in order of rank and usually indoors, drinking in sequence from a common cup. The term appears in the Old Saxon *Heiland*; in Norse, especially in the *Eddas*, in *Lokasenna*, and in *Hymiskviða*; and in Old English in *Beowulf, The Dream of the Rood* and *Judith*. The beverage served at *symbel* is never stated with certainty; it is usually vaguely described by the writers as beer, ale, mead, or wine; it is clear that no particular beverage was traditional for all feasts.[21] Apparently, however, distinctions among beverages were made in practice that are not evident in the literary record, as analysis of residues in the pair of horns from Skudstrup indicates that one was consistently used for barley beer and the other for mead.[22] Drink at *symbel* was also not merely a beverage consumed with a meal – food is not mentioned. The drinking itself appears to be the central but not the only activity; speech making and gift giving are clearly also significant. The speeches take two forms, the narrative of past events and the boast or promise, the *beot*. Such promises appear to be binding; it is the ritual context, the cup over which they are made, that gives them their binding power. It is at *symbel* in Heorot that Beowulf takes the oath to kill Grendel or be killed in the attempt.[23] And although this oath is spoken before the entire assembly, it is clearly Hroðgar to whom it is addressed. This pattern of usage is reflected in other literary sources and most probably reflects authentic early and traditional practices, whatever the date and venue we may assign the composition of the *Beowulf* poem.

It is the binding nature of the *beot* spoken at *symbel* that makes significant the presence of the horns in the grave of a king. Surely the king's thanes, his circle of warriors, were the core of the group to sit at *symbel* with the king, drink from the royal horns, and make promises to their royal war leader, but visiting dignitaries, exiled heirs to foreign thrones and others of rank resident in the court for any reason and for any length of time could scarcely have avoided participating in their host's *symbel*. Consequently, the royal drinking horns were probably more often than not the physical vehicle of the establishment of binding political alliances and social bonds, the fundamental matrix of royal power in early Anglo-Saxon England. Their presence in Mound One at Sutton Hoo should be reconsidered in this context.

To some extent, even the Romans recognized the role of ritual drinking in the political and ritual lives of the Germanic peoples they encountered. In discussing the Sutton Hoo horns, Bruce-Mitford brings to our attention the relief on the triumphal arch at Carpentras, Vaucluse, France.[24] Here, captive barbarians are depicted beneath two large drinking horns flanking what may be a cauldron. The large horns are ornamented at rim and tip, and are incised with a pattern suggesting the van dykes of the Sutton Hoo horns; they are also displayed with their tips crossed, as the Sutton Hoo horns may have been arranged when buried.[25] The rest of the arch is decorated with other trophies. Bruce-Mitford's interpretation of this relief suggests that the Romans depicted the horns because they were "typical" objects of German culture; as attributes to help identify the figures below; however, the inscriptive material on the arch would have left no doubt in anyone's mind as to over whom the Romans were here commemorating their victory. I am reminded, instead, of the objects from the Temple of Jerusalem carried in triumphal procession on the Arch of Titus. Here not just any objects are chosen for conspicuous and accurate depiction, but specifically those around which the collective identity and unity of the Jewish people were focussed, most particularly the Arc of the Covenant. Similarly, the horns at Carpentras may well have been singled out for conspicuous display because the social and political fabric they helped to weave together, and so had come to represent, had been conquered and subsumed into the Roman Empire and its broader network of bonds and alliances.

The East Angles were not, however, the only people in early Suffolk to whom drinking horns and drinking ritual were the physical vehicle of confirmation of social and political obligations. The Anglian and Saxon rulers of England held dominance over a Celtic subculture that not only survived the Anglo-Saxon conquest but interacted

---

[21]C. E. Fell, "Old English *beor*," *Leeds Studies in English*, n.s. 8 (1975), 76-95.

[22]J. Grüss, "Zwei Altegermanische Trinkhörner mit Bier- und Metresten," *Prähistorische Zeitschrift* 22 (1931),180-91.

[23]*Beowulf*, ll. 633-38; C. W. Kennedy, *Beowulf; The Oldest English Epic* (Oxford, London and New York 1950), 22.

[24]Bruce-Mitford, *The Sutton Hoo Ship Burial*, III, 383, fig. 277.

[25]*Ibid.*, fig. 226.

extensively with the ruling Germanic minority in the subsequent period. For the role of drinking ritual in Celtic society, we have both archaeological and literary evidence. In the recently excavated Hallstatt-period prince's grave at Hochdorf, dated about 500 B.C., eight gold-trimmed, aurochs-horn drinking horns were hung along the south wall of the tomb, along with one larger iron horn with bronze and gold trim, an assemblage not unlike the two great horns and six burrwood bottles at Sutton Hoo.[26] Of course, Celtic culture was not monolithic, nor can we assume that practices were unchanged from the Hallstatt Celts of sixth-century B.C. Germany to seventh-century England. However, we do have a source that brings the Celtic side of the picture into focus for the period of the Sutton Hoo ship burial, the *Gododdin*. Written by the poet Aneirin around A.D. 600, it chronicles a disastrous cavalry raid by north British warriors under their ruler, Mynyddog, from the region around Edinburgh south into Anglian Yorkshire, and laments those who did not return. One of the most consistently recurring motifs in the poem is the theme of Mynyddog's ale-feast, which was held over the entire year preceding the raid; the warriors who have drunk their warlord's ale, seated by rank at his ale bench, are obligated to follow him, even to their own deaths:

> The men went to Catraeth, they were famous; wine and mead in golden vessels was their drink for a year according to the honorable custom; three men and three score and three hundred wearing golden torques. Of those that hastened forth after the choice drink none escaped but three...[27]

Elsewhere, are numerous variations on the following: "He attacked in battle-stress in the forefront in return for mead in the hall and drink of wine..."[28]

Kenneth Jackson, who published the standard English translation of the poem, has stressed that the role of the intoxicants in the defeat of the Britons was not in the men being too drunk to fight well, but in that they were obligated to "earn their mead," to fight to the death, if need be, to serve their leader.[29] The *Gorchan of Tudfwlch* uses analogous structure: "In return for mead and ale the company went... across their boundary."[30] Certainly it was not quantity of mead and ale, unceremoniously guzzled, for which men paid with their lives, but the ceremonially consumed ale or mead of ale-feasts, of the Celtic equivalent of *symbel*. And indeed, the drinking horn appears in a list of treasures in *Culhwch ac Olwen*, which Doris Edel has convincingly suggested is an inventory of regnal regalia with its roots in the venue and period of the *Gododdin* rather than in the eleventh-century composition of the four branches of the *Mabinogian*, of which *Culhwch ac Olwen* is a part.[31]

Drinking horns also appear in later regnal contexts in Ireland. They occur frequently in the *Lebor na Cert*, the *Book of Rights*, among the tribute owed to the high king by provincial tribal rulers and among the stipends (*tuarastal*) owed to underkings by their overlords.[32] These horns are described in the genealogies as of wild ox horn (*cuirn buabull*).[33] A horn called "corne-cam-more" also figures as part of the regalia of the kings of Leinster.[34] The prescriptive prerogatives (*buada*) of the kings of Leinster also include the contents of the horn, the *coirm Chualann* or "ale of Cuala," mentioned in the genealogies in the encomium of Áed Dub and in an eleventh-century poem by Cúán ua Lothcáin.[35] The horn of the kings of Leinster, called the Charter Horn, was

---

[26]J. Biel, "Die Ausstattung des Toten," in D. Planck, *et al.*, *Der Keltenfürst von Hochdorf: Methoden und Ergebnisse der Landesarchäologie* (Stuttgart 1985), 92-93, 149, pls. 119, 168, 169.

[27]K. H. Jackson, *The Gododdin: the Oldest Scottish Poem* (Edinburgh 1969), 124-25.

[28]Jackson, *Gododdin*, 132.

[29]*Ibid.*, 36-37.

[30]*Ibid.*, 36.

[31]D. Edel, "The Catalogues in *Culwych ac Olwen* and Insular Celtic Learning," *BBCS* 30 (1983), 263-65.

[32]M. Dillon, *Lebor na Cert: The Book of Rights* (Dublin 1962).

[33]F. J. Byrne, *Irish Kings and High Kings* (London 1973), 153.

[34]R. Ó Floinn, "The Kavanaugh 'Charter' Horn," in D. Ó Corráin (ed.) *Irish Antiquity: Essays and Studies Presented to Professor M. J. O'Kelly* (Cork 1981), 268-78.

[35]Byrne, *Irish Kings and High Kings*, 152-53.

handed on to their descendants, the Kavanaughs of Garryhill and Borris House (Co. Carlow), and was acquired by the National Museum of Ireland in 1976.[36]

Certainly the king of East Anglia buried in Mound One at Sutton Hoo had Celtic subjects, some of whom may have fought in his warband. To them, the drinking horns would have been as potent a symbol of obligation as they were to their Anglian contemporaries. But there is an additional possible implication. Patrick Wormald has convincingly demonstrated that *bretwalda* or "ruler of the Britons," a term applied in late manuscripts of the *Anglo-Saxon Chronicle* to certain kings in Anglo-Saxon England whose territories extended beyond their tribal settlement areas, is historically dubious.[37] Nonetheless, Bede does mention, in the *Ecclesiastical History* (ii:5), that there were certain kings of the early Anglo-Saxon world who achieved a widespread if temporary hegemony over Angles, Saxons, and Britons alike, in regions that extended far beyond their inherited regional bases of power, often over several neighboring kingdoms.[38] Rædwald is one of these kings, the only ruler of East Anglia to achieve this distinction. If indeed Mound One at Sutton Hoo is his tomb or cenotaph, then we should not be surprised to find in it regalia of not only Anglian but also Celtic symbolic content. If indeed, as Martin Carver has phrased it, burial is a form of poetry, then the poem of Mound One at Sutton Hoo may well be about kingship.[39]

---

[36] Ó Floinn, "Kavanaugh 'Charter' Horn." I thank Michael Ryan, Keeper of Irish Antiquities, National Museum of Ireland, Dublin, for the references for the regnal context of drinking horns in Irish documentary sources and for the history of the Kavanaugh Charter Horn.

[37] P. Wormald, "Bede, the *Bretwaldas* and the Origin of the *Gens Anglorum*," in P. Wormald, D. Bullough and R. Collins (eds.) *Ideal and Reality in Frankish and Anglo-Saxon Society: Studies Presented to J.M. Wallace-Hadrill* (Oxford 1983), 99-121.

[38] Colgrave and Mynors, *Ecclesiastical History*, 148-51.

[39] M. Carver, "Commentary on Sutton Hoo: Past, Present and Future," 24th International Congress on Medieval Studies, Western Michigan University, May 4-7, 1989.

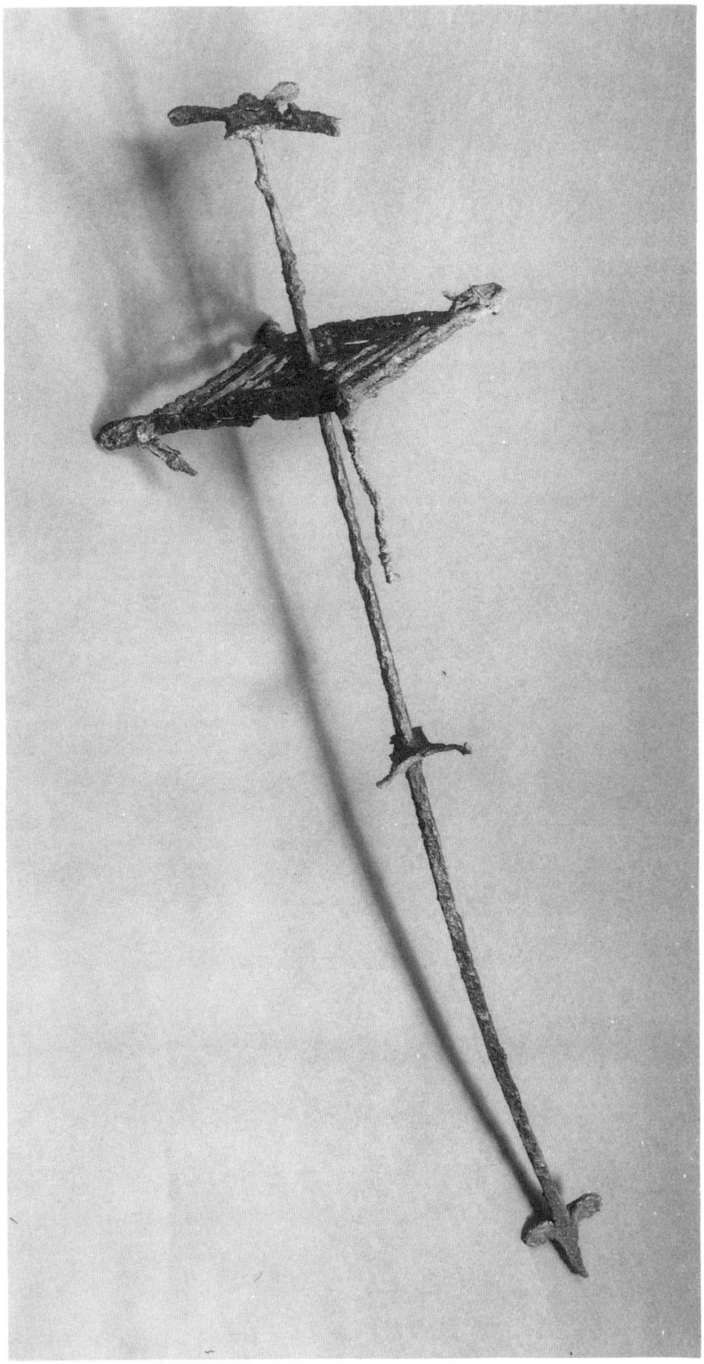

Pl. 1. Sutton Hoo, Mound One: the iron stand. London, The British Museum. (Photo: By permission of the Trustees, British Museum).

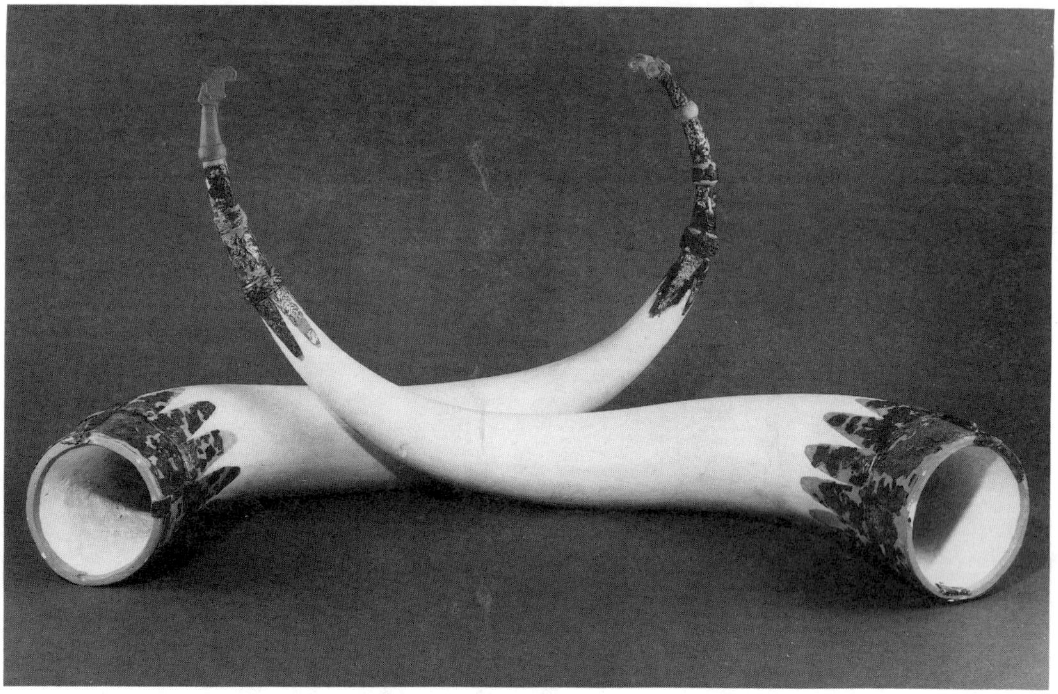

Pl. 2. Sutton Hoo, Mound One: drinking horns; reconstruction. London, The British Museum. (Photo: By permission of the Trustees, British Museum).

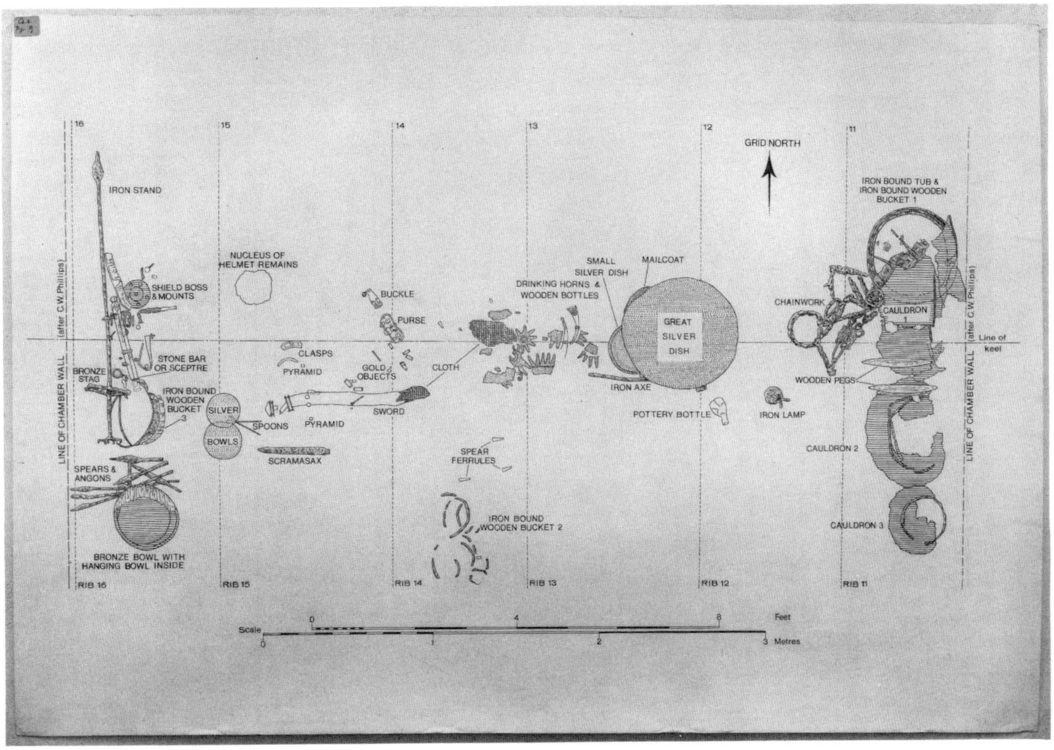

Pl. 3. Sutton Hoo, Mound One: diagram of finds. (By permission of the Trustees, British Museum).

Pl. 4. Sutton Hoo, Mound One: drinking horns; mouth mounts of one horn. London, The British Museum. (Photo: By permission of the Trustees, British Museum).

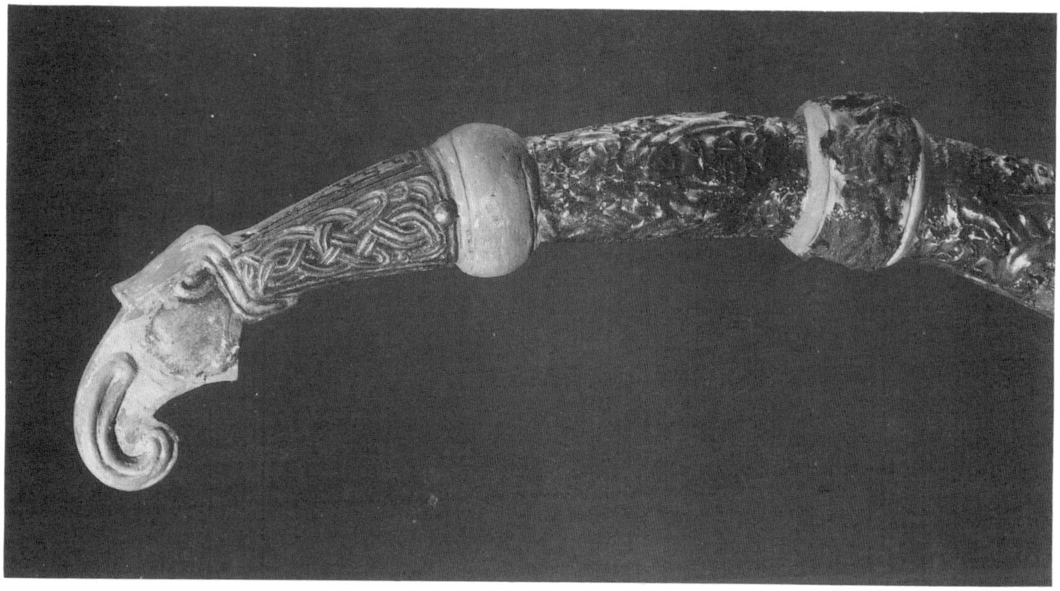

Pl. 5. Sutton Hoo, Mound One: drinking horns; terminal and end mount of one horn. London, The British Museum. (Photo: By permission of the Trustees, British Museum).

Pl. 6. Taplow: large drinking horns; reconstruction. London, The British Museum. (Photo: By permission of the Trustees, British Museum).

Death's Diplomacy: Sutton Hoo in the Light of Other Male Princely Burials

LESLIE WEBSTER

This paper will review the range of evidence presented by a (by no means exhaustive) number of Continental, Scandinavian and Anglo-Saxon burials, and thereby see how they might affect the way in which we judge Sutton Hoo as a statement of power. But first it is necessary to address the far from simple question of what constitutes a princely burial. This is, indeed, a minefield where only fools would tread, but we may at least begin with a few certainties. First of all, there can be no doubt that male princely burial itself (and its attendant rituals, of which we know virtually nothing) was an important symbolic expression of personal and/or dynastic power. Through it, the successors not only honored the dead man, but might also perform a range of other acts: claims to authority; claims to territory; expressions of cultural or religious ascendancy, or of political alignment. Even secret burial could be, in a real sense, for the record: when the body of Alaric I was interred with many treasures in the bed of the river Busento, which was temporarily diverted for the purpose, and those captives who had performed the labor were killed, this was just as much an expression of power – over nature as well as men – as more public burial.[1] Early medieval writers knew perfectly well the meaning of such burial, as Jordanes's description of the burial of Attila the Hun makes clear:

> In the secrecy of night, they buried his body in the earth. They bound his coffins, the first with gold, the second with silver, and the third with the strength of iron, showing by this means that these three things suited the mightiest of kings; iron because he subdued the nations, gold and silver because he received the honors of both empires. They also added the arms of freemen won in the fight, trappings of rare worth, sparkling with various gems, and ornaments of all sorts *whereby princely state is maintained*.[2]

Burials across Europe make manifest the simple fact that "princely state" is maintained by certain types and forms of possession and by certain modes of burial which express this concept as vividly in death as in life.

The iconography of male princely burial is, however, by no means static; thus, though weapons and jewelry and vessel assemblages, for instance, are widespread, this reflects the generality of Germanic burial practice rather than a distinguishing mark of royalty. Quality or quantity is the distinguishing feature, rather than the thing as such. Both the contents and the modes of interment may in fact vary widely, as factors of, for example, chronology, geography or religious persuasion. Nevertheless, it is evident that there are certain underlying features which are shared, in varying combinations, by these burials, whether inhumation or cremation, pagan or Christian, and even furnished or unfurnished.

For a closer examination of the topic, there can be only one starting point. Of the relatively numerous burials with grave-goods which might be classed as princely, only one is actually identifiable with any real certainty. This is, of course, the burial of Childeric (d. 481/82), which was found in 1653 by a deaf-mute stonemason beneath the later church of St. Brice in Tournai, Belgium.[3] Along with many rich grave-goods it contained a Roman-type seal-ring with the retrograde inscription CHILDERICI REGIS above a bust of a long-haired male wearing a Roman-style cuirass and *paludamentum* and carrying a spear – the weapon with which, according to Gregory of Tours, Merovingian kings were invested with royal authority. Unlike other rings with royal inscriptions, such a ring explicitly avows royal ownership, and it would be an unlikely chain of events which took the ring into some other's possession. The circumstances of the discovery were such, however, that one cannot be certain that all the other

[1] Jordanes, *History of the Goths*, trans. C. C. Mierow (Princeton 1915), 158.

[2] *Ibid.*, 258 (italics added).

[3] J. Chifflet, *Anastasis Childerici Primi* (Paris 1655).

recorded finds came from the king's grave rather than from adjacent ones, for which there is ample evidence. The crystal ball, for example, may well derive from a nearby female grave. It is also likely that other objects – ironwork, for instance – were overlooked during the investigation, and that still further pieces may have disappeared before Jacques Chifflet, the grave's remarkable chronicler, arrived on the scene. It seems however certain that most of the finds – the gold arm-ring, the gold and garnet belt-mounts and horse harness, the garnet inlaid sword and sea-fittings, as well as the purse with its Roman gold and silver coins – were indeed part of the king's royal equipment along with his *francisca* and lance. As such, they reflect both native Frankish custom and a wider relationship with Danubian Germanic metalwork of a type known from a scatter of other richly-furnished male graves in western Europe, and represented in the East by such rich graves as those at Apahida and Blučina.[4] The famous garnet-inlaid cicadas thought to have adorned the cloak (but which may actually have come from the horse-harness) also derive from Germanic sources. The cross-bow brooch, however, is a purely Roman object, signifying high office, and, like the signet-ring with its portrait of Childeric as a Roman general, it clearly suggests that this Frankish king was perceived as an heir of *Romanitas*. The two hundred silver and one hundred gold coins in his purse may also reflect this; not just a king's treasure, but a symbol of Roman-style *largitio*.

We know nothing of the burial of Childeric's Christianized successor Clovis,[5] but we know from Gregory of Tours that the emperor Anastasius bestowed on him the title of consul: Gregory gives a telling description of Clovis attired in a purple tunic and mantle and wearing a diadem, showering gold and silver among his subjects:[6] while Theodoric the Great (d. 526), perhaps the Empire's most effective Germanic heir, according to Cassiodorus also wore "the purple cloth of royalty studded with gems."[7] But the sense of conscious *Romanitas* implicit in Childeric's burial and these accounts clearly coexisted with a *Germanitas* made manifest in other ways, as the historical sources make plain.

Clovis and Theodoric were, of course, buried as Christians, Theodoric in a mausoleum of imperial intent. As a pagan, however, Childeric was buried in full-blown pagan style, probably under a burial mound which acted as a focus for a contemporary and subsequent Frankish cemetery. The grave may have contained a decapitated horse's head; and recent excavations nearby have revealed no fewer than three sacrificial pits, each containing the bones of a dozen horses, mainly stallions. Radiocarbon dates for these indicate that they may date between 440 and 540, making their association with the burial of Childeric very plausible.[8]

Such striking juxtapositions of Roman insignia alongside Germanic accoutrements and burial practices are not just fortuitous: they express in archaeological terms a belief that their owners were in some sense not only Germanic war-lords, but also the successors to Roman authority. And though the cross-bow brooch was to be superseded as an insignia of power, other Roman-style traditions were to succeed it. From at least the mid-sixth century for example, the traditions continue in princely graves, such as the princeling's grave from Cologne cathedral, and the chamber-graves, at Morken and Niederstotzingen.[9] It is at this point that, alongside other Roman-inspired symbols of power such as the wooden scepter in the Cologne boy's grave, helmets and body armor begin to appear in Frankish graves, evidently in imitation of the Byzantine imperial guard uniform, and no doubt with imperial echoes in mind. It is no accident after all, that the Byzantine *spangenhelmen* and the imperial parade helmets were the ultimate prototypes for the imperial crowns of the Middle Ages. What is perhaps more surprising is the extent to

[4]Apahida II: K. Horedt, "Das zweite Fürstengrab von Apahida: neue völkerwanderungszeit Goldfunde des 5 Jahrhunderts aus Siebenburgen," *Germania* 50 (1972), 174-220; Blučina: G. Bott (ed.) *Germanen Hunnen und Awaren, Schätze der Volkerwanderungszeit*, Ausstellungs-Kataloge des Germanischen Nationalmuseums (Nüremberg 1987), 374-75, pls. 56-57.

[5]Though recent work by Patrick Perin, "The Undiscovered Grave of King Clovis," in M. O. Carver (ed.) *Sutton Hoo Studies* (forthcoming 1992), brings together the evidence for its current location in Paris.

[6]Gregory of Tours, *The History of the Franks*, trans. L. Thorpe (Harmondsworth 1974), 38.

[7]Cassiodorus, *Variae*, XI, XX, XXXI.

[8]E. James, *The Franks* (Oxford 1988), 62-64.

[9]O. Doppelfeld and R. Pirling, *Fränkischen Fürsten im Rheinland: Die Gräber aus Kölner Dom, von Krefeld-Gellep und Morken* (Bonn 1966); P. Paulsen, *Alamannische Adelsgräber von Niederstotzingen (Kreis Heidenheim)*, Veröffentlichungen des Staatlichen Amtes für Denkmalpflege, Stuttgart, Reihe A, Vor- und Frühgeschichte, Heft 12/1 (Stuttgart 1967).

which not these, but functionally useless imitations of imperial parade helmets became potent symbols of power in some of the remoter corners of northwestern Europe.

The Sutton Hoo, Vendel and Valsgärde helmets, not forgetting the fragments from the royal site at Gamla Uppsala, have been shown by Rupert Bruce-Mitford to share a common source in late Antique parade helmets, reinterpreted for local consumption.[10] But though their decoration invokes Germanic myth, their form is unmistakably late Antique: it is, for example, no accident that when the carver of the Franks Casket came to depict the Roman general (later Emperor) Titus, he gave him one of these. Even in remotest Derbyshire, in the damaged seventh-century princely grave at Benty Grange, a flimsy horn-panelled helmet aping these more elaborate versions was felt to be an appropriate – if impractical – symbol of power.[11]

But these are not the only princely accoutrements on the wilder shores of Europe which held some glimmer of Roman *auctoritas*. The body armor at Sutton Hoo, and with it the shoulder-clasps from some form of cuirass, clearly belong in the same ambit, and so, ultimately, must the "scepter," for all its apparent ambiguities. Most striking of all, however, in this context are the purse and its coins and blanks; like the tally of three hundred coins in Childeric's purse, they seem to have been specially rounded up to a specific number, as well as having been carefully selected by mint. This is patently more than mere treasure per se; and whether or not one accepts Grierson's ingenious and plausible explanation of payment to oarsmen, there still lurks behind the coins the notion of *largitio* observed in Childeric's burial-purse and in Gregory's account of Clovis. Small wonder indeed that the East Anglian dynasty claimed descent from Caesar.

Equally important as a characteristic of princely burials is the concept of separateness, both physical and cultural. It is true that many of the fifth- and sixth-century burials of this type – sometimes distinguished by barrows – appear to represent the nuclei of cemeteries which grew up around them. Childeric's burial is one such; or to take an English example, the boat barrow at Snape in Suffolk may be another.[12]

But from the early sixth century, it was, for example, increasingly customary for the Franks of Gaul and the Rhineland to bury their elite not in *Reihengraberfelden*, but in churches, as the princely graves in a funerary chapel constructed in the atrium of Cologne cathedral and, somewhat later, that in the church at Morken show. It is thus hardly surprising that the newly Christianized Æthelbert of Kent and his Frankish wife adopted Continental custom and, instead of joining their forebears in some well-stocked cemetery such as King's Field, Faversham, Finglesham, Kingston, or Eastry, were buried – presumably without grave-goods – in the church of St. Peter and St. Paul at Canterbury. It is striking that at much the same time (i.e. around the year 600) other physically distinctive forms of elite burial were emerging in England, and it would seem, in northern Europe also. It seems, for instance to be around this time that the earliest of the imposing barrow burials at Vendel in Sweden belong, along with the princely cremations from the mounds at Gamla Uppsala and the magnificent burial from Åker, Norway, with its Frankish influenced buckle.[13] In England there is a twofold move to express status in burial construction around this time. First of all, in a number of normal cemeteries across the country, there is an observable and growing tendency to define higher-status graves by special structures – ditches, palisades, chambers and so on – often in presumed family groups at the edge of a cemetery. The St. Peter's, Broadstairs, and Spong Hill cemeteries are classic examples of the kind.[14] Like the Christian royal families, however, pagan families of *supra*-local importance were much more likely to be buried quite separately in other locations, specifically, in large barrows which were often in isolated and topographically prominent locations. The Sutton Hoo royal cemetery, none of which appears to predate A.D. 600 and which indeed probably focuses on Mound One, occupies a remote but

---

[10] R. L. S. Bruce-Mitford, *The Sutton Hoo Ship Burial*, vol. II (London 1978), 220-25.

[11] R. L. S. Bruce-Mitford, *Aspects of Anglo-Saxon Archaeology: Sutton Hoo and Other Discoveries* (London 1974), 223-42.

[12] *Ibid.*, 114-40.

[13] W. Slomann and A.-E. Christensen, "The Åker Find: Facts, Theories and Speculations," *Festskrift til Thorlief Sjøvold på 70-årsdagen*, Universitetets Oldsaksamlings skrifter, Ny rekke Nr. 5 (Oslo 1984), 173-90.

[14] St. Peter's, Broadstairs: A. C. Hogarth, "Structural Features in Anglo-Saxon Graves," *ArchJ* 130 (1973), 104-19. Spong Hill: C. Hills, *Spong Hill Part III: Catalogue of Inhumations* (*East Anglian Archaeology* 21) (Norfolk Archaeological Unit, Norfolk Museums Service 1984).

dominant position in a ridge overlooking the Deben valley. Similarly isolated and prominent positions may be observed in almost all the other rich primary barrows of this period – either overlooking natural boundaries as at Asthall, Benty Grange or Taplow, or situated by Roman roads like the barrows at Coombe Bissett and Caenby.

The great early seventh-century burial at Taplow is a particularly illuminating example: it consists of a massive mound, 75m in circumference and 5m high, standing alone above a cliff which drops down 30m to the river Thames below. From the mound itself, there is a wide view westwards across the Thames to the fertile, and in Anglo-Saxon times relatively populous, lands of the Upper Thames Valley. But the mound itself lies on a wooded gravelly terrace, the thin soils of which are inhospitable to agriculture and which in Anglo-Saxon times were very sparsely settled, as archaeological, toponymical, and documentary evidence combine to show. The implantation of such an exceptionally rich and imposing Anglo-Saxon burial on this windy plateau is a striking assertion of power in several ways: through the manner of burial itself and its contents; through its physical isolation, both as a prominent barrow on an otherwise flat plateau, and as a burial apparently separate from any conventional cemetery; and thirdly, and perhaps most interestingly, through a kind of cultural apartheid. The rich, exotic and Kent-oriented contents of the Taplow barrow have almost nothing in common with the prevailing culture of its nearest neighbors in the Thames Valley. The material culture is very different both in quality and in kind, even where richer burials are concerned.

This cultural distancing from the prevailing population is a marked feature of other princely Anglo-Saxon burials of the period. The Sutton Hoo barrow group has almost nothing culturally in common with either the great cremation fields or successor inhumation cemeteries of East Anglia. (The bizarre inhumation graves which cluster in alignment to the major barrows there are perceptibly different from the run of normal Anglo-Saxon burials in East Anglia, and seem to have been ritually chosen in some way.) The Sutton Hoo barrows dominate the ridge, in almost every way physically and culturally distinct from the hoi polloi about them, and expressing their separateness in the most ostentatious way available to them.

Cultural apartheid, however, may take other forms. In the huge barrow burial at Asthall (Oxfordshire) thought to be that of an implanted Mercian ruler, it surprisingly appears in the form of a cremation burial in a landscape otherwise accustomed to inhumations. (The melted remains, incidentally, indicated that several kilos of bronze and silver had been consumed on the pyre.)[15] At Beckum, in Westphalia, another version may be seen. Here a seventh-century Frankish princely warrior was buried with pagan splendor amid a sea of Saxons. He and his small troupe of lesser Frankish burials give every appearance of a lone Frankish outpost on the edge of Empire.[16]

The early seventh-century Kentish royal burials, on the other hand, were seemingly distinguished from the generality of contemporary Kentish burials by church burial without accompanying grave-goods.[17] Judged by the range and quality of its grave-goods, Kent was, of course, the richest of Anglo-Saxon kingdoms in the sixth and seventh centuries. In such a context, the absence of grave-goods may be just as much a matter of status as their presence, indeed especially so in a kingdom still in the throes of conversion, where paganism and Christianity are still very much face to face.

So in Anglo-Saxon England around the year 600 we see a development and subsequent acceleration of a trend to express the power of an elite through modes of burial which were ostentatious in their physical and cultural separateness. The reasons for this are not far to seek: the seventh century in Anglo-Saxon England was a period of major change in almost every aspect of life – economic, religious, social and political. It would be otiose to recount the evidence. In their various ways, the princely burials of this period seem to reflect some of these currents of change: a greater polarization in society; attendant territorial claims; and a concurrent emphasis on religious status. It is noteworthy in this connection that many ancient barrow sites, though *not*, in fact, Sutton Hoo, were later deliberately chosen for the location of Christian churches; Taplow is one such, and Gamla Uppsala and Vendel may stand for a number of Scandinavian pagan sites converted in the same way. The contemporary

---

[15]E. T. Leeds, "An Anglo-Saxon Cremation Burial of the Seventh Century in Asthall Barrow, Oxfordshire," *AntJ* 4 (1924), 113-26.

[16]C. Ahrens (ed.) *Sachsen und Angelsachsen*, Ausstellung des Helms-Museums, Hamburgisches Museum für Vor- und Frühgeschichte (Hamburg 1978), 471-72, 666-78.

[17]Presumably in the manner of Æthelbert and Bertha who were buried in the chapel of St. Martin, within the church of St. Peter and St. Paul at Canterbury: Bede, *Historia Ecclesiastica*, ii,5.

importance of these major pagan burial sites is readily seen in the fact that they were obviously perceived as conferring power to the new church.

To what extent that importance relied upon memory of the content of the burial as well as its appearance and location is impossible to assess. Nevertheless, even clandestine burial, as we saw in the cases of Alaric and Attila, was intended to impress. It is unlikely that the conspicuous consumption we observe at Sutton Hoo, Taplow, Tournai and Vendel was intended to be forgotten. After all, the grave-goods themselves held specific messages.

We have noted already now many of the Continental Germanic kings and princes chose to emphasize not only, as one might expect, their supremacy as leaders of, for example, Franks or Gepids, but also chose to assert their claims to be heirs to Roman authority and Roman land by wearing such Roman insignia of high office and military leadership as brooches, signet-rings, belt buckles, helmets and so forth. The potency of these symbols is clearly seen in the eagerness with which barbarians far beyond active Roman influence, indeed beyond the former Empire altogether, seized upon some of them to signify the special nature of their own authority. In this sense Sutton Hoo Mound One, Benty Grange, Vendel and Valsgärde are all the distant heirs of a great tradition.

But there were other messages, often complex and ambiguous, that the grave-deposits were intended to convey. For example, the great multiple assemblages of vessels for provisioning and feasting, which are so prominent at Sutton Hoo, Taplow, Broomfield, and in the Vendel and Valsgärde graves are patently *more* than a mere representation of the dead man's wealth, or indeed of what has been termed "the pagan banquet" in the afterlife. They also stand for the dead man's status as the provider of food and shelter for his followers and dependents, who had to be fed and feasted in the next world. Interestingly, though it is a patently good late Roman custom, the desire to provide the dead with a sufficiency of vessels seems to become much less apparent in the fifth century – Childeric's grave and those of his east European counterparts are notably unencumbered by them. But by c. 540, when the six-year-old prince was buried under Cologne cathedral, it had become customary to bury a range of drinking vessels and buckets with high-status burials; vessels were perceived as appropriate to princely burial in quantities beyond those due to normally rich burials. As with the Roman-style helmets, however, the idea was to reach its most florid expression on the more distant shores of northern and western Europe. The Cologne prince was buried with twelve vessels overall, a total easily outstripped by the twenty-eight vessels at Sutton Hoo Mound One and in some of the Uppland graves; but after that the Taplow burial heads the list, with some nineteen vessels altogether. Such displays were clearly messages for this world as well as the next, extravagant exhibitions of a princely power to command and the reciprocal responsibility to provide. They are indeed symbols of power just as much as a Roman-style helmet, or a gold belt buckle.

Finally, there are what some might think of as the specifically political implications of princely grave-goods. We have already seen something of this in the Asthill and Beckum burials. Here we may turn again to Taplow, where a close reading of the grave-goods shows that almost all the luxury items – the jewelry, the exotic imports, the claw-beakers, the drinking horns, the elaborate textiles – either derive from Kent or must have been transmitted through it.[18] This might be conveniently explained as a reflection of gift-exchange, were it not for the fact that it consists of a mix of pieces that were variously very old, old and brand-new at the time of burial.[19] Such a mix of old and new would raise no eyebrows in Kent itself, but out on that remote and woody plateau, miles from anywhere, it takes on a rather different complexion. While it is theoretically possible that the owner acquired it all in one fell swoop from a Kentish diplomatic mission eager to offload some outmoded equipment along with the new on a bunch of undiscriminating provincials, it is surely much more plausible that the Kentish assemblage at Taplow represents one family's accumulation over a considerable period of time. Thus it is evidence either for a long-standing local relationship with Kent, or for the burial of a noble of Kentish origin. The former hypothesis

[18] K. East and L. Webster, *The Anglo-Saxon Burials at Taplow (Bucks.), Broomfield (Essex) and Caenby (Lincs.)*, British Museum monograph (forthcoming).

[19] The cast of silver-gilt mounts with Style I decoration on the large pair of drinking-horns were perhaps as much as a century old when buried. They had certainly been refitted onto a fresh pair of horns when the originals were damaged, and it was no doubt at this point that additional repoussé mounts with Style II decoration were added. Other items such as the gold and garnet buckle have archaic features and show wear consistent with use over a period of time. At the other end of the chronological spectrum, the Style II gold sheeted clasps were virtually unworn at the time of burial which probably took place in the first quarter of the seventh century.

seems extremely unlikely in view of the burial's cultural and geographical isolation; the latter, however, would fit very well with what little we know of Kentish ascendancy in the South at the beginning of the seventh century, and may gain some support from Dr. John Blair's recent researches on the early kingdom of Mercia, which later in the seventh century seems to have stepped into a void in the region which seems to have been at least in part vacated by Kent.[20]

The Taplow burial, in its imposing construction and dominant location, was clearly intended to impose an image of authority onto the landscape; it seems equally likely from examination of the grave-goods that this authority was that of Kent, and that we see here a member or offshoot of the Kentish dynasty planted here on the very edge of Wessex. It would be more than unwise to propose any such reading of the Sutton Hoo grave-goods; but, given the relative proximity in date of the two burials, it is at least interesting to speculate on the routes which some of the contents of Mound One might have taken to the burial.

I should stress that at this period there is no archaeological evidence of proto-urban, *emporial*, activity at Ipswich though that was certainly advanced by the end of the seventh century. A number of Frankish and early Anglo-Saxon coins and other artefacts have been found at rural sites near Ipswich, but the precise nature of these sites has yet to be determined.[21] For the meantime, there is no obvious point of import into the East Anglian kingdom, nor much evidence from the ordinary sixth- and seventh-century cemeteries of any external traffic. (The contents of the boat barrow at Snape, and a few other isolated finds such as the Ixworth cross, are exceptional.) It is thus difficult to imagine the "Coptic" bowl from Mound One and the other Byzantine bronze vessels elsewhere in the immediate vicinity taking any route other than one through Kent, where their greatest concentration lies.

The silver Byzantine vessels must surely have followed a similar route. They are absolutely unlikely at this time to have formed a direct gift from the Emperor to some distant pagan: on the other hand, they are *exactly* the kinds of gifts one visualizes were brought back to the Frankish kings in their various diplomatic dealings with the East. Such things could very easily have passed to the Kentish royal family with its strong Frankish ties, and thence to East Anglia during the years of close diplomatic contact between the two dynasties, as recounted by Bede. This may also account for the other Frankish links observed in the Mound One grave group; links visible not only in the Merovingian coins and Frankish-type great gold buckle, but also in some of the motifs formerly held to be Scandinavian, but now seen as having a Continental dimension – as the spectacular recent find at Eschwege has reminded us.[22] Yet more intriguingly, it is a matter of record that, apart from the Sutton Hoo shield, the only other demonstrably Swedish artefact from early Anglo-Saxon England, a Gotlandic disc-on-bow brooch, comes from a rich grave at the royal center of Eastry in Kent.[23] One might, moreover, add that both Sweden and Norway were the recipients of glass vessels of Kentish type. The conclusion must be that, despite the marked differences of burial custom between the two kingdoms, on purely archaeological grounds one should suspect a close Kentish connection. How this is to be read in historical terms is, of course, quite another matter.

Mound One will, of course, always remain to some degree enigmatic; though the work of the Sutton Hoo Research Project, both on the site itself and in the regional survey, is extending our awareness of the cultural context in a remarkable way. I also hope, however, that in setting Sutton Hoo Mound One in the wider context of other royal and para-royal burials, we may see more clearly some of the ways in which this both extraordinary

---

[20]See J. Blair, "Frithuwold's Kingdom and the Origins of Surrey," in S. Bassett (ed,), *The Origins of the Anglo-Saxon Kingdoms* (Oxford 1989), 97-107. Dr. Blair's researches indicate a Mercian presence straddling the Thames from north Buckinghamshire down into northwest Surrey in the later seventh century. The charter evidence on which his argument is partly based also shows that Egbert of Kent only a few years earlier had founded the minster at Chertsey, Surrey, one of several hints that Kentish power extended into this area earlier in the seventh century. Thus if the Mercian hegemony in Surrey replaced an attested Kentish presence in that area, one may at least speculate that the same process was at work immediately north of the Thames. Certainly the "Kentish" character of the Taplow burial adds archaeological weight to this hypothesis.

[21]See J. Newman, "Barham, Suffolk – Middle Saxon Market or Meeting Place," and L. Webster, "Barham, Royston and Coddenham: Three Middle Saxon Sites Observed," in D. M. Metcalf (ed.) *Productive Sites: Proceedings of the Twelfth Oxford Symposium on Coinage and Monetary History* (forthcoming 1991).

[22]K. Sippel, *Neue Grabfunde des frühen Mittelalters aus Eschwege, Werra-Meissner Kreis*, Archäologische Denkmäler in Hessen 53 (1986).

[23]S. C. Hawkes, "Eastry in Anglo-Saxon Kent: Its Importance and a Newly Found Grave," *ASSAH* 1 (1979), 81-113.

and typical burial reflects traditional Germanic concepts of authority, and, perhaps more perilously, gain some hint of the shifts and adaptations necessary to the exercise of power in the rapidly changing society of early seventh-century Anglo-Saxon England.

The Sutton Hoo Ship Burial and Ireland: Some Celtic Perspectives

MICHAEL RYAN

The British Museum publication of the Sutton Hoo ship burial is a monument both intellectually and physically. The contents of the volumes contain material of profound interest for early medievalists, both archaeologists and historians, dealing with the Anglo-Saxon, the wider Germanic world and that of the other, Celtic, inhabitants of Britain and Ireland. The questions raised about trade, technology, diplomacy, the rise (or resurrection) of effective kingship, the identification of royal persons or places in archaeology, and pagan-Christian syncretism are endless. We are faced with the problems of particularism – who was he? when did he die? – and process – why that grave at that period?

This essay will examine some of those aspects of the Sutton Hoo grave which have often been described as "Celtic." I will retain the term because it has so frequently been used, but in this historical context something more specific, "Irish," "British," or "Pictish," would be appropriate. A great deal of the discussion of these aspects of the burial could become as subject to what R. B. K. Stevenson has called "the stresses of national mythologies"[1] as the debate about Insular illuminated manuscripts has been, but the exercise of attempting to isolate the origins of objects is not mere nationalistic self-indulgence. In a recent review of hanging bowls, Rupert Bruce-Mitford said of the largest vessel from Sutton Hoo:

> Wherever it was made, this bowl, because of its exceptionally high level of technical and ornamental development and its unique features (such as the fish) must have very important implications for the level of technical and artistic attainment of that region by as early as the end of the sixth century.[2]

Provenance has always been vital archaeological and art historical information.

Some of the results of the research in the British Museum have become known piecemeal in advance of the official publication. The redating of the coins[3] has had the result, from the Celtic point of view, of making St. Fursa's short-lived foundation in East Anglia in the mid 630s an unlikely mechanism for the arrival of the hanging bowls in Sutton Hoo, a theory advanced by Françoise Henry who believed all the enameled examples found in Anglo-Saxon graves to be Irish.[4] Surveys such as those by E. Fowler, D. Longley, R. B. K. Stevenson, and Bruce-Mitford's discussion of the Sutton Hoo bowls make the great complexity of the problem clear.[5]

In what follows I will concentrate on the whetstone scepter and the largest hanging bowl and will introduce some new information from Ireland, which, when fully assessed, may bring about a substantial rethinking of aspects of the art historical relationships between Ireland, northern Britain and the Anglo-Saxon world at the turn of the sixth century.

---

[1] R. B. K. Stevenson, "The Earlier Metalwork of Pictland," in J. V. S. Megaw (ed.) *To Illustrate the Monuments: Essays on Archaeology Presented to Stuart Piggott* (London 1976), 246.

[2] R. L. S. Bruce-Mitford, "Ireland and the Hanging Bowls – A Review," in M. Ryan (ed.) *Ireland and Insular Art A.D. 500-1200* (Dublin 1987), 35.

[3] See, R. L. S. Bruce-Mitford, *The Sutton Hoo Ship Burial*, vol. I (London 1975), 587.

[4] F. Henry, *Irish Art in the Early Christian Period to A.D. 800* (London 1965), 74-75.

[5] See, E. Fowler, "Celtic Metalwork of the Fifth and Sixth Centuries A.D.," *ArchJ* 120 (1963), 98-160; E. Fowler, "Hanging Bowls," in J. M. Coles and D. D. Simpson (eds.) *Studies in Ancient Europe* (Leicester 1968), 287-310; D. Longley, *The Anglo-Saxon Connection*, BAR Brit. Ser. 22 (Oxford 1975); Stevenson, "The Earlier Metalwork of Pictland"; R. L. S. Bruce-Mitford, *The Sutton Hoo Ship Burial*, vol. III (London 1983), 264ff.

Fig. 1. Location of principal Irish sites mentioned in the text.

THE SCEPTER

Bruce-Mitford's published description of the scepter (Pls. 1-3) makes a further detailed one here redundant.[6] The stone bar, which follows the form of a square-sectioned hone or whetstone, is 58.3cm long. With its metal mounts – at one end a bronze stag on a ring, at the other a cup-fitting, the total length is 82cm. Its present weight is 3.25kg, the stone alone being about 2.4kg, and it is quite clearly not something which could have been handled comfortably as a hone. The wear which occurs on it is consistent with handling in the middle of the stone and its cup-fitting is well-adapted for resting the object on the knee of a sitting person. Its identification as a scepter seems reasonable.

At each end of the stone bar is an onion-shaped knob, originally painted red. Below the knobs, on each side is a carved human face – four at each end (Pls. 2-3). The stone of the bar is an arkosic greywacke-grit of a general type used for finely-made whetstones found in Anglian contexts.[7] Petrological examination of the Sutton Hoo stone was confined to surface inspection, and one possible source suggested for it was southern Scotland or northwestern England, or drift derived from that area – an origin established for the material of other whetstones. Other possible origins lie in the Harz Mountains and in the Rhineland.

The scepter dimly reflects the staffs of office of Late Antique rulers. Bruce-Mitford summed up his view of the object thus:

> Its aspect and character, nevertheless seem thoroughly barbaric, and there can be no doubt as to its pagan inspiration. The elaborately presented stag at the top must have been an emblem of special significance...[8]

The whetstone has inspired a great deal of debate.[9] Some of it has focussed on its possible mythological significance,[10] and some has strayed very far from the archaeological evidence and introduced matter of doubtful relevance.[11] Certain assumptions have been given widespread currency best summed up by the assertion that the whetstone-scepter represents a survival of Celtic royal practice adopted by the Anglo-Saxons perhaps as part of a legitimation process. It is difficult to underestimate the importance of the object in influencing the interpretation of the burial as a whole and in clinching, for some, the argument about the identity of the person whose grave it was. Bruce-Mitford was quite satisfied that it was the East Anglian king, Rædwald's insignia as *Bretwalda*.[12] He was the only member of his dynasty to achieve that shadowy status and, as he was not succeeded by a kinsman, Bruce-Mitford argues that it was fitting that his scepter should have been consigned to the grave and not passed to a successor.[13] In the first volume of the publication Bruce-Mitford took the scepter to be the decisive object in identifying the grave as a king's burial.[14] The magnificent jewelry and the "standard" were helpful only. As the

---

[6] R. L. S. Bruce-Mitford, *The Sutton Hoo Ship Burial*, vol. II (London 1978), 311-93.

[7] V. I. Evison, "Pagan Saxon Whetstone," *AntJ* 55 (1975), 79.

[8] Bruce-Mitford, *The Sutton Hoo Ship Burial*, II, 346.

[9] K. Hauck, "Halsring und Ahnenstab als herrscherliche Würdezeichen," in P. E. Schramm (ed.) *Herrschaftzeichen und Staatsymbolik*, Schriften der Monumenta Germaniae Historica 13.1 (Munich 1954), 145-212; W. Berges and A. Gauert, "Die eiserne 'Standarte' und das steinerne 'Szepter' aus dem Grab eines angelsachischen Konigs bei Sutton Hoo," in P. E. Schramm (ed.) *Herrschaftzeichen und Staatsymbolik*, Schriften der Monumenta Germaniae Historica 13.2 (Munich 1954), 238-80; C. Neuman de Vegvar, "The Iconography of Kingship in Anglo-Saxon Archaeological Finds," in J. Rosenthal (ed.) *Kings and Kingship*, *Acta* 11 (Binghamton 1986), 1-15.

[10] Hauck, "Halsring und Ahnenstab als herrscherliche Würdezeichen"; J. Simpson, "The King's Whetstone," *Antiquity* 53 (1979), 96-101.

[11] S. L. Cohen, "The Sutton Hoo Whetstone," *Speculum* 41 (1966), 466-70; M. J. Enright, "The Sutton Hoo Whetstone Sceptre: A Study in Iconography and Cultural Milieu," *ASE* 11 (1983), 119-34.

[12] Bruce-Mitford, *The Sutton Hoo Ship Burial*, II, 347.

[13] Bede (*H.E.* II.V) says of Rædwald only that he obtained the imperium over the other English provinces south of the Humber. On the doubtful status of the term *Bretwalda* see, P. Wormald, "Bede, the *Bretwaldas* and the Origins of the *Gens Anglorum*," in P. Wormald, D. Bullough and R. Collins (eds.) *Ideal and Reality in Frankish and Anglo-Saxon Society: Studies Presented to J. M. Wallace-Hadrill* (Oxford 1983), 99-129.

[14] R. L. S. Bruce-Mitford, *The Sutton Hoo Ship Burial*, vol. I (London 1975), 689.

"office" of *Bretwalda* passed from ruler to ruler by "force or power" not by agreement, the symbols were not passed on. He contended that the scepter argues especially for the *Bretwalda* Rædwald as the person buried in the ship.[15]

The object shows more than one period of work. The grooves in the stone knob at the top do not fit well with the metal strips now holding the stag assembly in place.[16] The stag model was old, perhaps an heirloom, when mounted. It may have been of Celtic manufacture. While the scepter can be linked in general terms with Late Antique examples, Bruce-Mitford noted significant contrasts – its great weight, the fact that it is made of stone, the red paint and the treatment of the faces, the number (eight) of human face-masks, four of them inverted when in use and finally the square cross-section. He failed to find convincing parallels for the object as a whole in the Germanic world.

The human heads in their pear-shaped fields are, however, entirely Germanic in feeling and Bruce-Mitford lists an impressive set of parallels – not only on the Sutton Hoo metalwork but on other pieces such as the Valsgärde Grave 8, shield 1, and Grave 12, shield boss flanges, the head formerly on a wooden shaft from Vimose and the Søholdt, Denmark staff which was topped by a bronze ring and bore on its sides a mask and a human figure.[17] Although the heads are Germanic in style the use of stone suggested a Celtic background to Bruce-Mitford. Whetstones with human heads and apparently ceremonial function, he stated, seem to be characteristic of the Celtic "background" in the British Isles and are not found on the Continent.[18] Bruce-Mitford briefly mentioned in this context, two small possibly amuletic, Viking-age whetstones from the "black earth" of Birka, Sweden, one 2.5 the other 5cm long. The longer stone tapers to one end which is perforated, the shorter has an angular waisted outline. But after discussing some comparanda he concludes that the geological background and habit of carving stone bars with faces seem to provide a British context for the Sutton Hoo scepter "although there is no real parallel to it." This conclusion then, in an argument which seems tainted by circularity, leads Bruce-Mitford to regard the scepter as that of a *Bretwalda* – a ruler of Britain – who had some claim to hegemony over all the peoples of the island. It is important, therefore, to examine the possibility of a Celtic background for the object. Historians must decide on what reality lies behind the title *Bretwalda*.

Seven parallels to the scepter are cited by Bruce-Mitford. A plain stone bar (46.2cm long and 5cm in thickness) with a slight taper towards either end was associated with late sixth- early seventh-century graves at Uncleby, Yorkshire.[19] The bar showed wear consistent with holding in the hand but not with use as a hone. It was found upright in a barrow. From Hough-on-the Hill came a small human bust on a stone bar. Although in marked relief, the features are not pronounced. There is concentric circle decoration on the breast, shoulders and back. It was made of material similar to the Sutton Hoo object but it is a stray find without independent dating evidence. A head carved on a portion of a stone bar from Lochar Moss, Dumfriesshire is also a stray find from a bog.[20] The head, a simple face with bulging eyes, was carved in relief on a portion of a stone bar. It is undated but might be compared with the pebble-carving of a face from a ring-fort at Trabolgan, Co. Cork (Pl. 4). There is no evidence cited that the Lochar Moss object is a whetstone. The Welsh parallel from Llandudno is a head in relief on a portion of a curved, round-sectioned basalt.[21] A small, elongated stone, almost 14cm. long, possibly from Portsoy, Banffshire, Scotland carries two crudely incised opposed human heads one at either end; a cross, fish and other symbols are also simply engraved on it.[22] This object also lacks a context. A small conical shaped stone with a human face carved at the top was found at the Broch of Main, Shetland and was tentatively identified as a chessman

---

[15]*Ibid.*, 717.

[16]Bruce-Mitford, *The Sutton Hoo Ship Burial*, II, 349.

[17]*Ibid.*, 359-60.

[18]*Ibid.*, 361-62. M. J. Enright goes so far as to suggest that the scepter is of Celtic manufacture (see, Enright, "The Sutton Hoo Sceptre").

[19]Evison, "Pagan Saxon Whetstone," 79-81.

[20]Bruce-Mitford, *The Sutton Hoo Ship Burial*, II, 369.

[21]*Ibid.*, 368, fig. 269a-d.

[22]R. Smith, *A Guide to the Anglo-Saxon and Foreign Teutonic Antiquities in the Department of British and Medieval Antiquities* (London 1923), 128, fig. 163; C. Thomas, "The Interpretation of the Pictish Symbols," *ArchJ* 120 (1963), 38, fig. 1, 3-5.

- it is c. 4.2cm high and 1.9cm in diameter at the base.[23] A purplish-brown fine-grained whetstone from Church Island, Lough Currane, Co. Kerry is preserved in the British Museum.[24] It is square-with-rounded-corners in section and tapers to one rounded end; the opposite end bears a projecting human face defined by a rope-pattern which also encircles the end of the stone. Within this is an incised saltire. The stone is 12.19cm long and 3.3cm in maximum width and it weighs 212.625gr.[25]

As Bruce-Mitford states, none of these provides a satisfactory parallel for the stylistic traits of the Sutton Hoo scepter.[26] Some of the carvings are very informal indeed, and the opposed heads of the Portsoy stone can probably be interpreted as doublets which find their parallels on Insular fine metalwork of the eighth century and later.[27] Reginald Smith wisely stressed the likeness of the Portsoy carving to trial or motif pieces.[28] A whetstone fragment from Lough Gur, Co. Limerick, now in the National Museum of Ireland was used as a motif piece;[29] it is carved with interlace ornament. Interlaced human figures occur on a tabular shale motif-piece from Garryduff, Co. Cork.[30]

There is no firm dating evidence for any of these objects nor are they all whetstones. It cannot be asserted as Enright does that: "One may conclude unless or until further evidence demonstrates otherwise, that the head-on-whetstone motif was comparatively familiar to the Celts, but was less known to the seventh-century Anglo-Saxons..."[31] The earliest firmly-dated whetstone bearing carved heads is that from Sutton Hoo. The parallels quoted from Bruce-Mitford very likely come from various periods and various cultural contexts, and to speak of them as "known to the Celts" is meaningless.

Did whetstones figure as regalia in the Celtic world? The ancient laws of Ireland are completely silent on this question. One of three early laws of status, the eighth-century *Crith Gablach*, lists possessions appropriate to the various grades of society, and only one – the *mruigfer* (the highest grade of free farmer but not noble) – is described as having a grinding stone (*lia forcaid*) and it occurs in a list of domestic equipment.[32] There is no reference to whetstones in the later *Book of Rights*, an antiquarian, probably twelfth-century text, which deals exhaustively with the material attributes of kings.[33] The sagas and all other texts are likewise devoid of references. Only one Welsh source, the story of Culhwch and Olwen, contains a number of catalogues, one of which mentions a whetstone in a list of kingly possessions which includes a sword, knife, drinking horn, cauldron, draughtboard, mantle, etc.[34] For people who carried swords and knives a small whetstone may well have been an everyday piece of equipment, particularly when some tools and weapons were made of metal which was easily blunted. One has to be cautious in identifying all such personal items as regalia. Not one of the Irish tales quoted by Enright sheds any light on the question of whetstones.

Whetstones which may have something of an amuletic or symbolic nature do occur in Ireland. The finest example was recently discovered at Newtownlow, Co. Westmeath (Pl. 5). It is a beautifully formed square-sectioned stone tapering at either end. The stone is 20.8cm long, and it weighs 309.47gr. At one end there is a short bronze chain and hook. The chain is attached to a loop which springs from two metal tangs formed by folding a single piece.

---

[23] Anon, "Proceedings; Monday, 10th December 1923; Donations to the Museum," *PSAS* 58 (1923-24), fig. 5.

[24] Anon., "Medieval Hone From Ireland," *AntJ* 7 (1927), 323-24.

[25] Another large whetstone of unidentified stone from the cemetery at Faversham, Kent, is described by Evison as "large and similarly well-shaped, 28.8 x 3.5 x 3.5cm., but with a perforation at one end" but it was not discussed by Bruce-Mitford. See Evison, "Pagan Saxon Whetstone," 79.

[26] Bruce-Mitford, *The Sutton Hoo Ship Burial*, II, 369.

[27] Examples occur on the "Tara" and Cavan brooches but there are many others in a context heavily influenced by Anglo-Saxon traditions.

[28] Smith, *Guide to the Anglo-Saxon and Foreign Teutonic Antiquities*.

[29] U. O'Meadhra, *Motif Pieces From Ireland*, Theses and Papers in North-European Archaeology 7 (Stockholm 1979), 25.

[30] M. J. O'Kelly, "Two Ringforts at Garryduff, Co. Cork," *PRIA* 63 (1962-64), 78-80.

[31] Enright, "Sutton Hoo Whetstone Sceptre," 121.

[32] D. Binchy, *Crith Gablach* (Dublin 1941), 7.

[33] M. Dillon, *Lebor na Cert: The Book of Rights* (Dublin 1962).

[34] D. Edel, "The Catalogues in *Culhwch ac Olwen* and Insular Celtic Learning," *BBCS* 30 III and IV (1983), 264-65.

These are neatly sunk into the stone and held in place by a rivet. They carry incised cross decoration. The chain consists of two "S"-shaped links of bronze wire with the ends crimped to suggest animal heads. The hook is very elegantly modelled and terminates in a beast head; it has bulging eyes and a moustache. The back of the hook bears incised interlocking "T" shapes within elegant mouldings.[35] It was found on the site of a destroyed crannóg. Though I originally assigned this piece to the tenth century A.D., I welcome the opportunity to recant and suggest that it belongs to a version of the Ringerike style and should properly be regarded as eleventh-century.

An unlocalized whetstone (Pl. 6) of purplish stone in the National Museum of Ireland follows the same pattern as the Newtownlow example with related decorated metal fittings for a chain which is now lost. It is 22.4cm long, and 2.8cm in maximum width. It has, in addition, a plain applied bronze ferrule at the other end. A plain whetstone with the rebates cut for metal fittings was found in a bog near Listowel, Co. Kerry. It is 12.1cm long, and 2.2cm in maximum width. The faces and ends are described as having been polished to a very smooth finish.[36] None of these whetstones show any signs of use. Bruce-Mitford illustrates two perforated whetstones of high quality from a ringfort at Coleraine.[37] One of them clearly belongs to the series in question, as does the example from Lough Currane described above. A very large whetstone, 45.08cm long with an iron suspension loop was found at Loughpairc Crannóg, Co. Galway.[38] It appears to be a crude version of the finer examples cited. It occurs in a domestic context. The same site produced a much finer but unperforated hone.[39]

A number of relevant whetstones have come from late Viking-age contexts in Dublin. A diminutive example, now broken, was found in a twelfth-century context in Christchurch Place (National Museum of Ireland (NMI) E122:1670). It has a bronze chain crimped in the manner of the Newtownlow example. An eleventh-century deposit at Fishamble Street (NMI E179:1599) yielded a hone which is closely comparable to the perforated one from Birka (see above p. 86). An exceptionally beautiful hone (NMI E81:9139) from Winetavern Street is made of a reddish stone and appears not to have been used. It is very small and may be an import from eastern Scandinavia where similar whetstones were in circulation. A miniature whetstone, unlocalized but probably found in Dublin (NMI 1897:48), has seen intensive use (Pl. 7). At one end however, a silver (or silvered) beast head finial in the Ringerike style is fitted. It dates probably to the eleventh century.

In the light of recent finds, one can only suggest that metal-mounted, fine whetstones in Ireland belong to the Viking-age and the Dublin ones, in particular, can belong to no other period. Some of these whetstones had seen no use and may have functioned as amulets or, in the case of the larger examples, as insignia of rank. The largest of the fine Irish whetstones are, however, well within the range of size for comfortable, practical use as hones. The archaeological evidence does not appear to support the notion of regalia-whetstones as an original Celtic phenomenon.

It is also questionable to assert that the occurrence of human heads on the scepter is likewise a Celtic phenomenon. Multiple-headed sculptures were known in Iron Age Ireland and in Britain[40] but they were either two-headed or three-headed and there is no convincing evidence for continuity into the medieval period. Of the heads on the Sutton Hoo scepter those at the top have exposed chins and may be intended to be read as beardless (Pl. 3). At the other end, three have beards and two of them moustaches (Pl. 2). Beneath the jawline of those with exposed chins is a pattern of ribbing identical in treatment with the beards which might have been intended as off-the-chin beards. Alternatively, they might be read as female. No two of the heads are exactly alike. All the heads are contained within pear-shaped mouldings which terminate in low, flat bosses below the chin. These have been most unconvincingly compared by Karl Hauck with the insigniae worn by the imperial bodyguard in the mosaic of

---

[35]M. Ryan, Catalogue entry, in M.Ryan and M. Cahill (eds.) *Irish Gold 4000 Years of Personal Ornaments* (Melbourne 1988), 29 No. 82.

[36]D. C. Twohig, "Pendant Whetstone," *Jnl. of the Kerry Archaeol. and Hist. Soc.* (1977), 143-44.

[37]Bruce-Mitford, *The Sutton Hoo Ship Burial*, II, 365, fig. 266.

[38]R. A. S. Macalister, *et al.*, "The Excavation of Loughpairc Crannog near Tuam," *PRIA* 32C (1914-16), 150.

[39]*Ibid.*, pl. xvii, No. 24.

[40]A. Ross, *Pagan Celtic Britain* (London 1967), 74.

the emperor Justinian at San Vitale, Ravenna.[41] The pear-shaped field defined by a moulding has sufficient antecedents in Germanic metalwork not to require such a specific origin nor does its disposition over the head particularly suggest the suspension chain of a medallion. Not only are the heads stylistically Germanic, but we can find convincing parallels for the iconography of the scepter in approximately contemporary or earlier Germanic work.

Staffs decorated with human figures are known. Bruce-Mitford, following Hauck, compared the scepter with the wooden staff from a grave mound, Søholdt, Lolland, Denmark which bore a human figure and separately, a human head.[42] In the Vimose find there was a repoussé face-mask within billeted mouldings made for attachment to a backing. A bronze bust of a bearded man from Haglunda, Öland, appears to have been the finial of a staff or other similar object: on the breast of the figure are two additional human faces.[43] Hauck notes the tradition that Tassilo on his deposition surrendered to Charlemagne his dukedom together with a staff "*in cuius capite similitudo hominis erat scultum.*"[44]

More precise parallels for the Sutton Hoo iconography may be found in the Germanic world from the Migration Period to the Viking-age. A bronze stylus of the eleventh century from Hagested, near Holbaek, Jutland, is surmounted by a quadruped; below it are four human masks (Pl. 8).[45] A similar arrangement of heads occurs on a tiny four-headed silver pin from a fifth-century Alemannic girl's grave at Eschborn in Taunus, Germany.[46] A Viking-age pin from Praestegaarden, Nordland, Norway now in the Bergen Museum bears an arrangement of four heads below an openwork disc-head.[47] Two bone objects, perhaps handles, are preserved in the Statens Historiska Museum, Stockholm. One from Tunby, St. Ilian's parish, Västmannland, is carved with four heads in relief. The other, from a tenth-century cremation in Väsby, Vallentuna cemetery, Uppland, now has two of its heads missing.[48] Also from the Viking-age is the small carved antler tip from Ireland published by Sir William Wilde:[49] at one end are four human face-masks, and at the point, an elegant Ringerike beast (Pl. 9).[50] A particularly interesting composition occurs on the Bregentved, Zealand, harness strap-distributor (Pl. 10). Each of its four links bear two distinct opposed heads. The links are cast from the same model and produce an effect not unlike that of the whetstone in their arrangement.[51]

Jan-Peder Lamm has surveyed multiple-headed figures in the Baltic area, especially among the Slavs where generalized parallels for the Sutton Hoo scepter iconography may be found.[52] He instances the description of the god Suantovitus at Arkona by Saxo Grammaticus – a large four-headed wooden sculpture – and the limestone column found at Zbrucz on the Dneister.[53] A small wooden idol and a whetstone with a bronze finial, both from Wolin repeat the four-headed iconography.[54] These are much later than Sutton Hoo and the trading and other links of the Vikings make discussion of these southern Baltic examples difficult in the present context. Much more

---

[41] Hauck, "Halsring und Ahnenstab als herrscherliche Würdezeichen," 206.

[42] See, Bruce-Mitford, *The Sutton Hoo Ship Burial*, II, 359-60; Hauck, "Halsring und Ahnenstab als herrscherliche Würdezeichen"; M. B. Mackeprang, "Menschendarstellungen aus der Eisenzeit Danemarks," *Acta Archaeologica* 6 (1935), 245.

[43] J. P. Lamm, "On the Cult of Multiple-headed Gods in England and the Baltic Area," *Prezglad Archeologiczny* 34 (1987), 229.

[44] Hauck, "Halsring und Ahnenstab als herrscherliche Würdezeichen," 209.

[45] Cohen, "The Sutton Hoo Whetstone," pl. II.

[46] H. Ament, "Eschborn, Main-Taunus-Kreis," in *Führer zu archäologischen Denkmälern in Deutschland: Frankfurt am Main und Umgebung*, Nordwestdeutschen und West- und Suddeutschen Verband für Altertumsforschung, Band 19 (Stuttgart 1989), 210 and 209, fig. 65b.

[47] Lamm, "Cult of Multiple-headed Gods," 230, fig. 28.

[48] *Ibid.*, 228-29.

[49] W. R. Wilde, *A Descriptive Catalogue of the Antiquities of Animal Materials and Bronze in the Museums of the Royal Irish Academy* (Dublin 1861), 339.

[50] Anne Ross (*Pagan Celtic Britain*, 77-78) wrongly assigns the object to the Iron Age La Tène tradition.

[51] Mackeprang, "Menschendarstellungen aus der Eisenzeit Danemarks," 236, fig. 6.

[52] Lamm, "Cult of Multiple-headed Gods."

[53] *Ibid.*, 222, fig. 4. This comparison is also cited by Cohen ("Sutton Hoo Whetstone," pl. III).

[54] Lamm, "Cult of Multiple-headed Gods," 223, fig. 5 and 224, fig. 9.

relevant is the widespread use of the human head in early Germanic ornament – on the great Gotlandic collars, or on Kentish square-headed brooches, placed between beasts in back-to-back arrangements.[55] Roman and Byzantine imperial coinage widely admired, used, and copied in the Germanic world could have provided a ready source for the association of the human head with concepts of royalty in the minds of barbarian artists.

The scepter is an Anglo-Saxon product; its immediate background is Germanic. Like many Migration Period prestige-objects, it represents an adaptation of a Late Antique prototype although, at first sight this ancestry may not be obvious. There is no discernable Celtic influence in its style and manufacture.[56] Comparisons with the Pfalzfeld pillar, references to the Celtic practice of headhunting, or appeals to the status of the smith in ancient Ireland[57] do nothing to supply the lack of evidence for a Celtic connection. Petrologically its raw material was easily obtainable within the Anglian kingdom of Northumbria. It follows, therefore, that the scepter cannot be used to underpin the theory that Sutton Hoo Mound One was the grave of a *Bretwalda* who claimed hegemony over both Celtic and Germanic peoples in Britain and whose claim found its physical embodiment in his regalia.

THE LARGEST HANGING BOWL

The Sutton Hoo burial contained three hanging bowls. These are vessels fitted with hooks for suspension, often decorated in a "Celtic" style, the vast majority of which have been found in Anglo-Saxon graves of the period A.D. c. 550 - c. 650.[58] No early example has been found in Ireland although a decorated openwork escutcheon of one came from the River Bann in the northeast. A mould for a similar openwork escutcheon was found at Craig Phadrig in Invernesshire, Scotland, demonstrating that at least one site in Pictland was producing bowls. Françoise Henry argued very strongly that the majority of hanging bowls in Anglo-Saxon graves were manufactured in Ireland where garment fasteners ("latchets," penannular [gapped-ring] brooches, and long decorated stick pins called "hand-pins") provided a technical and aesthetic background for them.[59]

In the opinion of Bruce-Mitford certain details of the largest vessel (Pls. 11-12) do re-open the argument that it, at least, was made in Ireland.[60] The largest bowl is 31 cm in diameter, and it carries an exceptional number of decorative escutcheons – one for each suspension hook (3), square ones on the body of the bowl (3), and circular ones on the base (2), one internal, carrying a model bronze fish rotating on a pedestal, and one external. In addition, below each hook-escutcheon is an applied bronze boar head, snout upwards. There are two silver-gilt repairs one with Salin Style II birdheads, obviously added locally. The bowl was old when deposited in the grave.

The ornament of the escutcheons can be summarized as follows: champlevé enamel with fine-line reserved scrollwork, both zoomorphic and otherwise; millefiori glass platelets; and, on the internal escutcheon, niello or silver inlay. An exceptional feature of the enamels is the inlaying of the champlevé with other enamel. The square escutcheons have inlaid corner lentoids with internal patterning.

The escutcheon frames are highly distinctive.[61] All are of whitish copper-alloy with a high tin content. The circular frames have vertical outer faces decorated by continuous inward curves on either side of a central grooved line. The inner face carries a continuous, tripartite cast scheme of closely-set fine lines. The square escutcheons have the same scheme inside and out.

It is an exceptional object. Hanging bowl 1 is the only example with eight escutcheons and the only one in the sixth – seventh-century series to have the purely decorative square escutcheons. It is the only bowl with large inlays of blue glass and possibly the only one with green enamel. It is also the only one with silver or niello inlay. The appliqué boars' heads are not unique; related examples occur on the Manton Common (Scunthorpe), the Hildersham

---

[55]Bruce-Mitford, *The Sutton Hoo Ship Burial*, II, 369-70, fig. 270.

[56]*Pace* Enright ("Sutton Hoo Whetstone Sceptre") and Neuman de Vegvar ("Iconography of Kingship"), 12.

[57]Enright, "Sutton Hoo Whetstone Sceptre."

[58]Bruce-Mitford, "Ireland and the Hanging Bowls."

[59]F. Henry, "Hanging Bowls," *JRSAI* 66 (1936), 209-46.

[60]Bruce-Mitford, "Ireland and the Hanging Bowls."

[61]Bruce-Mitford, *The Sutton Hoo Ship Burial*, III, 229-31.

and Lullingstone bowls. Bowl 1 uses 208 millefiori insets on its eight escutcheons; its closest parallel is the Manton Common bowl with 115 inlays on five escutcheons. A further link between these two bowls is the use of the sunburst pattern in millefiori and a millefiori inlay of blue crescents in white squares, which is approximated on the Manton Common bowl.

The fine line style of the escutcheons is paralleled on a number of pieces from Ireland – the "latchet" from Dowris, Co. Offaly and an unprovenanced example in the National Museum of Ireland;[62] a zoomorphic penannular brooch, probably from the River Shannon (NMI) and its mould-sibling or near-sibling in the Ulster Museum, Belfast;[63] in Pictland, the Gaulcross, Morayshire and Norries Law, Fife, handpins.[64] To these may be added the scrollwork on the distinctive disc-headed pins from Ireland.[65] Lentoids on the "tail" of the Dowris latchet provide parallels for those on the Sutton Hoo escutcheons as both contain internal ornament. The massed use of millefiori occurs on the well-known brooch from Ballinderry Crannóg No. 2, Co. Offaly[66] (Pl. 13), and on a mount from Lagore Crannóg, Co. Meath. A similar use of millefiori survives on thirteen penannular brooches of H. Kilbride-Jones's classes from Ireland.[67] In Ireland, however, according to Bruce-Mitford, fine-line style and millefiori have so far not been found together on the same piece.

Of the millefiori patterns on Bowl 1, the sunburst can be singled out as providing an important link with the bowl from Manton Common. Bruce-Mitford recognized the same pattern on an unprovenanced hand pin from Ireland but variants of it are much more widespread than that. An example occurs on the Bartrauve, Co. Mayo hand pin.[68] An unprovenanced penannular brooch (National Museum of Ireland 1906:78) carries now damaged sunburst millefiori – a red core with blue and white radii (Pl. 14). Another unlocalized example (NMI 1886:6) has millefiori set in red enamel (Pl. 15). The bronze of the brooch has been drilled to receive the inlays – the radii are yellow and blue with a red core. An unusual mount from Lugacaha, Co. Westmeath (NMI 1984:65) has a great deal of millefiori including sunbursts (blue and white with red cores), blue crosses of squares, yellow and blue hexafoils and white-and-blue half squares. A series of incised leaf scrolls around the central setting can be read as long-snouted beasts of general Salin Style II tradition.

The Ballinderry Brooch (Pl. 13) has fine ornament on its ring which matches the Sutton Hoo escutcheon frames closely (Pls. 11-12). The parallel is reinforced by the half-cylindrical length of similar moulding in a grayish metal from the same site which might well have been manufacturing scrap (Pl. 16, top).[69] Bruce-Mitford, following Stevenson, compares the outer aspects of the round escutcheons to possible knife handles in the Norries Law hoard and also to the Gaulcross handpins.[70] In 1983, although he thought it plausible to attribute Bowl 1 to an Irish workshop, he was inclined to emphasize the openwork Manton Common escutcheon and its links with the Craig Phadrig mould as evidence against an Irish origin, particularly as there is little to choose between Irish and Pictish fine line style. But the source was not Pictish either as millefiori "does not register" in Pictland.[71] He concludes, "the source must have been the politically lively but to us archaeologically blank kingdoms of Wales or the North-west of Britain." He argues further that the state of art achieved in Bowl 1 could hardly have been reached in Ireland at A. D. c. 600 without leaving its reflection in manuscripts, and there is no indication of it in the *Cathach* of St. Columba or the Bobbio texts.[72]

---

[62]M. Ryan, Catalogue entries, in M. Ryan (ed.) *Treasures of Ireland: Irish Art 3000 B.C. to 1500 A.D.* (Dublin 1983), 111-12.

[63]*Ibid.*, 116-17.

[64]Bruce-Mitford, *The Sutton Hoo Ship Burial*, III, 271-72.

[65]Ryan, *Irish Gold*, 25.

[66]H. Hencken, "Ballinderry Crannóg No. 2," *PRIA* 47C (1942), 34-40.

[67]H. Kilbride-Jones, *Zoomorphic Penannular Brooches* (London 1980).

[68]*Ibid.*, fig. 74, 222.

[69]Hencken, "Ballinderry Crannóg No.2," 45 No. 641.

[70]Bruce-Mitford, *The Sutton Hoo Ship Burial*, III, 274; Stevenson, "Earlier Metalwork of Pictland."

[71]Bruce-Mitford, *The Sutton Hoo Ship Burial*, III, 280.

[72]*Ibid*, 294.

In his 1987 paper, Bruce-Mitford returned to the issue and laid particular stress on the scrap-moulding from Ballinderry as being crucial in deciding if the Sutton Hoo Bowl 1 was made in Ireland. If its analysis matched Sutton Hoo's then the Irish origin of the bowl would be clinched. This is a non-sequitur because the Ballinderry fragment is not unique. There are now three other mouldings from the Irish midlands with identical, or near identical, patterns. From Toneymore, Lough Kinale, at or near a crannóg, came a piece not unlike the Ballinderry fragment, which formed part of the arc of a circle (Pl. 16, second from bottom). It is "C"-shaped in cross-section. A cylindrical bead with the same decoration from Auburn, Co. Westmeath, from a crannóg, is 2.3cm long and 5.5mm in diameter (Pl. 16, second from top). A fragment of a similar moulding was found at the royal site of Clogher, Co. Tyrone.[73] A cast bronze moulding from Lagore is of similar type, but its pattern is merely one of criss-cross lines (Pl. 16, bottom). Analysis of the Sutton Hoo escutcheons shows a copper content of between 68% and 73.8% with a high admixture of tin (varying between 21% and 29%) and a small amount of lead (3.3% - 4.8%). Analyses by the X-ray diffraction method for the Irish objects are as follows:

Object	Copper	Zinc	Silver	Lead	Tin%
Ballinderry scrap moulding (front)	63.052	0.462	5.942	4.071	14.039
Toneymore Lough Kinale (front)	24.329	0.216	12.708	6.676	17.073
Auburn Co. Westmeath	47.410	0.563	11.401	6.080	23.943

The Ballinderry moulding certainly falls near the lower end of the range of the Sutton Hoo escutcheons. The other pieces are noteworthy for their relatively low copper and high silver and tin contents.

Fine ribbing with horizontal and criss-cross patterns occurs widely on penannular brooches in Ireland, but the precise Sutton Hoo pattern crops up again on the edge of frames of a complex object thought to be the metal components of a saddle found in recent years on the bed of the River Shannon near Athlone. Found in twenty-six pieces, this remarkable object, not yet conserved and only conjecturally reconstructed, consists of elements of a metal frame with clips (Pl. 17), a very decayed metal ring which carried four tripartite studs with sunburst ornaments (Pl. 18), a disc with fine-line scrolls and a central blue-glass stud (Pl. 19), stylized vaguely anthropomorphic heads, and other metal mountings with hexafoil and petal decoration. Two animal heads with glass eyes appear to have formed the ends of a decorative moulding. If my colleague Eamonn Kelly's proposed reconstruction based on the Frankish analogue from Wesel-Bislich Grave 446 is right,[74] then the form of this piece owes a great deal to the Germanic world, although its ornament is predominantly that of the hanging bowls and zoomorphic penannular brooches. An almost exact analogue for features of the ornament is the brooch from Moystown Demesne, Co. Westmeath (National Museum of Ireland 1956:446) (Pl. 20). Another comparison, to which my colleague Raghnall Ó Floinn has drawn my attention, is the moulding, also from the River Shannon, published by Wilde.[75] This has not only the petal ornament but also ribbing very like the Norries Law handles

---

[73] Richard Warner, pers. comm.

[74] W. Janssen, "Die Sattelbeschläge aus Grab 446 des frankischen Graberfeldes von Wesel-Bislich, Kreis Wesel," *Archäologisches Korrespondenzblatt* 11 (1981), 149-69.

[75] Wilde, *Descriptive Catalogue*, 631.

and Gaulcross hand pin.[76] If the date for Sutton Hoo Bowl 1 is about right at A.D. c. 600, then the saddle and the other objects mentioned from Ireland belong to the same general period. Clearly the chronology and relationships of major categories of object, especially penannular brooches, in both Ireland and Scotland must be re-assessed. The distribution of the distinctive frame pattern is widespread in Ireland and this must weigh heavily in identifying the origin of the large bowl from Sutton Hoo.

The location of important workshops in Ireland in the sixth and seventh century is beyond dispute – the excavations at Garranes, Co. Cork revealed an area in which penannular brooches were cast and millefiori and enamelling carried on.[77] Brooches were fabricated at Clogher, Co. Tyrone, a royal site.[78] An interesting link with the Sutton Hoo standard was found there – a small wrought-iron horned bull-head, which in its form and even its curled projection of the underside, matches the beasts from Sutton Hoo. The sandhills settlement at Dooey, Co. Donegal, produced a motif piece with hexafoils, a diaper pattern of lozenges and scrollwork very similar to that which appears on latchets, penannular brooches, and related objects.[79] A tiny ringed pin found there carries two opposed eared beasts which seem to belong to the same general type as those adapted to manuscript painting in the Book of Durrow (Pl. 21). A piece of experimental gold filigree, almost certainly an attempt at Anglo-Saxon technique, came from a foundation deposit of the royal crannóg of Lagore, which later produced evidence of fine metalworking. The slave-collar from Lagore has interesting parallels with the cauldron chain from Sutton Hoo.[80] Also from Lagore is a small cast fragment of animal ornament which has clear Anglo-Saxon overtones. In some ways the most underrated evidence is the carved schist monolith from Mullaghmast, Co. Kildare, with its patterns from the repertoire of the brooch-maker. Its two large lentoids on one face contain internal patterns.[81] It stands 1m high and was clearly not a portable object (fig. 2).

The evidence cited shows that workshops capable of producing the Sutton Hoo bowl existed in Ireland, but does not prove that it was produced there. More importantly, it provides a context of production and contact with Pictland and Anglo-Saxon England, which makes the appearance of the great Christian art of the later seventh century no surprise. In this connection, the Book of Durrow with its solitary page of Anglo-Saxon ornament is by no means an incongruous artistic phenomenon in the Irish midlands. The contacts with Scotland go back to the prehistoric Iron Age.[82] A striking instance is provided by the seventh-century Ardakillen brooch from Co. Roscommon with its fleshy ridged scrollwork which is closely matched on silver bosses in the Norries Law Hoard.[83] The decorative trick is distinctive and can be seen on Irish Iron Age repoussé discs.[84] The contacts suggested clearly predate the Irish missions originating in Iona (founded in A.D. 563). The evidence now points to interaction between the Irish and the Anglo-Saxons before, and independent of, the Irish missions to Northumbria of the 630s. General Anglo-Saxon-Celtic contact began, of course, much earlier within Britain.[85]

It is always tempting to particularize, and here the temptation to attribute the increased interaction between Ireland and the Anglo-Saxon world to the activities of Northumbrian political exiles in Iona and Ireland from the later seventh century onwards is difficult to resist.[86] The workshop sites of the midlands which we have mentioned fall

---

[76]Stevenson, "Earlier Metalwork of Pictland," 248.

[77]S. P. Ó Ríordáin, "The Excavation of a Large Earthen Fort at Garranes, Co. Cork," *PRIA* 47C (1942), 77-150.

[78]R. Warner, "The Clogher Yellow Layer," *Medieval Ceramics: Bulletin of the Medieval Pottery Research Group* 3 (1979), 37-40; R. Warner, "A Case study: Cloghar Macc Daimini," *Bulletin of the Ulster Placename Soc.* 4 (1981-82), 1, 27-31.

[79]A. B. Ó Ríordáin and E. Rynne, "A Settlement in the Sandhills at Dooey, Co. Donegal," *JRSAI* 91 (1961), 58-64.

[80]B. G. Scott, "Iron 'Slave Collars' from Lagore Crannog, Co. Meath," *PRIA* 78C (1978), 223-26. But see Laing (L. Laing, "The Romanization of Ireland in the Fifth Century," *Peritia* 4 [1985], 268), who regards the similarities as cognate developments from a common late-Roman blacksmithing tradition.

[81]E. P. Kelly, Catalogue Entry, in M. Ryan (ed.) *Treasures of Ireland*, No. 37 109-11.

[82]R. Warner, "Ireland and the Origins of Escutcheon Art," in M. Ryan (ed.) *Ireland and Insular Art*, 19-22.

[83]Stevenson, "Earlier Metalwork of Pictland," 249.

[84]See, B. Raftery, *A Catalogue of Irish Iron Age Antiquities* (Marburg/Lahn 1983), figs. 208, 210, 212.

[85]D. Longley, *The Anglo-Saxon Connection*, BAR Brit. Ser. 22 (Oxford 1975), 35.

[86]H. Moisl, "The Bernician Royal Dynasty and the Irish in the Seventh Century," *Peritia* 2 (1983), 103-26.

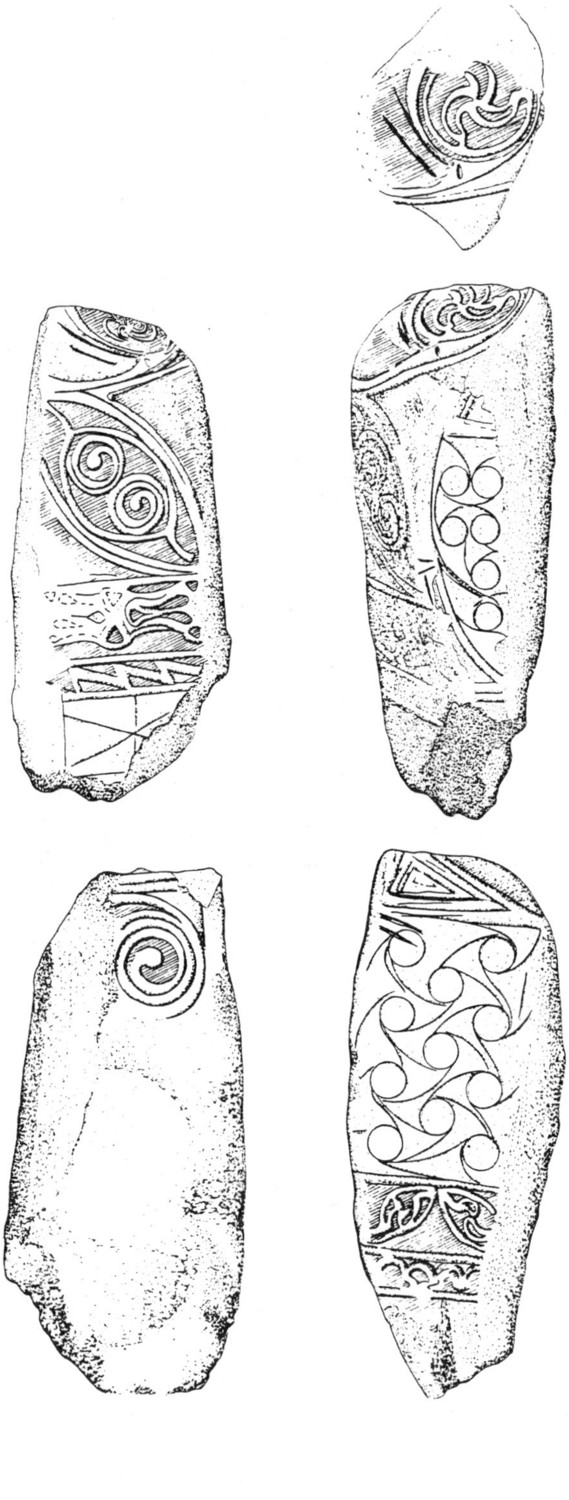

Fig. 2. The Mullaghmast Stone (after Coffey, with revisions).

mainly within the sphere of influence of the Uí Néill dynasties who were enlisted as allies by the Dal Riada (of northeastern Ireland and western Scotland) as a counterweight to the claims of their Ulaid overkings. Strong tradition asserts that Aldfrith, king of Northumbria from A.D. 685 was half Irish and a kinsman of the Uí Néill. Have we, therefore, in the largest hanging bowl an example of a diplomatic gift? It is perfectly possible but it cannot be definitely decided. The rise of powerful kings with extra-territorial influence distinguished from their traditionalist predecessors seems to have developed along parallel lines in both Anglo-Saxon England and pre-Viking Ireland. It is very likely that such powerful figures on neighboring islands would have come to each other's notice. Given the contacts provided in northern Britain between the Irish, Picts, and Angles such intercourse was a certainty even without the church missionaries. Contact between the peoples of the two islands appears to have been long and continuous. Exchange or trade is a much more likely way in which Celtic objects could have been brought to Sutton Hoo than, say, booty. The custom-made millefiori on the otherwise purely Anglo-Saxon jewelry may be a very particular instance of cross-fertilization between Celtic and Germanic metalworkers, something which could occur naturally in a world where exchange of goods and even of craftsmen was somewhat freer than we have previously thought. In this context does it follow that the Celtic elements in the great ship burial derive from the fact that the deceased was a *Bretwalda*? I doubt it.

Pl. 1. Sutton Hoo, Mound One: the whetstone. London, The British Museum. (Photo: By permission of the Trustees, British Museum).

Pl. 2. Sutton Hoo, Mound One: the whetstone; upper end, stone bar. London, The British Museum. (Photo: By permission of the Trustees, British Museum).

Pl. 3. Sutton Hoo, Mound One: the whetstone; lower end, stone bar. London. The British Museum. (Photo: By permission of the Trustees, British Museum).

Pl. 4. Pebble-carving from Trabolgan, Co. Cork. (Photo: National Museum of Ireland).

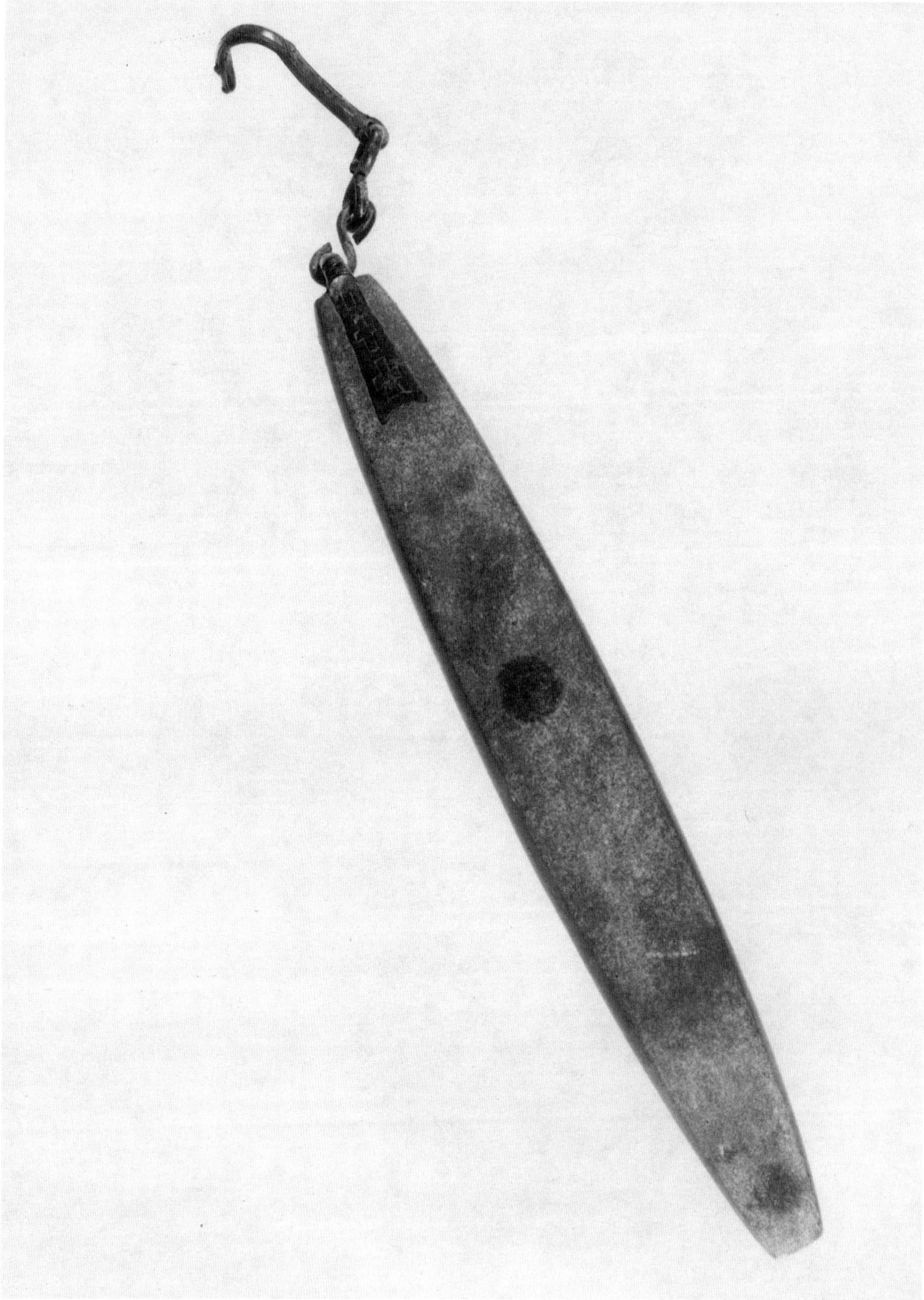

Pl. 5. Whetstone from Newtownlow, Co. Westmeath. (Photo: National Museum of Ireland).

Pl. 6. Whetstone, provenance unknown. (Photo: National Museum of Ireland).

Pl. 7. Whetstone (NMI 1897:48). (Photo: National Museum of Ireland).

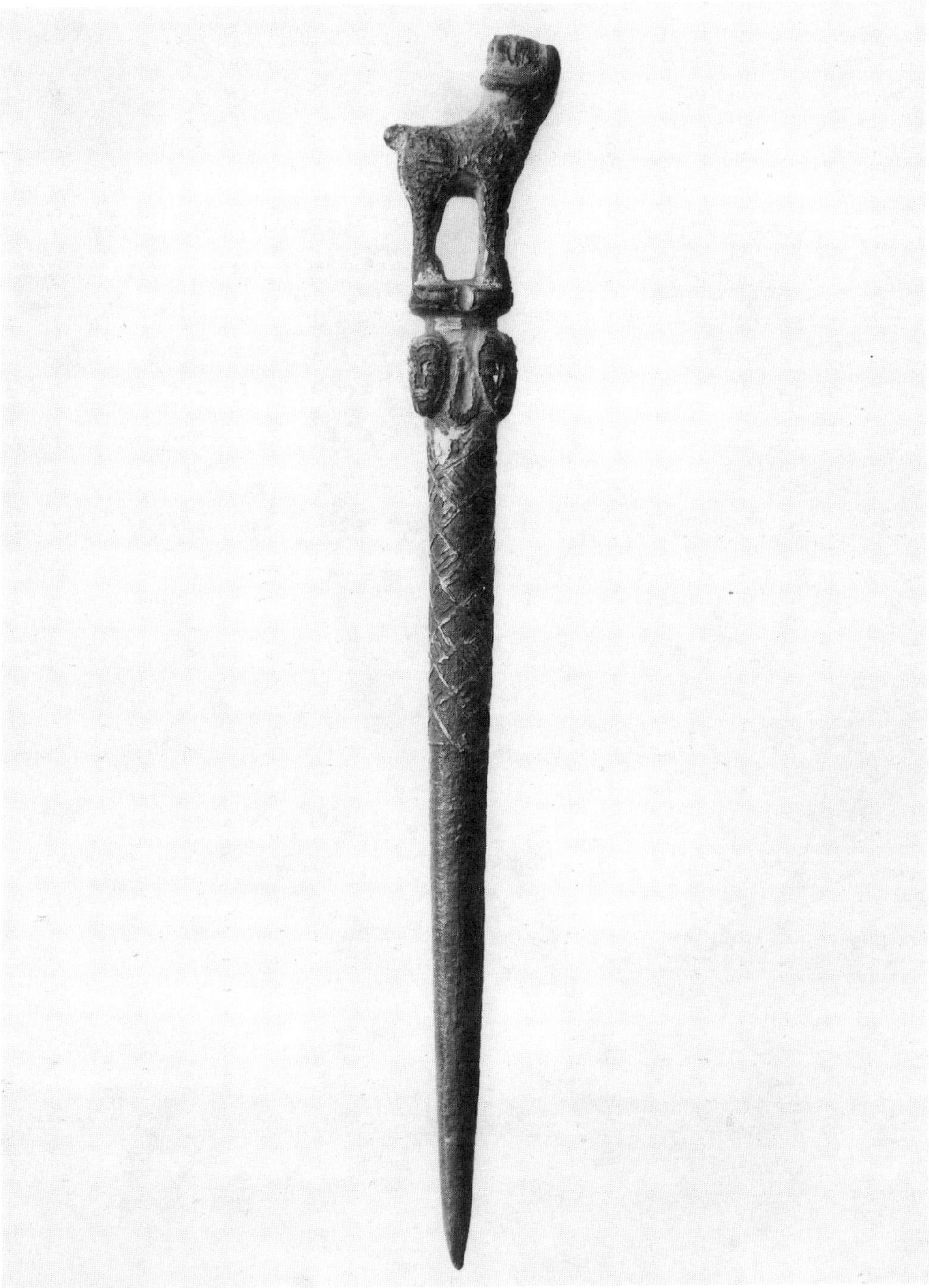

Pl. 8. Bronze stylus from Hagested, Jutland. (Photo: Nationalmuseet København).

Pl. 9. Carved antler tip, Viking age. (Photo: National Museum of Ireland).

Pl. 10. Harness strap-distributor, Bregentved, Zealand. (Photo: Nationalmuseet København).

Pl. 11. Sutton Hoo, Mound One: large hanging bowl; complete escutcheon. London, The British Museum. (Photo: By permission of the Trustees, British Museum).

Pl. 12. Sutton Hoo, Mound One: large hanging bowl; escutcheon; detail. London, The British Museum. (Photo: By permission of the Trustees, British Museum).

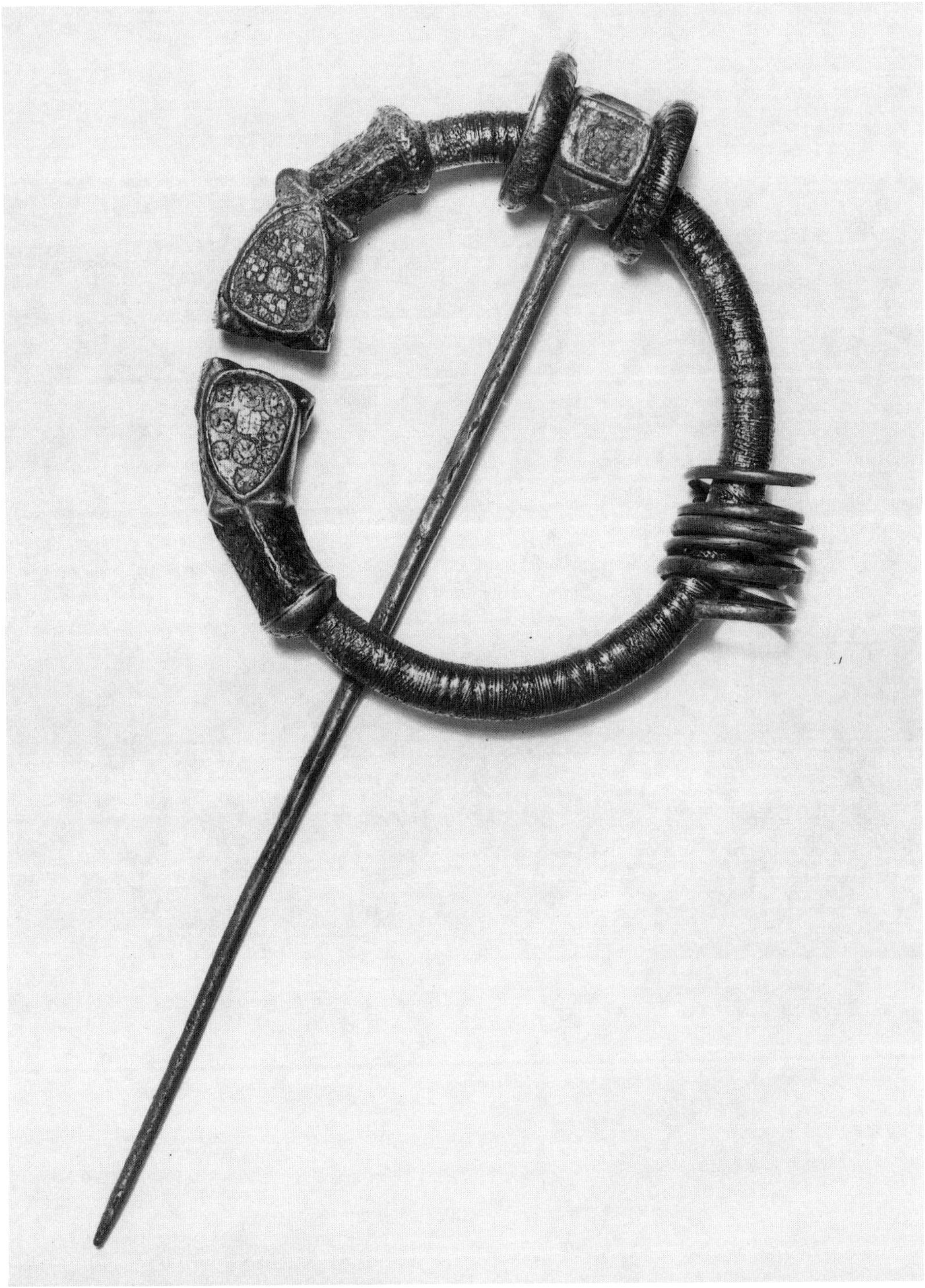

Pl. 13. Brooch from Ballinderry Crannóg No. 2, Co. Offaly. (Photo: National Museum of Ireland).

Pl. 14. Penannular Brooch (NMI 1906:78), provenance unknown. (Photo: National Museum of Ireland).

Pl. 15. Penannular Brooch (NMI 1886:6), provenance unknown. (Photo: National Museum of Ireland).

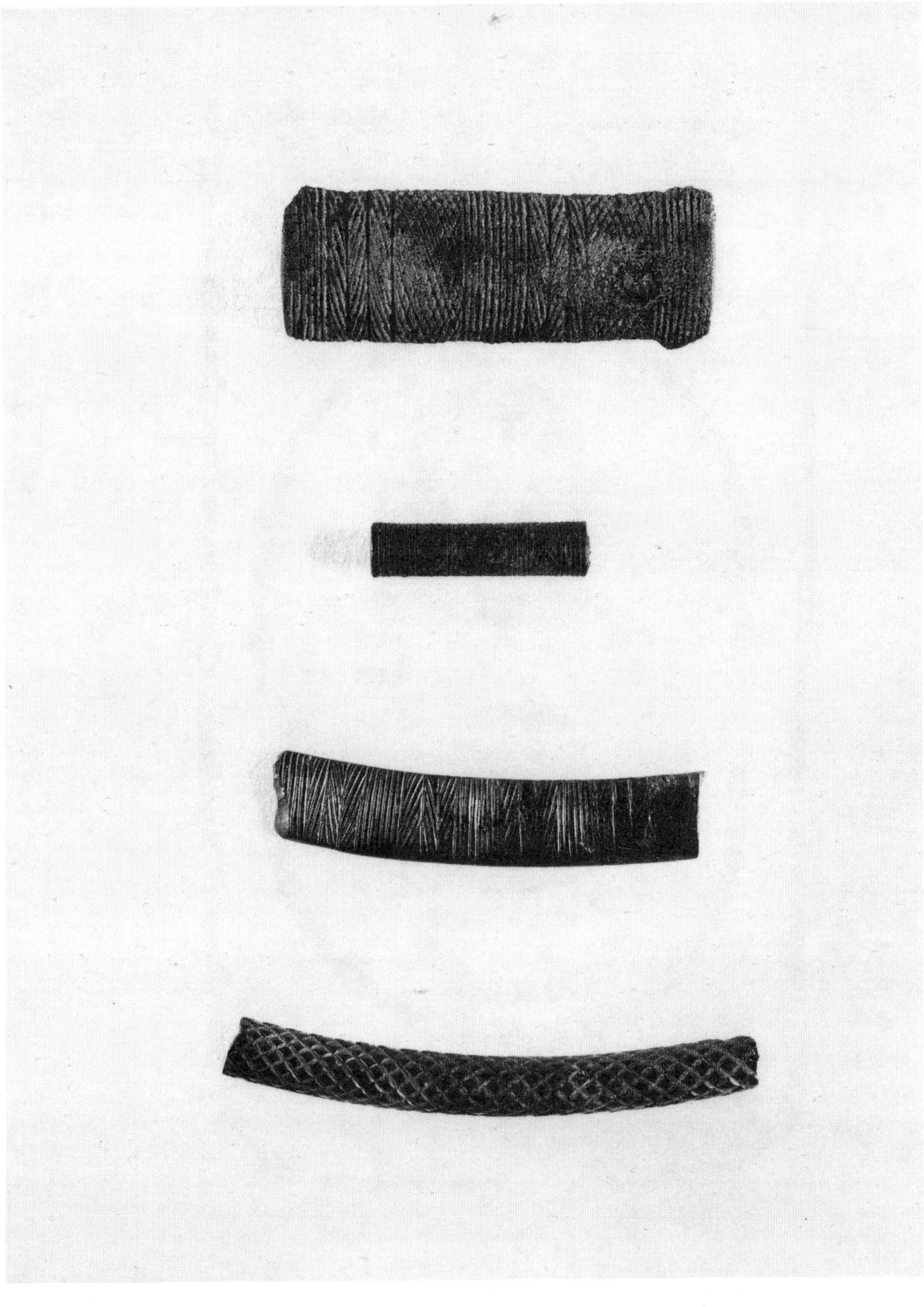

Pl. 16. Top: moulding fragment: Ballinderry Crannóg No. 2, Co. Offaly. Second from top: cylindrical bead, Auburn, Co. Westmeath. Second from bottom: moulding-fragment, Toneymore, Lough Kinale. Bottom: bronze moulding, Lagore. (Photo: National Museum of Ireland).

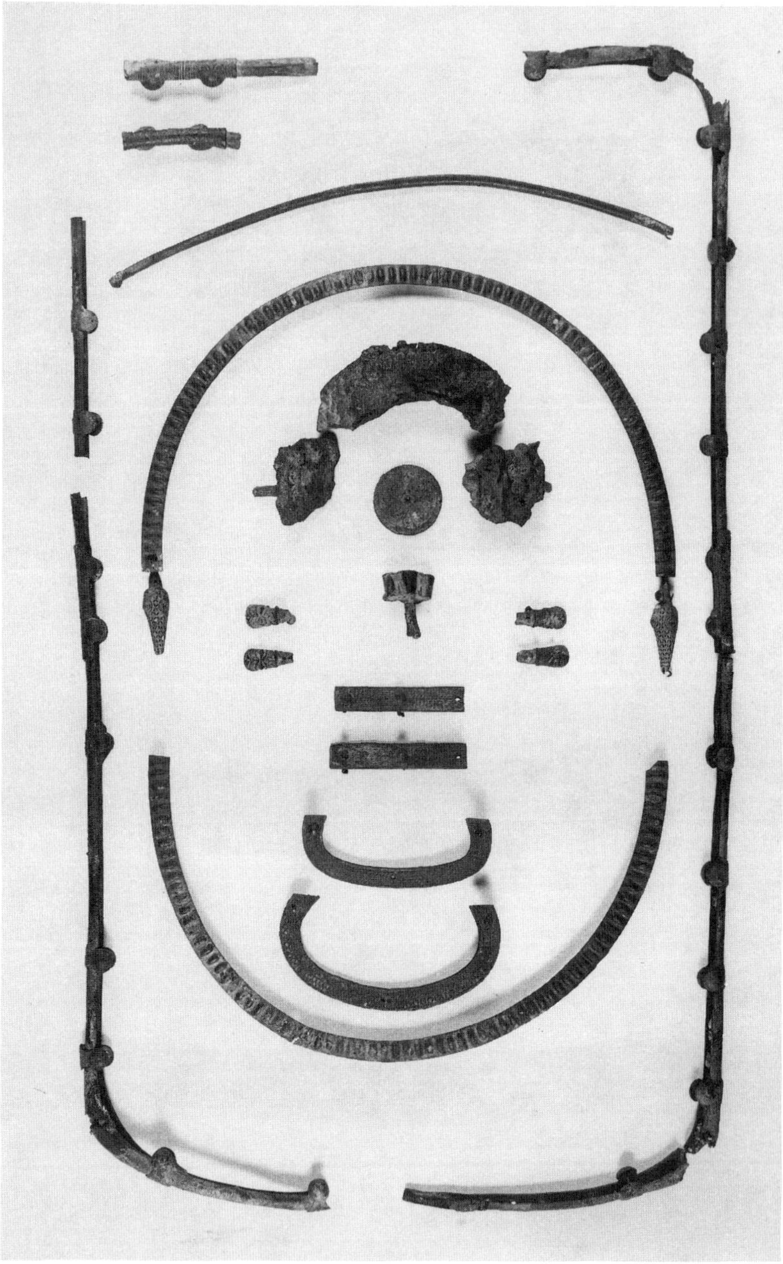

Pl. 17. Fragments of a saddle from the River Shannon. (Photo: National Museum of Ireland).

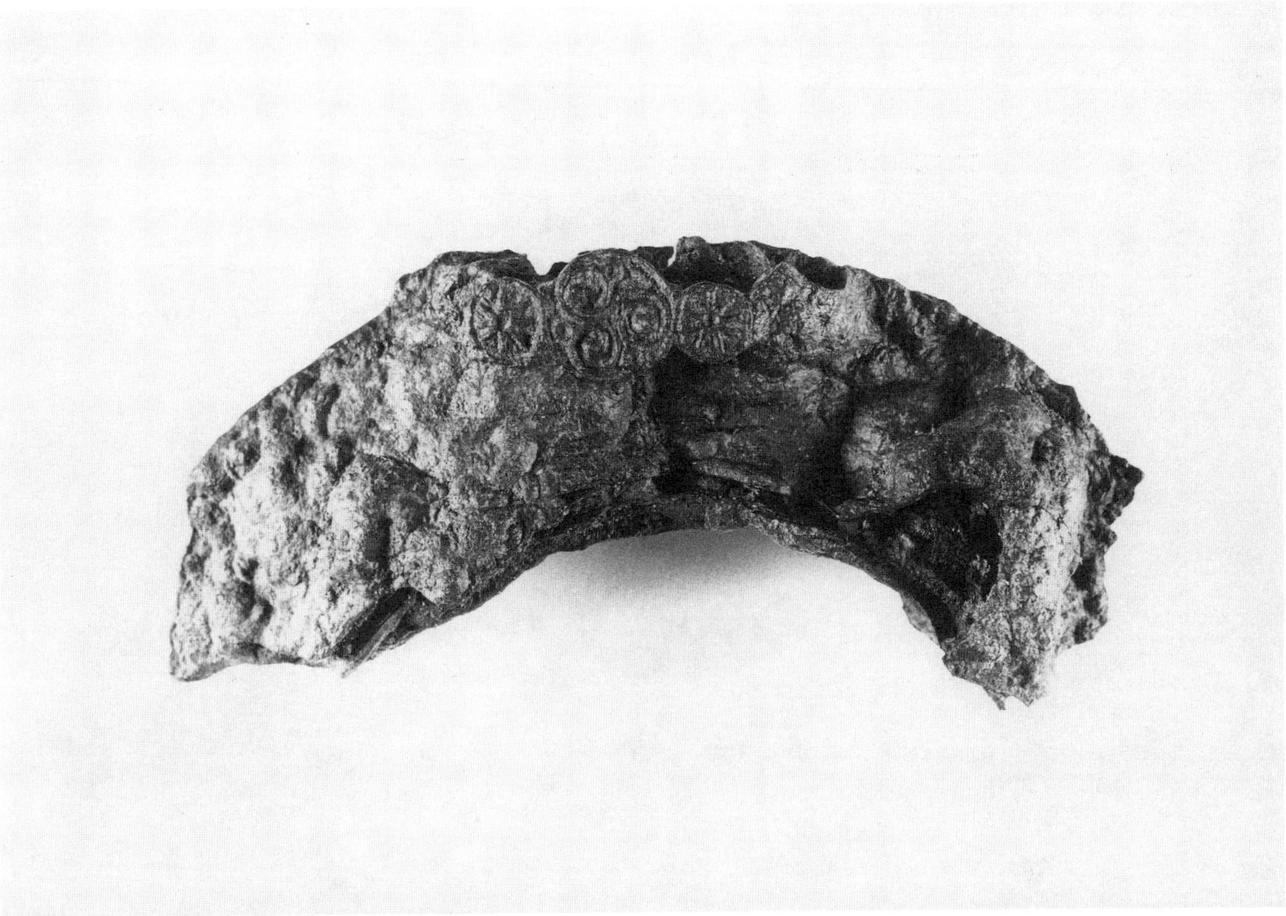

Pl. 18. Shannon saddle, detail of metal ring. (Photo: National Museum of Ireland).

Pl. 19. Shannon saddle, detail of metal disc. (Photo: National Museum of Ireland).

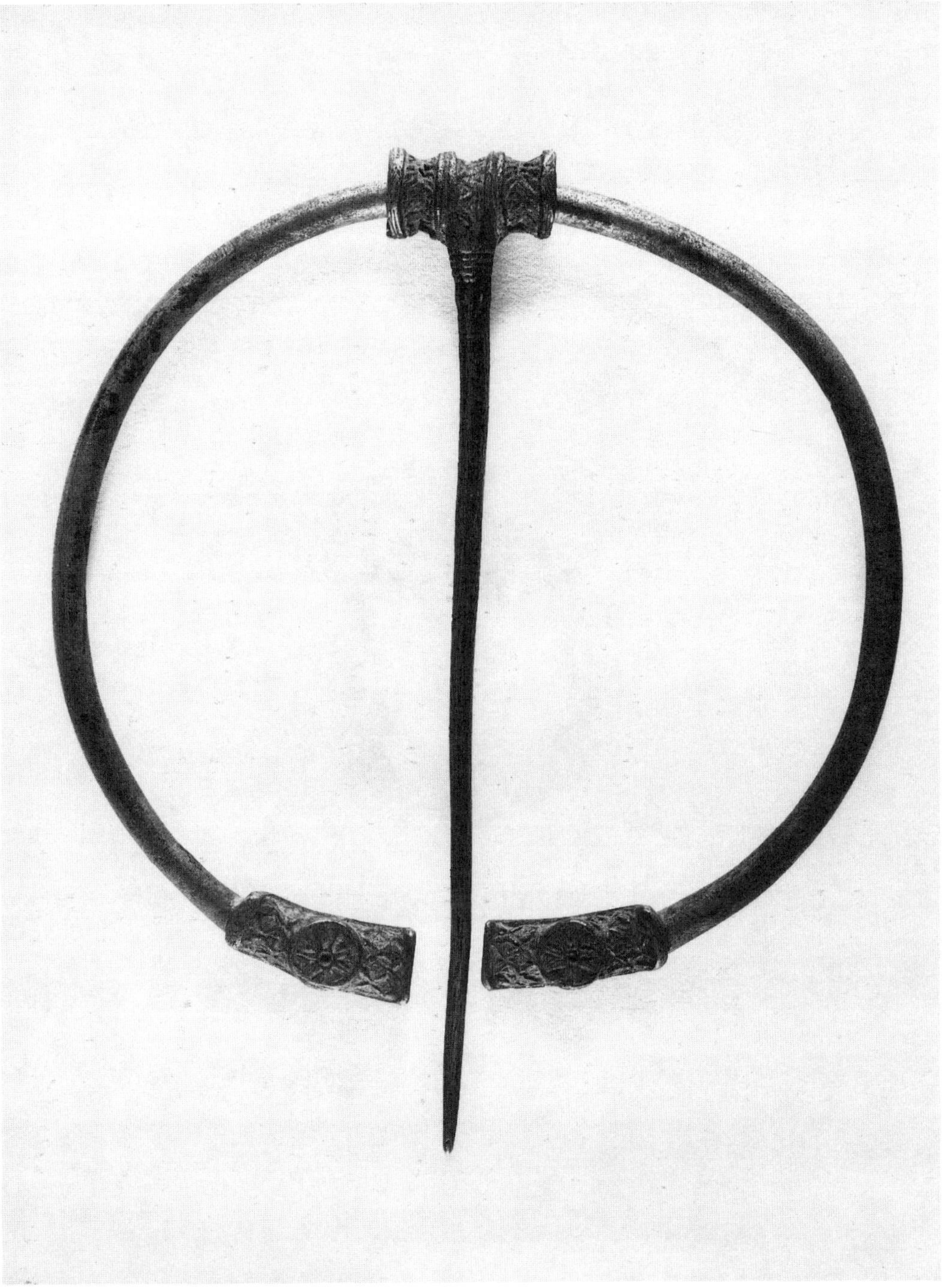

Pl. 20. Penannular Brooch, Moystown Demesne, Co. Westmeath (NMI 1956:446). (Photo: National Museum of Ireland).

Pl. 21. Ringed pin, Dooey, Co. Donegal. (Photo: National Museum of Ireland).

The Mediterranean Perspective

DAVID WHITEHOUSE

My task is to comment on aspects of seventh-century Britain from the point of view of an archaeologist working on the Mediterranean in the first millennium A.D. Since Michael Ryan has examined the Celtic perspective, I shall glance at western Britain as well as the east. Seen from the Mediterranean, the dominant impression of Britain in the early seventh century is how un-Roman it had become. This is surprising. After all, lowland Britain had been part of the Roman Empire for nearly four hundred years. Its inhabitants paid taxes to Roman officials, were drafted into the Roman army, and sought justice in Roman courts. Although farther from the core of the empire than any other province, Britain acquired from Rome the basic features of civilization: organization at the level of the state, urbanism, and literacy. It also encountered, to an unknown extent, the everyday use of money and relatively advanced technology, such as monumental construction in brick and stone and the harnessing of water as a source of energy. Britain, in short, had been part of the political realm and the world economy of Rome. Italian aristocrats, such as Melania the Younger, owned property in Britain in c. 400; British bishops attended church councils at Arles in 314 and Rimini in 359. We debate the degree of integration of Britain into the Roman Empire, but it would be perverse to deny that integration occurred.

In the fourth century, the Roman Empire was divided in two. In the fifth century, the western half disintegrated and was replaced by a series of independent chiefdoms and states. The Visigoths invaded Italy in 401 or 402, looted Rome in 410, and eventually settled in Spain. The Vandals invaded the Maghreb and created a kingdom based on Carthage. In the course of the century, western Europe was overrun by Huns, Franks, and others, many of whom carved out for themselves territories, which they ruled as independent or quasi-independent chiefdoms and states.

By this time, Britain had been abandoned. In 367, Picts, Scots, and Attacotti had overrun parts of the province, which was recovered in 369. In 383, Magnus Maximus took troops to support his bid for power in Gaul. Stilicho withdrew further detachments to defend Italy in 401. Within the decade, stripped of government forces, Britain ceased to belong in any meaningful sense to the Roman Empire.

After the fifth century, lowland Britain presents an almost completely un-Roman appearance. Excavations at Canterbury, London, Lincoln, and York show that, although some of the former cities were still occupied, the inhabitants lived in communities that were no longer urban. There is little or no evidence for the survival of Christianity or Roman paganism, or for the use of money or the most advanced technology introduced by the Romans. We debate the degree of contrast between Roman and post-Roman England, but we agree that the contrast exists.

As soon as we examine the archaeological evidence for contact between Britain and the Mediterranean immediately after the Roman period, we encounter a paradox. Evidence of contact exists, but it is markedly stronger in western Britain (which had been relatively or wholly un-Romanized) than in the heart of the former provinces. The most obvious evidence consists of pottery: amphorae, which arrived filled with wine and perhaps other perishable foodstuffs, and tableware. The amphorae fall into at least five groups, which Charles Thomas, expanding the typology proposed by C. A. R. Radford, labels BI-II and BIV-VI.[1] The following table presents a concordance of Thomas' nomenclature and the names used by D. P. S. Peacock and D. F. Williams in *Amphorae and the Roman Economy*,[2] which provides us with up-to-date information on places of manufacture and chronology:

[1] C. Thomas, *A Provisional List of Imported Pottery in Post-Roman Western Britain and Ireland* (Redruth 1981); C. A. R. Radford, "Imported Pottery found at Tintagel, Cornwall," in D. B. Harden (ed.) *Dark Age Britain* (London 1956), 59-70.

[2] D. P. S. Peacock and D. F. Williams, *Amphorae and the Roman Economy* (London 1986).

Thomas	Peacock & Williams	Place of Manufacture	Date
BI	43	Aegean (?)	4th- early 7th centuries
BII	44	Eastern Mediterranean	5th- mid 7th centuries
BIV	45	Eastern Mediterranean	late 1st- 6th centuries
BV	34	Central Tunisia	late 2nd- 5th centuries
BVI	49	Gaza	4th- 6th centuries

The occurrence of these and other, unidentified varieties of amphora is as follows:

Region	Number of Find-places					
	BI	BII	BIV	BV	BVI	Others
SW England	14	14	6	3	1	11
Wales	4	1	2	1	-	2
Ireland	2	1	-	-	-	2
Scotland	1	5	-	-	-	-
Rest of England	-	-	6	6	2	-
Total	21	21	14	10	3	15

If we ignore types BIV and BV, some of which were imported long before the end of the Roman occupation, we find that the great majority of the amphorae occur in western Britain. Two-thirds of the find places of BI and BII amphorae are in southwestern England, and if we combine the figures for BI, BII, and BVI (i.e. amphorae that cannot be earlier than the fourth century), we find that only two find-places lie outside southwestern England, Wales, Ireland and Scotland – and that one of these (Wroxeter) is far closer to Wales than to southeastern England.

A second feature of the corpus is equally striking: the eastern origin of the amphorae. Seventy percent of the finds, including those of unknown origin, were made in the eastern Mediterranean; if, as above, we count only BI, BII, and BVI, the percentage is 100. This eastern bias is not restricted to the amphorae. Seventy-four percent of the Mediterranean tableware also comes from the east, although the repertoire also includes pottery from Tunisia, and southern and western France.

Our understanding of the occurrence of objects from the eastern Mediterranean in western Britain in general (and southwestern England in particular) is aided by a passage in the Life of John the Almsgiver, Patriarch of Alexandria, who died in 617.[3] The passage refers to a voyage from Alexandria to Britain, in the course of which the captain exchanged a cargo of grain either for cash – which seems improbable – or bullion (presumably gold; the Greek text uses the word *nomisma*), and for tin. If Alexandrian ships were in the habit of visiting Britain to acquire gold (from Ireland or Wales) and tin around the year 600, they provide an explanation for both the existence of imports from the eastern Mediterranean, and the concentration of finds in southwestern England, the source of the tin. Some of the pottery from France could have been acquired en route, in much the same way that Roman traders in the Indian Ocean bought and sold goods at several stopping-places between their home ports in the Red Sea and their final destinations in India or Sri Lanka,[4] although I certainly would not deny the possibility of direct trading up and down the Atlantic seaboard.[5]

Western Britain, therefore, had direct, if intermittent, contact with the Mediterranean between the fifth and the seventh centuries. What about the east? Objects from the Mediterranean certainly arrived in eastern England; they are represented most spectacularly at Sutton Hoo itself. Here, I will touch on four categories of object found in fifth- to seventh-century contexts that either originated in the Mediterranean or traveled through it: coins, "Coptic" metal vessels, amethysts, and cowrie shells.

The find-places of imported gold coins were summarized by S. E. Rigold, who recorded twenty-six fifth- to early eighth-century gold coins struck in the Mediterranean, either by the Byzantine emperor in the east or by a western ruler imitating Byzantine custom.[6] The most tantalizing find consists of at least ten *tremisses* of Justin I (518-527), discovered at Kingston-on-Thames in 1848; unfortunately, only a summary description exists and the coins themselves cannot be located. If we add to the list eastern Gallic issues of Theodobert I, Gallic derivatives of Byzantine heavy *tremisses*, and Visigothic, Spanish, and southwestern Gallic pre-royal *tremisses*, the total number of imported gold coins found in England, apart from Sutton Hoo, is forty-five. Twenty-four of these (53%) were found in Kent, twelve or more (27%) in the Thames valley, and four (9%) in East Anglia.

The so-called Coptic vessels are very much rarer. I say "so-called" because, as Joachim Werner anticipated, the term "Coptic" gives a mistaken sense of precision to their place of manufacture.[7] While some of the objects, including most of the cast examples, are Egyptian,[8] the others, including most of the beaten examples, were made elsewhere in the eastern Mediterranean and in Italy.[9] Regardless of where in the Mediterranean they were made, their occurrence at Sutton Hoo and in the rich burial at Taplow in the Thames valley shows that in the eyes of the Anglo-Saxons they were objects of high prestige.

The ultimate source of the amethysts was India and for this reason Meaney suggested that they reached Britain in the hands of traders who brought the "Coptic" metalware.[10] In a recent discussion of imported objects from Anglo-Saxon graves, J. W. Huggett noted the strong Kentish bias of find-places, with no fewer than 60% of all amethyst beads coming from a single cemetery: Faversham.[11]

The cowrie shells are more difficult to assess, since only some of the species recorded from Anglo-Saxon graves inhabit the warm waters of the Mediterranean or the Red Sea. *Cypraea europea*, for example, is found in British waters and specimens have been identified from Anglo-Saxon contexts at Driffield and Dunstable. Large species,

---

[3]G. Monks, "The Church of Alexandria and Economic Life," *Speculum* 38 (1953), 349-62.

[4]L. Casson (trans. and ed.) *The Periplus Maris Erythraei* (Princeton 1989), 11-43.

[5]See, for example, M. Rouche, *L'Aquitaine des Wisigoths aux Arabes*, 418-781 (Paris 1979), 258-60.

[6]S. E. Rigold, "The Sutton Hoo Coins in the Light of the Contemporary Background of Coinage in England," in R. L. S. Bruce-Mitford, *The Sutton Hoo Ship Burial*, vol. I (London 1975).

[7]J. Werner, "Italienisches und koptisches Bronzgeschirr des 6. und 7. Jahrhunderts," in *Mnemosyne Th. Wiegand* (Munich 1938), 74-86.

[8]See H. Roth, "Urcei alexandrini: zur Herkunft gegossenen 'koptischen' Buntmetallgerätes auf grund von Schriftquellen," *Germania* 58 (1980), 156-61, for a reference to *urceos Alexandrinos* at the abbey of St. Wandrille at Fontanelle some time between 753 and 787.

[9]P. M. Richards, "Byzantine Bronze Vessels in England and Europe: The Origins of Anglo-Saxon Trade," unpublished Ph.D. thesis, Cambridge University (1980); M. C. Carretta, *Il catalogo del vasellame bronzeo italiano altomedievale*, Ricerche di archeologia altomedievale e medievale 4 (Florence 1982), 16.

[10]A. L. Meaney, *Anglo-Saxon Amulets and Curing Stones* (Oxford 1981), 76. E. T. Leeds had suggested that they were scavenged from Roman graves (E. T. Leeds, *The Archaeology of the Anglo-Saxon Settlements* [Oxford 1913], 131-32).

[11]J. W. Huggett, "Imported Grave Goods and the Early Anglo-Saxon Economy," *MA* 32 (1988), 66-68.

such as *Cypraea tigris* and *Cypraea arabica*, on the other hand, live exclusively in warm water, and the finds from Sarre, Alfriston, Haslingfield, and other sites undoubtedly came from, or through, the Mediterranean.[12]

The inventories provided by Rigold, Richards, and Huggett add up to a trickle of more or less prestigious objects from the Mediterranean arriving in eastern England between the fifth and seventh centuries. As in the Roman period, when very much larger quantities of objects reached consumers all over England, there is nothing to suggest direct importation; most of the objects, I assume, arrived indirectly by way of Gaul and Germany.

I will examine the points of entry by which these objects arrived by considering one of the largest categories of early Anglo-Saxon imports from the continent: glass vessels. The classic survey of glass in early medieval Britain is by D. B. Harden.[13] Although the number of objects has increased and the chronology has been refined, Harden's typology, tables, and distribution maps still have much to tell us. Harden divided the vessels from Anglo-Saxon cemeteries of the fifth to seventh centuries into eleven basic types. Finds from Germany, Belgium, and France show that most, but not all of the objects were made on the Continent; indeed, it is very likely that glassmaking was a lost art in fifth- to sixth-century England. Next, Harden divided the English finds into two groups: (A) objects probably made or imported to Britain in the Roman period, which were antiques at the time of burial; and (B) objects made between the fifth and seventh centuries. Group B was subdivided into three chronological stages: Bi, fifth- to early sixth-century; Bii, sixth-century; and Biii, late sixth- to seventh-century. The final stage in Harden's analysis was to list the objects by the counties in which they were found and the subgroup to which they were attributed. Here, abstracted from his publication, are the figures for Group B:

County	5th-early 6th century	6th century	late 6th-7th century	Total
Kent	27	27	105	159
Surrey/Sussex	13	2	1	16
All others	13	11	24	48
Total	53	40	130	223

If we convert the numbers to percentages per period, the following pattern emerges:

County	5th- early 6th century	6th century	late 6th- 7th century
Kent	51	68	71
Surrey/Sussex	25	5	7
All others	25	28	22
Total	101	101	100

One thing is immediately obvious: the preponderance in all three stages of finds from Kent. To some extent, this preponderance may be due to the likely presence in the seventh century of glassmakers at or near Faversham, which

[12] *Ibid*, 72.

[13] D. B. Harden, "Glass Vessels in Britain and Ireland, A.D. 400-1000," in D. B. Harden (ed.) *Dark Age Britain* (London 1956), 132-67.

has produced more than 70% of all the fifth to seventh century glass from England. Even so, the figures point unequivocally to Kent as the main recipient of glass from the continent. We have already seen similar sets of figures for Byzantine coins, amethyst beads, and cowrie shells. I draw the conclusion that the principal entry-point for imports from the Continent was in Kent.

Indeed, Richard Hodges may be correct when he points to Sarre on the Isle of Thanet as a likely entrepot.[14] The now-silted Wantsum Channel between Thanet and the mainland of Kent would have afforded a sheltered landing-place, protected by the Roman forts at Reculver and Richborough (the find-place of two Byzantine coins).

If East Anglia possessed an entrepot at this date, the strongest candidate for its location is Ipswich, where excavations have revealed evidence of late sixth- or early seventh-century occupation and two cemeteries: in Hadleigh Road[15] and at the Butter Market.[16]

The principal routes by which Mediterranean objects reached the other side of the North Sea and the English Channel were identified nearly thirty years ago by Werner on the basis of the find-places of two types of object: gold coins minted in the Mediterranean, especially those of Theodoric (493-526) and Justinian (527-65), and bronze vessels.[17] The distribution of the coins and the vessels led Werner to identify a trade route from Ravenna at the head of the Adriatic, through the Alps to the upper Rhine, and thence westward to northern France and the North Sea. The evidence suggests that the route may have been busiest in the second and third quarters of the sixth century, the period of Justinian's reconquest of Italy, of the establishment of Ravenna as the seat of the Byzantine viceroy, and of relatively intense diplomatic activity between the Byzantines and the Franks. A second route followed the Rhone valley from Marseille to central France and beyond.

The crossing to Kent and other entry-points is unlikely to have been the monopoly of any one group, although the Frisians are accorded pride of place in the literature, thanks partly to Bede, who noted their presence in London in 679. The importance of the Frisians is underlined by the relative abundance of Byzantine gold coins in Friesland; P. C. J. A. Boeles lists two coins of Justin I (518-27), eight of Justinian (527-65), two of Justin II (565-78), three of Maurice Tiberius (582-602), two of Phocas (602-10) and four of Heraclius and Heraclius Constantine (c. 613/4-30 or later) – more than from the whole of Francia.[18]

I have sketched the way in which minor *objets de luxe*, such as amethyst beads, probably arrived in eastern England in the sixth and early seventh centuries. The bronze vessels may have been part of this commercial or semi-commercial network, although I think it is more likely that the majority arrived as gifts.[19] Be that as it may, one group of objects from Sutton Hoo includes items that almost certainly were gifts: some, or all, of the silver. The silver comprises sixteen pieces from the Mediterranean, made at Constantinople or some other major center in the east.[20] I find it impossible to follow W. Levison who, writing of the fair of St. Denis, near Paris, stated: "We may imagine that at such gatherings the so-called 'Coptic' bronze vessels found in Saxon graves were acquired by English traders, and conjecture a similar source for silver objects such as those discovered... [at] Sutton Hoo..."[21]

The objects are simply too splendid to have been bartered at St. Denis, or any other Dark Age market. The most spectacular silver object at Sutton Hoo is a dish, 72cm across, which weighs 5.64kg (Pl. 1). It bears the control stamps of the emperor Anastasius (491-518). A fluted bowl with drop-handles, decorated with a female head, is of similar date, or slightly earlier (Pl. 2). In other words, both objects were at least a hundred years old

---

[14]R. Hodges, *Dark Age Economics* (London 1982), 69.

[15]N. G. Layard, "An Anglo-Saxon Cemetery at Ipswich," *Archaeologia* 60 (1907), 325-52.

[16]M. M. Mango, *et al.*, "A Sixth-Century Mediterranean Bucket from Bromeswell Parish, Suffolk," *Antiquity* 63 (1989), 295-311.

[17]J. Werner, "Fernhandel und Naturalwirtschaft im östlichen Merowingerreich nach archäologischen und numismatischen Zeugnissen," *Bericht der Römisch-Germanisch Kommission* 42 (1961), 307-46.

[18]P. C. J. A. Boeles, *Friesland tot de Elfde Eeuw* ('s-Gravenhage 1951), 500-24; see also, J. Laufaurie, "Trouvailles de monnaies des VIe-VIIe siècles de l'Empire d'Orient en Gaule mérovingienne (resumé)," *Bulletin de la Société Française de Numismatique* 97.5 (1972), 206-07.

[19]See, Mango, *et al.*, "Sixth-Century Mediterranean Bucket."

[20]R. L. S. Bruce-Mitford, *The Sutton Hoo Ship Burial*, vol. III (London 1983), 1-165.

[21]W. Levison, *England and the Continent in the Eighth Century* (Oxford 1946), 7-8.

when they were buried. We have no means of knowing, of course, what happened to the vessels between the time they were made and their burial. They may have been given to their latest owner by a fellow-ruler, or have been inherited by him (did they reach western or northern Europe as gifts from Anastasius to a barbarian ally?), or taken as booty.

We reach firmer ground with ten bowls with cruciform designs, evidently the product of a single workshop and kept together as a set (Pl. 3). Parallels in the Lampsacus treasure and other Byzantine hoards suggest a date around 600. A similar date is suggested for the pair of spoons bearing the names *Saulos* and *Paulos* (Pl. 4). These twelve items, therefore, do look like gifts to the king with whom they were buried. Indeed, Rupert Bruce-Mitford has suggested that, if indeed the king was Rædwald, they may have been presented to him on the occasion of his conversion in Kent, some time before 618.[22]

The inventory of silver objects is completed by a ladle and a plain bowl, both of which could have been new, or fairly new, at the time of burial.

If the spoons and the set of bowls arrived in England as gifts, they were not without precedent. Silver vessels, in fact, were among the preferred gifts of late Roman and Byzantine emperors to loyal associates, and displaying a large collection of plate was an accepted way of advertising one's status. Written records and a handful of objects show that the Merovingians adopted this custom.[23] The will of Didier of Cahors, which is earlier than 655, mentions gold and silver, which he inherited from his parents or received at the royal court and from princes whom he had served (*Aurum vel argenteum, quod ex successione parentum habeo, vel quod in regia aula et in servitio principum elaboravi*).[24] Evidently, kings and princes were still rewarding subordinates with gifts of plate.

The largest collections of silver plate were enormous; in 621, bishop Didier of Auxerre bequeathed to his cathedral more than one hundred items of silver with a combined weight of nearly 140kg.[25] The objects included four *missoria* (dishes) with a combined weight of 44kg. These must have been colossal, for the Great Dish from the Mildenhall Treasure weighs a mere 8.3kg.[26]

The evidence of the documents overshadows the handful of objects that survive.[27] The most impressive survivor is the "Shield of Hannibal," a silver dish of the fifth or sixth century, comparable in size to the Anastasius dish from Sutton Hoo, which was discovered at Passage (Izère) in 1714.[28] It bears the scratched inscription: + *Agnerico Sum* +.[29] A sixth-century silver strainer, which a former owner acquired in Angers, bears the name *Albinus*, perhaps Albinus who was bishop of Angers from 529 to c. 550.[30] Similarly, one of the silver bowls from Valdonne in the Bouches du Rhône, which date from the first half of the seventh century, bears the name *AR/BAL/DO*, whom Werner identifies as Haribaldus, a *vir inluster* in Provence.[31]

The Sutton Hoo silver, therefore, was by no means the only high-status silver in post-Roman Europe. Indeed, it was not the only silver plate in England in the seventh century, for Bede (*HE* 3.6) refers to a large silver dish at the court of Oswald, king of Northumbria.

In conclusion, let us consider the background to the arrival of Byzantine plate in western Europe. An essential part of this background was the *imitatio imperii* of certain western rulers, which consisted not only of perpetuating

---

[22]Bruce-Mitford, *Sutton Hoo Ship Burial*, III, 145.

[23]E. Knögel, "Schriftquellen zur Kunstgeschichte der Merowingerzeit," *Bonner Jahrbücher* 140-41 (1936), 1-258.

[24]Rouche, *L'Aquitaine*, 200-01 and 573, n. 114.

[25]*Ibid.*, 199-200 and 573, n.111.

[26]J. M. C. Toynbee and K. S. Painter, "Silver Picture Plates of Late Antiquity: A.D. 300 to 700," *Archaeologia* 198 (1986), 22-24, no. 1.

[27]F. Baratte and K. S. Painter, *Trésors d'orfèvrerie gallo-romains* (Paris 1989), 254-82.

[28]*Ibid.*, no. 243.

[29]J. Vezin, "L'inscription du 'Missorium' d'Agnéric," *Bulletin de la Société Nationale des Antiquaires de France* (1972), 147-54.

[30]J. P. Caillet, "La passoire liturgique de Saint-Aubin d'Angers," *Bulletin monumental* 144 (1986), 295-304; Baratte and Painter, *Trésors*, no. 248.

[31]J. Werner, "Arbaldo (Haribaldus). Ein merowingischer Vir Inluster aus der Provence," in *Mélanges de numismatique, d'archéologie et d'histoire offerts à Jean Lafaurie* (Paris 1980), 257-63; Baratte and Painter, *Trésors*, no. 247.

traditions derived from late Roman practice but also of imitating contemporary Byzantine emperors.[32] The following is a sample of occasions in the sixth and seventh centuries when prominent westerners (regardless of their motives) had direct contact with the emperor or imitated imperial practices. In Italy, the Lombard king Agilulf (590-616) possessed a helmet, the decoration of which showed him enthroned, flanked by courtiers and Victories, and approached by figures bearing crowns: a scene reminiscent of late Roman diptychs and *missoria*.[33] According to Paul the Deacon (*Hist. Lang.* 4.30), the same king had his son proclaimed co-ruler in the circus at Milan, an imitation of a Byzantine ceremony.[34] As Chris Wickham noted, "Agilulf, clearly, was concerned to establish, through a fairly eclectic set of images, a late Roman aura of kingship."[35]

In the Frankish kingdom, Clovis was declared an honorary consul by Anastasius in 508. As Procopius (*BG* 3.33.5) complained, Theodobert I (533-48) usurped imperial prerogatives by presiding over circus games at Arles and issuing gold coins of Byzantine type. Chilperic (561-84) presided over games at Soissons and Paris. According to Gregory of Tours (*Hist. Franc.* 5.34), Chilperic's queen Fredegunde owned gold, silver, precious stones, collars, and other imperial ornaments (*imperialia ornamenta*). Radegonde asked for, and received, a relic of the True Cross from Justin II in 569. Arnegunde, whose early seventh-century jewelry shows that she cannot have been the eponymous consort of Chlotar I, was buried at St. Denis in a red silk gown with gold-thread embroidery, apparently imported from Constantinople.[36] At about the same time, Dagobert (sole king, 629-39) was on sufficiently amicable terms with Heraclius to promulgate an imperial decree, and communications with the Mediterranean were sufficiently close for news of Heraclius's victory over the Sasanians in 628 to be known at the Burgundian court within a year.[37] Later in the century, an aristocratic female, probably Bathilde, wife of Clovis II, was buried at Chelles in a gown embroidered with a parure consisting of collar, pectoral cross, and chain, which as H. E. F. Vierck has shown, is a close copy of the regalia of a Byzantine princess.[38]

Rather than a gift from a Mediterranean dignitary, therefore, I prefer to conjecture that the spoons and the set of bowls, and perhaps other pieces of silver, from Sutton Hoo may have arrived in England as gifts from a Frankish court – reinforcements, perhaps, of the kind of alliance created when Aethelbert king of Kent (c. 560-616) married Bertha, a Frankish princess. Seen in this perspective, the silver from Sutton Hoo is remarkable not so much because of its bullion value (which is dwarfed by the astonishing gold and silver grave goods from the mid seventh-century tomb at Malaja Pereshchepina in the Ukraine,[39] by a number of Roman and Byzantine hoards, and by the treasures of Didier of Auxerre) but because it may be the result of gift-exchange in imperial style far beyond the western frontier of the Byzantine Empire.

ACKNOWLEDGEMENTS

I am grateful to Kenneth Painter and Michael Ryan for information on silver, to Alan Stahl for information on coins, and to fellow-participants in the meetings at Kalamazoo for comments and criticism. Unfortunately, I learned of the existence of R. W. Higginbottom's thesis too late to consult it before completing my text,[40] and Michael

---

[32] H. E. F. Vierck, "La 'Chemise de Sainte-Bathilde' à Chelles et l'influence byzantine sur l'art de cour mérovingien au VIIe siècle,' in *Centenaire de l'Abbé Cochet, 1975. Actes du colloque international d'archéologie* (Rouen 1978), 521-64.

[33] A. Melucco Vaccaro, *I Longobardi in Italia* (Rome 1982), 146-49.

[34] B. Ward-Perkins, *From Classical Antiquity to the Middle Ages. Urban Public Building in Northern and Central Italy, A.D. 300-850* (Oxford 1984), 107-08.

[35] C. Wickham, *Early Medieval Italy* (London and Basingstoke 1981), 34.

[36] J. Werner, "The Frankish Royal Tombs in the Cathedrals of Cologne and St. Denis," *Antiquity* 38 (1964), 201-16.

[37] S. H. Wander, "The Cyprus Plates and the *Chronicle* of Fredegar," *Dumbarton Oaks Papers* 29 (1973), 345-46.

[38] Vierck, "La 'Chemise de Sainte-Bathilde'."

[39] J. Werner, "Der Grabfund von Malaja Pereščepina und Kuvrat, Kagan des Bulgaren," *Bayerische Akademie der Wissenschaften*, phil. -hist. Klasse Abhandlungen, neue folge 91 (1984).

[40] R. W. Higginbottom, "Anglo-Saxon Contact with the Eastern Mediterranean A.D. 400-700 and its Context," unpublished M.A. thesis, University of Manchester, 1975; M. G. Fulford, "Byzantium and Britain: a Mediterranean Perspective on Post-Roman Mediterranean Imports in Western Britain and Ireland," *MA* 33 (1989), 1-6.

Fulford's discussion of direct links between Constantinople and Britain in the sixth century appeared after I had consigned it to the editors.

Pl. 1. Sutton Hoo, Mound One: silver salver with stamps of Anastasius I. London, The British Museum. (Photo: By permission of the Trustees, British Museum).

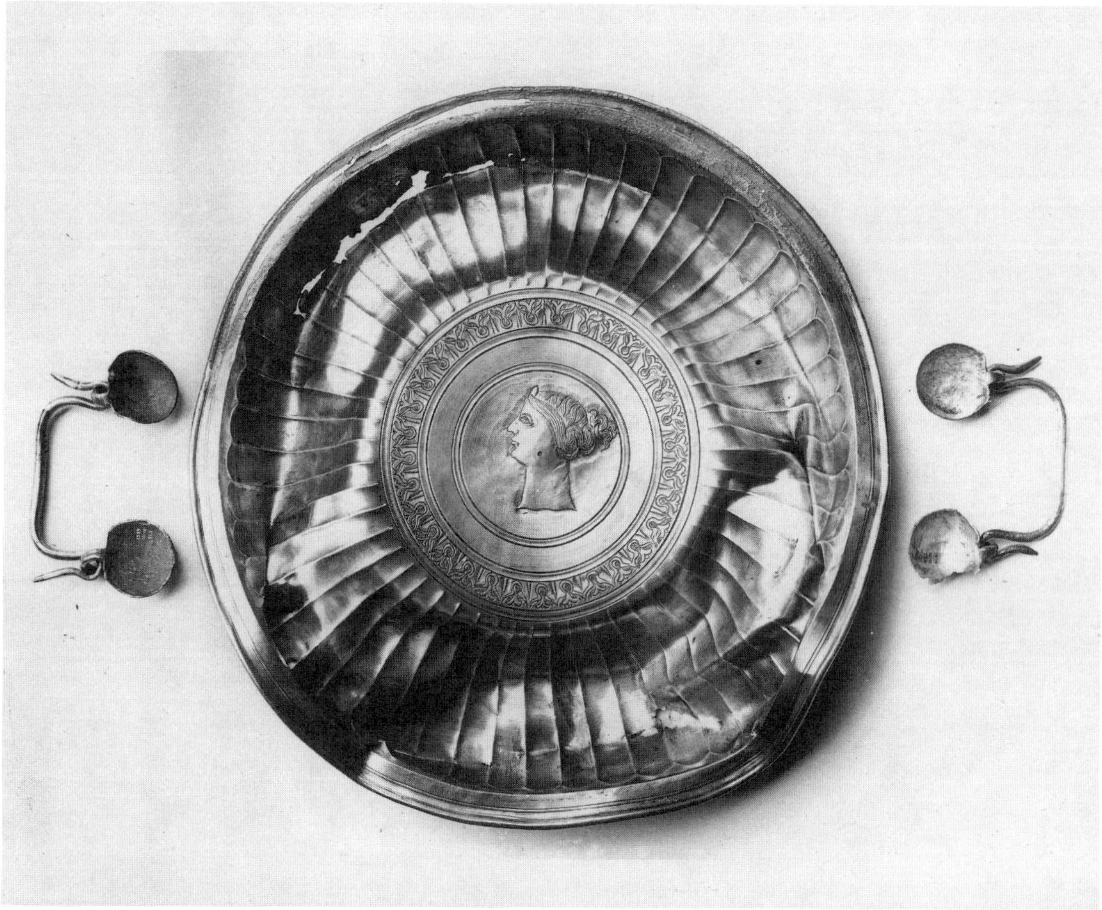

Pl. 2. Sutton Hoo, Mound One: fluted silver bowl. London, The British Museum. (Photo: By permission of the Trustees, British Museum).

Pl. 3. Sutton Hoo, Mound One: two of set of ten nested silver bowls with cruciform ornament. London, The British Museum. (Photo: By permission of the Trustees, British Museum).

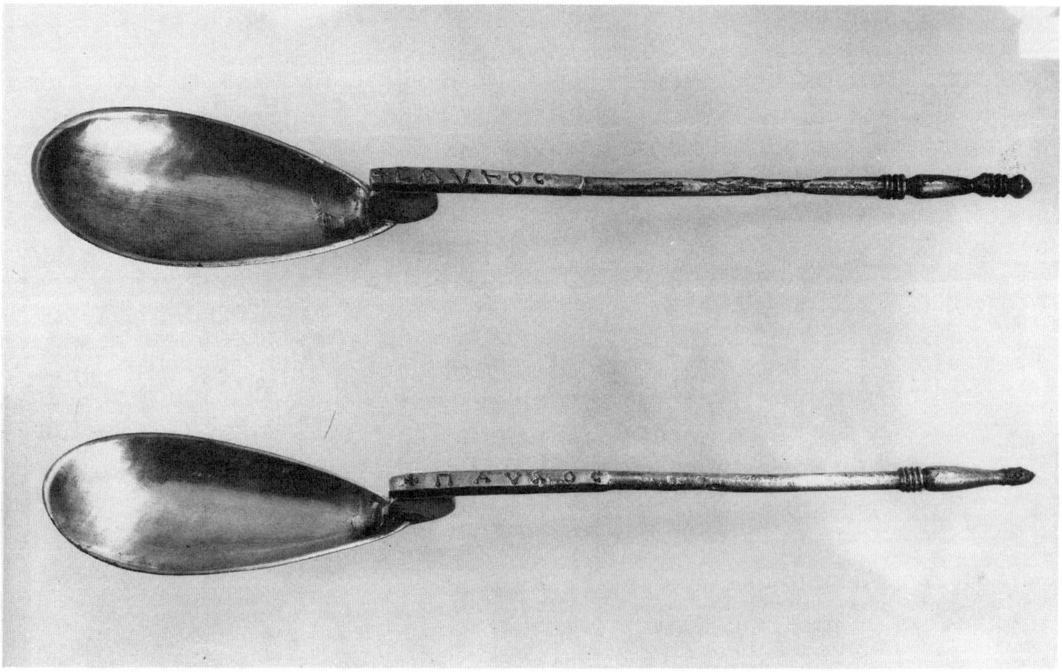

Pl. 4. Sutton Hoo, Mound One: the two silver spoons. London, The British Museum. (Photo: By permission of the Trustees, British Museum).

The Date of the Sutton Hoo Coins

ALAN M. STAHL and W. A. ODDY

Thirty-seven gold coins were found in the purse of the Sutton Hoo burial, all apparently minted in Merovingian France.[1] Only four of these coins bear the name of a ruler. Three are coins in the name of the Byzantine emperor Maurice Tiberius, bearing the mint signatures of the French town of Arles [SH.27], Valence [SH.26] and Venasque [SH.11].[2] As it is unlikely that these coins were minted under any effective Byzantine authority, they are known as quasi-imperial issues (Germanic imitations of Byzantine coins with no mint attributions are known as pseudo-imperial coins). Their value for chronology is to place the gathering of the Sutton Hoo coins some time after Maurice's accession in 582. Provençal coins in the name of Maurice appear to have been minted in two phases; first, with a simple cross reverse, and, then with a circle separating the cross from the legend. The transition from type one to type two has been dated to about 595.[3] As two of the Sutton Hoo coins are of the later type, we have a tentative *terminus post quem* of 595 for the parcel.

The only coin in the group with the name of a Frankish ruler identifies a king Theodebert and has no mint designation [SH.2]. There were two Merovingian kings of this name: Theodebert I, in the first half of the sixth century, and Theodebert II, 595-612. Coins clearly of Theodebert I are closely modelled after those of his Byzantine contemporaries, and, like them, have a winged figure on the reverse. The Sutton Hoo piece bears a reverse cross, which is unknown in Mediterranean gold coinage until the fourth quarter of the sixth century.[4] If the Sutton Hoo coin were to be attributed to Theodebert I, the cross would have to be seen as an innovation of his which was then ignored for several decades and then widely revived. It is more likely that this coin is of Theodebert II, following prototypes of Byzantine and quasi-imperial issues. This would give the only royal coin in the Sutton Hoo parcel a date of post-595, consistent with the two coins from the second period of the coinage of Maurice from Provence.

While these four coins give a date of 595 after which the Sutton Hoo hoard must have been deposited, they are less useful for giving a date before which the parcel was assembled. The coins in the name of Maurice are from Provence, in the south of Frankish Gaul, so they may well be earlier than the bulk of coins, which were minted nearer England. In so small an assemblage, the lack of later dated coins cannot be taken to demonstrate a burial during or soon after the reign of Maurice or Theodebert; to determine a date for the parcel as a whole, it is necessary to establish some sort of chronology for the other, non-royal, coins.[5]

It is a peculiarity of Merovingian coins that few of them identify the ruler under whose authority they were minted; rather they identify a minting place on one side and an individual, sometimes qualified with the word *monetarius*, on the other. This is conveniently termed the "mint-and-minter" type as distinct from the "royal" coins, which bear the name of a king, and "quasi-imperial" coins, which bear the name of an emperor. Several hundred

---

[1]This paper is based to a great extent on data developed by Oddy for the 1975 Sutton Hoo publication, which are published with references for the first time in the Appendix, below. The analysis and chronological inferences are the contribution of Stahl. The Sutton Hoo coins are published in J. P. C. Kent, "The Coins and the Date of the Burial," in R. L. S. Bruce-Mitford, *The Sutton Hoo Ship Burial*, vol. I (London 1975), 578-647; the best general introduction to Merovingian coinage is P. Grierson and M. Blackburn, *Medieval European Coinage*, vol. I, *The Early Middle Ages* (Cambridge 1986).

[2]Sutton Hoo coin 1 [SH.1] has an obverse legend which appears to be a garbled version of the name Justin or Justinian. It is identified by S. E. Rigold as a derivative of coins of Justin II and dated by him to around 590. See S. E. Rigold, "An Imperial Coinage in Southern Gaul in the Sixth and Seventh Centuries?," *NChron*, ser. 6, 14 (1954), 123, #10.

[3]Rigold, "Imperial Coinage," 113.

[4]*Ibid.*, 96; W. Hahn, *Moneta Imperii Byzantini*, vol. II, Österreichische Akademie der Wissenschaften, Phil. -Hist. Kl., Denkschriften 119 (Vienna 1975), 52-53.

[5]In this discussion, the Sutton Hoo coins are treated as a hoard, that is a representative and random sample of circulating coins, rather than as a consciously selected group. This assumption is based on considerations discussed in A. M. Stahl, "The Nature of the Sutton Hoo Coin Parcel," in C. B. Kendall and P. S. Wells (eds.) *Voyage to the Other World: The Legacy of Sutton Hoo*, Medieval Studies at Minnesota 4 (Minneapolis forthcoming), 3-14.

mint names on Merovingian coins have been identified with settlements, ranging from the important political and ecclesiastical centers of the realm to small villas and vici.

Of the hundreds of minters' names on such coins, only one has been securely identified with an individual known from other sources. The minter Eligius was originally a goldsmith and became treasurer to king Chlothar II about 625.[6] He also served under Dagobert I and Clovis II, and in 641 became Bishop of Noyon. It is for his works in this latter post that he merited a nearly contemporary hagiographic biography, which is one of our few sources relating to Merovingian coinage. The name Eligius as *monetarius* appears on coins with each of the three kings he is documented to have served; other coins which have only his name and various mint names can be generally dated to 625-641. No coins of Eligius are in the Sutton Hoo find.

With no explicit guidelines for dating, most Merovingian coins have to be dated more-or-less like other archaeological artefacts, using criteria of stylistic development, context, and technology for establishing a chronology. In the nineteenth century, style was the chief criterion used for developing chronologies of Merovingian coins. There was a general assumption of a movement from styles close to late Roman and Byzantine models to increasingly barbarous imagery. For the dating of the Sutton Hoo coins, the most important such inference derived from observations concerning the "anchored-cross" reverse type, common on coins of the region around Paris and appearing on nine of the Sutton Hoo coins [SH.17-25]. It was observed a century ago that this reverse is usually paired with an obverse bust of a distinctive style (termed *à l'appendice perlé*) which was considered so barbarous that it had to come towards the end of the series, i.e. in the second half of the seventh century.[7] Following such an argument, the first specialist in Merovingian coinage to examine the Sutton Hoo coins dated the assemblage, which he thought to represent the earliest phase of the anchored cross issue, to the 640s.[8] Similar stylistic arguments pushed the date of the hoard well into the second half of the seventh century.[9] But styles that are termed barbarous degenerations by some are seen by others as crude first attempts, and stylistic analysis is best used to associate coins into groups that may be geographical or chronological, but not to provide an *a priori* basis for ordering such groupings.

Few Merovingian coins have been found in controlled excavations, and the usual context for dating coins is the association of a group of coins found together, that is a hoard, rather than the association of coins to other artefacts. Documented hoards of Merovingian gold coins are few and small. The Sutton Hoo excavation is the only find of more than a handful of such coins since the beginning of this century. It is one of only a dozen documented hoards of seventh-century Frankish coinage and the only one whose entire contents are known with certainty. In view of the enormous diversity of Merovingian issues, the hoard evidence can be used to give only the most general chronology to major developments.

The basic outline of development of Merovingian coinage is, however, reasonably clear.[10] For most of the sixth century, Frankish rulers issued pseudo-imperial coins, which bore the name and image of a Byzantine emperor on the obverse and a winged figure and occasional monograms on the reverse; the signed coins of Theodebert I were an exception to this practice. Most of these coins were of gold and the weight of the Byzantine *solidus* or *tremissis* (one-third of a *solidus*). Towards the end of the century, some cities of Provence, near the Mediterranean coast, used a cross for their reverses flanked by the initials of the mint, creating the quasi-imperial series. Early in the seventh century, these Provençal mints began using the name of a Merovingian monarch on their *solidi* and *tremisses*. In the rest of Gaul, the pseudo-imperial coins gave way to a mint-and-minter coinage almost exclusively of gold *tremisses*; royal names appear only exceptionally on Merovingian coins outside of Provence. The mint-and-minter *tremisses* display a large variety of typological and stylistic groupings, some of which are clearly geographical in distribution and some of which appear to be of limited chronological duration. In the last few

[6] J. Lafaurie, "Eligius Monetarius," *Revue Numismatique*, ser. 6, 19 (1977), 111-51.

[7] G. de Ponton d'Amécourt, *Recherche des monnaies mérovingiennes du Cenomannicum* (Mamers 1883), 89.

[8] P. Le Gentilhomme, "Aperçu sur quelques apects du monnayage des peuples barbares," *Revue Numismatique*, ser. 5, 4 (1940),33-35.

[9] R. L. S. Bruce-Mitford, "Sutton Hoo – A Rejoinder," *Antiquity* 26 (1952), 76-82.

[10] Grierson and Blackburn, *Medieval European Coinage*, 111-38.

decades of the seventh century, the mint-and-minter gold *tremisses* gave way to a coinage of silver *denarii*, with few legible legends.

The only dates that can be assigned to Merovingian hoards with certainty are *termini post quem* taken from accession dates of the most recent rulers identified. Of the dozen known hoards of mint-and-minter coins, all but one have at least one "datable" coin in them, either Byzantine, quasi-imperial, Merovingian royal, Visigothic royal, or of the minter Eligius. Most of these hoards are small – for none are more than sixty-five coins known with certainty – so arguments from the absence of later reigns are unreliable for providing *termini ante quem*. In the case of the quasi-imperial coins of Provence, it is not certain that a coin was struck during the lifetime of the ruler identified on its obverse. Most Byzantine and royal coins can be dated only to within the entire reign of the person identified, but for Merovingian kings who ruled only a part of Gaul, a coin can be dated to the period in which that king ruled the sub-kingdom containing the mint identified.

When grouped by their latest datable coins, the Merovingian hoards present a reasonably consistent picture.[11] Two are from the third quarter of the sixth century: the Monneren (Lorraine)[12] and Velsen (Netherlands)[13] hoards represent the end of pseudo-imperial coinage; both have imitation *tremisses* in the name of Justinian (527-65) and no quasi-imperial or mint-and-minter coins.

The next phase dates to the end of the sixth century. The Escharen (Netherlands) hoard has Byzantine coins of Maurice Tiberius (582-602) and quasi-imperial coins in his name of the first type, without reverse circle.[14] The Faversham (Kent) grave find of looped coins likewise has Provençal coins in the name of Maurice of type one.[15] Both have mint-and-minter coins; the Escharen hoard includes coins of central Gaul of the anchored cross/*appendice perlé* style and others with a style of obverse portrait produced in mints of northeast Gaul and referred to as the "Group II" style.[16] None of the reverses of these mint-and-minter coins has a circle separating the cross from the legend.

As we have seen, the Sutton Hoo hoard includes a coin of Theodebert II in addition to Provençal issues in the name of Maurice. Two of the quasi-imperial coins are of the second type, and seven of the mint-and-minter coins also bear circles on the reverse [SH.28-34]. Like the Escharen hoard, the Sutton Hoo parcel has coins with the anchored-cross reverse [SH.17-25]. It also has a coin [SH.4] of Group II style from the same dies as one in the Escharen hoard; these dies were considerably more worn by the time of the striking of the Sutton Hoo specimen than for that in the Escharen hoard. The Sutton Hoo hoard appears, then, to be somewhat later than the Escharen and Faversham finds.

Three hoards have coins that give them a *terminus post quem* in the 610s. The Buis (Burgundy) hoard[17] has a coin of Marseille in the name of Chlothar II (613-629) as well as one in the name of Maurice; in addition to anchored cross and Chalon-type coins (a derivative of the second Provençal type, with a wreath circling a cross flanked by letters) it is the only hoard to contain coins of the Group III, "Magnentius Head", style.[18] The Nietap

---

[11]The chronology of hoards of Merovingian gold coins was first worked out by Lafaurie in his study of the Escharen Hoard (J. Lafaurie, "Le trésor d'Escharen [Pays-Bas]," *Revue Numismatique*, ser. 6, 2 [1959-60], 153-210) and elaborated in his Spoleto presentation (J. Lafaurie, "Les routes commerciales indiqués par les trésors et trouvailles monétaires mérovingiens," in *Moneta e scambi nell' alto medioevo*, Settimane di studio del Centro italiano di studio sull' alto medioevo 8 [Spoleto 1961], 231-78). His chronology and that of Grierson and Blackburn (*Medieval European Coinage*) attempt to estimate the date of assemblage of the various hoards; the discussion here considers only the minting date of the few "datable" coins in each.

[12]W. Reinhart, "Die früheste Münzprägung im Reiche der Merowinger," *Deutsches Jahrbuch für Numismatik* 2 (1939), 50-56.

[13]P. O. Van der Chijs, *De munten der Frankische- en Duitsch-Nederlandsche Vorsten* (Harlem 1866), 353-60.

[14]Lafaurie, "Le trésor d'Escharen," 197-209.

[15]S. E. Rigold, "The Sutton Hoo Coins in the Light of the Contemporary Background of Coinage in England," in R. L. S. Bruce-Mitford, *The Sutton Hoo Ship Burial*, I (London 1975), 668-77.

[16]J. Yvon, "Note sur deux groupes de monnaies mérovingiennes du Nord-Est de la Gaule," *Revue Numismatique*, ser. 5, 15 (1953), 67-77.

[17]P. Le Gentilhomme, "Les monnaies mérovingiennes de la trouvaille de Buis," *Revue Numismatique*, ser. 5, 2 (1938), 154-68; reprinted in P. Le Gentilhomme, *Mélanges de numismatique mérovingienne* (Paris 1940), 95-130.

[18]Lafaurie, "Le trésor d'Escharen," 157-58. The contention that an Islamic coin in the Bibliothèque Nationale was part of this hoard is totally circumstantial (J. Lafaurie, "Nouvelles recherches sur le trésor de Chissey-en-Morvan (Saône-et-Loire) l.d. Buis," *Bulletin de la Société*

(Netherlands) hoard has a light-weight *solidus* of the joint reign of Heraclius and Heraclius Constantine (616-632) as well as a Provençal issue in the name of Maurice; its mint-and-minter *tremisses* include Chalon types and coins of Frisian manufacture referred to as the Dronrijp type.[19] The Wieuwerd (Netherlands) hoard of jewelry and looped and mounted coins has as its latest datable pieces Marseille coins of Chlothar II, a *tremissis* of the Visigothic king Sisebut (612-21), and light-weight *solidi* of the joint rule of Heraclius and Heraclius Constantine.[20] The only two mint-and-minter coins in the hoard are of Maastricht.[21]

Three hoards have their most recent datable coin in the 620s. A small hoard found in 1820 in Mons (Belgium)[22] includes coins in the name of Phocas and Heraclius as well as a *tremissis* of the Visigothic king Suinthila (621-631); it also has mint-and-minter coins of Soissons and Trier, as well as Frisian coins of the Dronrijp type.[23] The hoard found at Crondall (England)[24] contains a coin of Paris of the minter Eligius, whose activity in the royal court there is documented as starting before 629.[25] In addition to Anglo-Saxon gold issues, the Crondall hoard contains Merovingian *tremisses* of the anchored-cross and Chalon types, as well as Frisian coins of the Dronrijp type. A hoard from Saint-Aubin (Lorraine)[26] has a coin of Charibert II of Aquitaine (629-632) and two of Dagobert I (622-639) of uncertain mints; it also contains mint-and-minter coins of the anchored-cross and Chalon types.

The huge hoard found in 1810 in La Baugisière (Vendée)[27] has a Marseille coin in the name of Sigebert III (634-656), and, among the recorded non-royal coins, anchored-cross coins with the *appendice-perlé* bust type. The Merovingian hoard of gold *tremisses* with the latest datable coin is the Bordeaux hoard of 1803.[28] Its latest datable coins are of the Visigothic king Wamba (672-80); its Merovingian coins include royal coins from Dagobert I (629-39) to Childeric II (662-75) and mint-and-minter coins of a variety of types.[29]

We can then line up most of the Merovingian hoards by their datable coins and so establish a relative chronology which appears reasonably consistent in its placement of certain stylistically defined groups of mint-and-minter coins. The anchored-cross/*appendice-perlé* style appears in the earliest hoards of mint-and-minter coins and continues through the chronology. The Group II style appears among hoards whose last datable coin bears the name of Maurice. The circle dividing the reverse cross from the legend is found on the Sutton Hoo coins in the name of Maurice and first appears on mint-and-minter coins in this hoard. The Chalon reverse type, bearing a cross flanked by letters surrounded by a wreath, is first seen in the next series of hoards, those with coins datable to the 610s; the "Magnentius head" and Dronrijp types are also first seen in these hoards.

Française de Numismatique 32 [1977], 211-16); the piece (H. Lavoix, *Catalogue des monnaies musulmanes de la Bibliothèque Nationale, Khalifes orientaux* [Paris 1887], 7, #26) is clearly from the end of the seventh century, long after the Merovingian coins of the Buis Hoard (M. L. Bates, "The Coinage of Syria under the Umayyads, 692-750 A.D.," in M. A. Bakhit and R. Schick [eds.] *The Fourth International Conference on the History of Bilad al-Sham during the Umayyad Period* [Amman 1989], 196-203.

[19] A. Pol, "De 7e-eeuwse muntvondst Nietap," *Jaarboek voor Munt- en Penningkunde* 62-64 (1975-77), 23-62.

[20] J. Lafaurie, *et al.*, "Le trésor de Wieuwerd," *Oudheidkundige mededelingen uit het Rijksmuseum van Oudheden te Leiden* 42 (1961), 78-107.

[21] The argument (Lafaurie *et al.*, "Le trésor de Wieuwerd," 100) that the Chlothar coin is a replacement in its mount ignores the fact that a coin of Phocas (602-610) is in a similar mount.

[22] J. Lelewel, "Vingt-trois pièces des monétaires mérovingiennes, et une du roi wisigoth Swintilla," *Revue Numismatique* 1 (1836), 324-25.

[23] Grierson and Blackburn, *Medieval European Coinage*, 125-26.

[24] C. H. V. Sutherland, *Anglo-Saxon Gold Coinage in the Light of the Crondall Hoard* (Oxford 1948).

[25] Lafaurie, "Eligius," 115-16.

[26] L. Maxe-Werly, "Trouvaille de Saint-Aubin (Meuse)," *Revue Numismatique*, ser. 3, 8 (1890), 12-53.

[27] B. Fillon, "Tiers de sol mérovingiens inédits," *Revue Numismatique* 10 (1845), 14-25.

[28] P. Le Gentilhomme, "Trouvaille de monnaies d'or des Mérovingiens et des Wisigoths faite à Bordeaux en 1803," *Revue Numismatique*, ser. 4, 39 (1936), 87-133; reprinted in Le Gentilhomme, *Mélanges de numismatique mérovingienne*, 5-51.

[29] Two coins from the hoard share obverse dies with coins from Sutton Hoo, #123 (St. Stephen of Bordeaux with SH.22) and # 128 (Ussom with SH.33); the appearance of coins of the same dies in hoards which seem so distant chronologically is probably best explained as the result of a long use of dies at these very small mints.

The limitations of such a chronology based on hoards are clear: the minting of most "datable" coins can be placed only within a fairly broad range of years; the length of time from the striking of a coin to its inclusion in a hoard is a variable that cannot be inferred or assumed to be equivalent for different hoards;[30] with so few datable coins in each hoard, the lack of later issues cannot be used as a *terminus ante quem*; and, such a chronology is applicable only to coins in hoards, while the vast majority of mint-and-minter coins are without known provenance and cannot be dated by hoard association.

For the Sutton Hoo coins, the hoard-based chronology places the parcel after the Faversham and Escharen finds, which represent the very beginning of mint-and-minter coinage and have no clearly seventh-century issues. It comes before the Nietap, Wieuwerd, and Crondall hoards, all northern finds with coins datable to the 610s and 620s. The lack of such clearly later coins in the Sutton Hoo parcel suggests a date for it near the beginning of the seventh century, but the numbers are too small to be more than suggestive.

To control such a hoard-based chronology, the publishers of the Sutton Hoo burial sought a dating criterion based on technical measurements, and established a chronology based on declining purity of the gold of Merovingian *tremisses*. It has long been recognized that some Merovingian coins are of a much paler gold than others, and, by analogy with countless other historical coinages which underwent progressive debasements, it has been supposed that the baser coins are generally later than the finer ones. The problems with deriving a chronology from such an observation are manifold. First of all, there must be some non-destructive method of measuring the fineness of the coins. Secondly, it must be demonstrated that there was, in fact, a consistent decline in gold content over time. Finally, enough data must be incorporated into a graph that a given undated coin or coins can be compared to the curve of debasement and be given a date within an acceptable range of years.

After some investigation, it was determined that Merovingian coins are, for the most part, binary alloys of gold and silver; thus specific gravity can be used to achieve an acceptably precise gold content.[31] A preliminary survey of datable Merovingian coins confirmed a general decline in standard, and comparison of the gold contents of four hoards of Merovingian mint-and-minter coins found a declining gold content consistent with the chronology established independently on the basis of datable coins: Escharen, Sutton Hoo, Nietap, Crondall.[32] Subsequent research has demonstrated a progressive decline in the fineness of late seventh- and early eighth-century Byzantine gold coinage of Italian mints[33] and a coherent pattern of alteration in the gold content of seventh-century Visigothic royal *tremisses*.[34]

The chief difficulty in applying such data to the analysis of the Sutton Hoo hoard is the paucity of datable Merovingian coins with which to establish and calibrate a curve of debasement. Of the small number of Merovingian coins with royal names, the great majority of them are of the single mint of Marseille on the Mediterranean coast, far from the centers of Merovingian power and from the mints of most of the coins in the Sutton Hoo parcel. Moreover, most of the remaining royal coins are from other Provençal mints. In analyzing the gold content of tested coins, J. P. C. Kent discovered that coins of Provence were generally finer than coins in the name of the same king from mints in the Merovingian heartlands to the north; moreover, he determined that

[30]Like other medieval gold coins, Merovingian *tremisses* seldom show patterns of wear which might be compared to estimate their amount of circulation before burial.

[31]R. F. Coleman and A. Wilson, "Activation Analysis of Merovingian Gold Coins," in E. T. Hall and D. M. Metcalf (eds.), *Methods of Chemical and Metallurgical Investigation of Ancient Coinage*, Royal Numismatic Society, Special Publication 8 (London 1972), 88-92.

[32]W. A. Oddy, "The Analysis of Four Hoards of Merovingian Gold Coins," in Hall and Metcalf, *Methods*, 112-25; together with this article are tables headed "Analyses of the Sutton Hoo Gold Coins," pp. 96-99, and "Analyses of Merovingian Coins in the British Museum," pp. 100-07.

[33]W. A. Oddy, "The Debasement of the Provincial Byzantine Gold Coinage from the Seventh to Ninth Centuries," in W. Hahn and W. E. Metcalf (eds.) *Studies in Early Byzantine Gold Coinage* (New York 1988), 135-42.

[34]L. Olson, "Visigothic Coin Hoard Structure," paper read at the 24th International Congress on Medieval Studies, Western Michigan University, 1989; we are grateful to Mr. Olson for sharing with us his unpublished data and for offering his valuable suggestions for the revision of this paper.

there were two different standards within Provence.[35] Since most of the Sutton Hoo coins, like those of other hoards, are from northern mints, they can only be dated by comparison with royal coins outside of Provence.

Outside of Provence, the distribution of mint names on datable Merovingian coins is far from even. Of the twenty tested datable coins of Neustria, the mints of Tours, Amiens and Orléans are represented by one coin each. The remaining seventeen specimens are of Paris and all bear the name of the moneyer Eligius with or without a royal name as well. Austrasian mints are identified on only two tested royal coins, one from Toul and one from Acauno (St. Moritz in Switzerland). The two tested Burgundian coins are both from Chalon-sur-Saône. From Aquitaine, there are five coins of Arvernus (Clermont-Ferrand), one from Rodez, and fifteen from Banacciaco (Banassac). The town of Banassac is far to the south of France, much closer to the Provençal mints whose coinage is excluded from Kent's calculations than to the mass of mints represented in the mint-and-minter coins of the Sutton Hoo and other northern hoards. It is more likely to have been on a Mediterranean standard than on that of mints near the centers of royal Merovingian authority. Like those of Provence, royal coins from the mint of Banassac are therefore excluded from this attempt to calibrate a gold content curve to which the Sutton Hoo mint-and-minter coins can be compared.

In addition to coins with royal names, Kent included in his calculations coins with a "regal moneyer." These are mint-and-minter coins which bear the name of a minter whose name also appears on a coin with a king's name. Kent justified this by noting that, "Added to the discussion are the undated coins of moneyers who also strike dated pieces. It is understood that the undated coins may not be exactly contemporary with the dated ones, but they are unlikely to be far removed in time."[36] He then cited the case of Eligius, whose working life of twenty years he considers "probably rarely attained." The validity of assuming that all the coins of a minter (even from a single mint) can be considered equivalent to those with a royal name is challenged by the case of Eligius himself. The coins with his name from the mint of Paris range from 27.9% to 79.9% gold with no apparent modal fineness; those bearing his name along with that of Clovis II (who had reigned less than two years when Eligius became a bishop), have a range from 27.9% to 47.4% gold.[37]

The unreliability of such data becomes even more apparent when mint-and-minter coins of one mint are considered "datable" because the minter's name appears on a royal coin of a different mint. In the column of figures for "regal moneyers" under Theodebert II,[38] Kent included non-royal coins with the minter's name Maniliobo from Mouzon in Austrasia for the reason that the same name, spelled differently, appears on a coin of Theodebert from Clermont-Ferrand in Aquitaine. The use of stylistic similarity to justify such an inclusion represents a confusion between the identity of the *monetarius* and that of the die engraver. That such individuals cannot be assumed to have been the same is demonstrated by the diversity of style of coins in the name of Eligius[39] and many even clearer examples such as the *monetarius* Leodio of Toul, whose known coins could not possibly be from the same engraver's hand.[40] In general, the use of mint-and-minter coins with no royal name to establish a chronology of gold contents is unreliable and will not be included in the discussion which follows.

Despite the paucity of evidence, Kent constructed a curve for royal coins outside of Provence which not only shows debasement, but indicates a sudden, precipitous fall and partial restoration of standard, all within the 630-640 decade.[41] A later attempt by another scholar to "smooth out" this improbable curve was hampered by the fact that

---

[35] J. P. C. Kent, "Gold Standards of the Merovingian Coinage," in Hall and Metcalf, *Methods*, 69-74.

[36] J. P. C. Kent, "The Date of the Sutton Hoo Hoard," in Bruce-Mitford, *The Sutton Hoo Ship Burial*, I, 592.

[37] *Ibid.*, Table 35, 599.

[38] *Ibid.*, Table 34, 597-98.

[39] Lafaurie, "Eligius."

[40] A. Stahl, *The Merovingian Coinage of the Region of Metz*, Publications d'histoire de l'art et d'archéologie de l'Université Catholique de Louvain 30 (Louvain-la-Neuve 1982), 148.

[41] Kent, "Gold Standards," 72.

the specific data used by Kent to construct his curve had not been published.[42] These data are published in the Appendix, below, and allow a thorough re-examination of Kent's inferences.

Kent admitted that Merovingian coins from before 575 were not of uniform gold content.[43] The published figures for coins of the Velsen hoard, which appears to date to the middle of the sixth century, range from 47.8% to 94.7% gold, with no apparent concentration of readings.[44] A coin of Reims with the name of Sigebert (Prou 1028), has a reverse type of a winged figure so is probably to be attributed to Sigebert I (561-575); its gold content of 73.0% gives the single usable figure for before 575.[45]

The earliest royal coins outside of Provence whose fineness Kent reported are two of Childebert II (575-595).[46] The 93.4% reading corresponds with W. A. Oddy's analysis of Bibliothèque Nationale 304, a coin of Tours attributed in Prou's catalogue to Childebert III (695-711).[47] The coin with the 84.7% gold content is Brussels 142, a coin of Arvernus (Clermont-Ferrand) attributed by Hugo Vanhoudt to Childebert, son of the Major Domo Grimoald, who usurped the Austrasian throne from 656 to 657.[48] To these can be added Fitzwilliam 433 with a fineness of 92.6%[49] and ANS 9, with a fineness of 91.9%.[50] By ignoring some previous attributions, four coins can then be assigned to the reign of Childebert II and to the decades from 575 to 595, three with about 92-93% gold and one about 85%.

Two coins can be assigned to the reign of Theodebert II (595-612); the Sutton Hoo coin with no mint name and 85.2% gold, and one from Clermont with 85.9% gold. Three coins outside of Provence can be assigned to the reign of Chlothar II. Two of these are from Chalon-sur-Saône in Burgundy, so must be from the period 613-629; for the early part of his reign Chlothar ruled only Neustria, and Burgundy appears to have been firmly in the hands of the Austrasian rulers;[51] these have respectively 68.8% and 62.7% gold. Bibliothèque Nationale 60 has no mint name, so may date from any time in Chlothar's long total reign of 584-629; it has 71.6% gold. Brussels 217 is attributed by Vanhoudt to Chlothar III,[52] and with its 28.6% gold content is best left out of these calculations.

We then have a total of nine Merovingian coins outside of Provence and Banassac that can convincingly be dated between Childebert II's accession in 575 and Dagobert I's Austrasian accession in 622; none of these coins can be dated to a shorter range than sixteen years. There are no coins of Chlothar II from Austrasian mints, so no specimens can securely be dated to the decade from 613 to 622. Far more coins are available for the reigns of Dagobert I (622-639), thirteen tested specimens, and Clovis II (639-657), ten specimens. With the inclusion of those with the name of Eligius, fourteen non-royal coins tested, the only datable moneyer (c. 625-641), the numbers become significant, especially for the decades of the 620s and 630s. The data are presented in the Appendix, below, and summarized in Figure 1. In this graph, each horizontal line represents a single tested specimen; its height indicates its percentage of gold as tested by specific gravity and its extent indicates the date range during which its minting may have taken place.

---

[42]D. Brown, "The Dating of the Sutton Hoo Coins," in D. Brown, J. Campbell and S. C. Hawkes (eds.) *ASSAH*, BAR Brit. Ser. 92 (Oxford 1981), 71-86.

[43]Kent, "The Date of the Sutton Hoo Hoard," 592-93.

[44]Oddy, "Analysis of Four Hoards."

[45]A coin of Sigebert I from Toul, also in the Bibliothèque Nationale (Prou 978) is holed and was not tested by Oddy. A specific gravity determination using less precise instrumentation reported it to be 82% gold (Stahl, *Merovingian Coinage*, 148, #C1a).

[46]Kent, "The Date of the Sutton Hoo Hoard," 597.

[47]M. Prou, *Catalogue des monnaies françaises de la Bibliothèque Nationale; Les monnaies mérovingiennes* (Paris 1892), 72.

[48]H. Vanhoudt, "De merovingische munten in het Penningkabinet van de Koninklijke Bibliotheek te Brussel," *Revue Belge de Numismatique* 128 (1982), 144-45.

[49]Grierson and Blackburn, *Medieval European Coinage*, 479.

[50]D. P. Dickie and R. D. Parrott, "Merovingian Coins in the Collection of the American Numismatic Society," *American Numismatic Society Museum Notes* 4 (1950), 93.

[51]E. Ewig, "Die fränkischen Teilungen und Teilreiche (511-613)," *Akademie der Wissenschaften und der Literatur, Mainz, Geistes- und Sozialwissenschaftliche Klasse*, Abhandlungen 9 (1952), 163.

[52]Vanhoudt, "Merovingische munten," 166.

A general trend is evident. The six pieces datable between 575 and 613 have about 84% gold; none of the clearly later pieces are this fine. The three pieces of Chlothar II fall between 62% and 72%, which is within the very broad range of gold contents for pieces datable to the 620s and 630s. Dozens of coins are datable between 622 and 641, ranging from about 18% gold to about 81%. Kent interpreted the data as indicating a decline until about 630, then a restoration of standard followed by rapid decline and subsequent restoration around 640, then a renewed decline. As most coins cannot be dated to less than a ten-year period, it is difficult to understand how such a unilinear and precise curve could be derived. The twenty-point range of values for the two year minting by Eligius for Clovis II at Paris (639-641) is strong evidence that even at a single mint, presumably under direct royal control, the gold content of individual pieces was poorly regulated.[53] In general, it can be said that most of the royal coins minted between 622 and 641 have between 30% and 80% gold fineness, but a more precise standard cannot be derived from these data. Most of the pieces datable after 639 have below 55% gold content, with a decline suggested for the decades following.

How do the Sutton Hoo coins fit into this picture? All of them have more than 70% gold content (one ingot has 69.2%). Thirty of the thirty-seven coins are above 81% gold content which is the highest measured for a coin datable after 622. These coins can then be assigned before that date and, for the most part, correspond in fineness to the few pieces datable between 575 and 613. There remain the seven Sutton Hoo coins whose gold content lies between 70% and 81%. It is not possible to rule out the possibility that these too were minted before 613; the comparative data are far too few to be significant. The 70% to 81% range of fineness may have been the standard of the undocumented decade from 613 to 622, but there is no evidence to demonstrate this. While there are coins in the 70% to 81% range of Dagobert I from Neustria, which must have been minted between 629 and 638, other coins from the same period have well below 50% gold content. The seven Sutton Hoo coins with less than 81% fineness could then have been minted either before 613, in the period 613-622, or after 622; there is no valid basis for deciding which of these alternatives is correct. What can be said is that thirty of the Sutton Hoo coins resemble in fineness datable coins from the period before 613 and there is no clear evidence that the other seven were minted after that year.

This conclusion, based on admittedly very slim evidence, is consistent with the chronological inferences drawn from the hoard analysis above. The Sutton Hoo hoard contains four coins datable to before 613, when Chlothar II extended his rule over all of France; it contains none datable after that date. Such later coins are present in the Crondall hoard of England and the Nietap and Wieuwerd hoards of the Netherlands, so they would have been available in the North Sea region. In a similar way, the Sutton Hoo parcel contains no coins whose gold content would place them clearly after 613. The evidence adduced here then leads to a conclusion that at least some of the Sutton Hoo coins were minted after 595, and they may all have been minted before 613.

[53]This situation might be explained by supposing that coins with the name of Eligius were minted after his designation in 641 as Bishop of Noyon, but to hypothesize such an "immobilization" of status recognition would also leave the possibility of "memorial" royal coins and thereby undermine the whole premise of "datable" Merovingian coins.

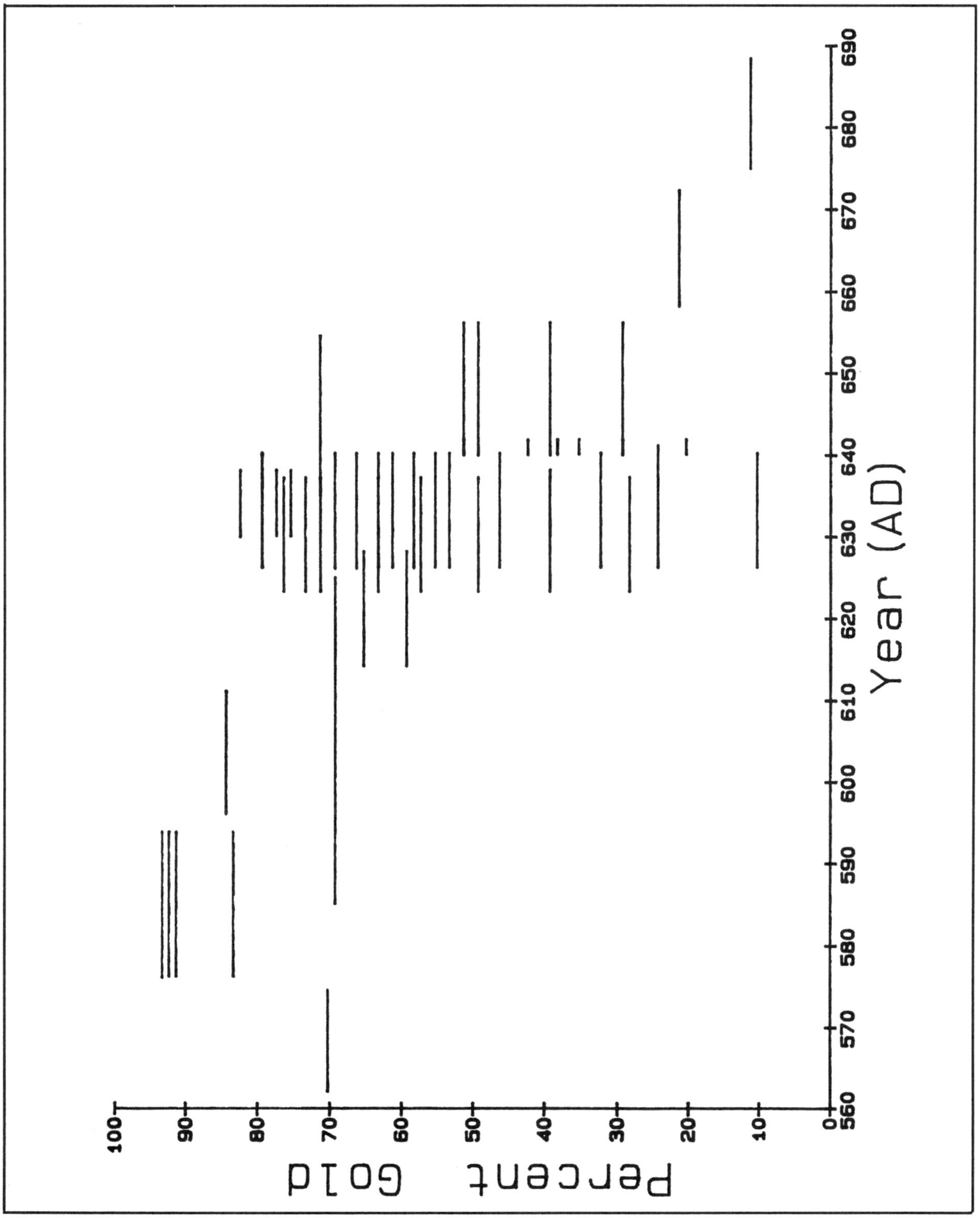

Fig. 1. Gold content of datable Merovingian coins from other than Mediterranean mints.

APPENDIX

Gold content of datable Merovingian Coins

The data presented below are almost all the results of measurements made by Oddy around 1970, in preparation for the 1975 publication of the Sutton Hoo coins.[54] The exceptions are the coins labelled ANS, in the collection of the American Numismatic Society, New York, which were measured by Stahl. All are the results of specific gravity determinations according to the method outlined in Oddy and Hughes.[55] The accuracy of the specific gravity method has been discussed by Oddy and Blackshaw.[56] There are two factors to be taken into consideration: first, the accuracy of measurement of specific gravity, and second, the conversion of the measured specific gravity into a gold content.

The accuracy of the measurement of specific gravity has been shown to have a maximum likely error of 0.6 and a standard deviation of 0.2 for twenty measurements of the same coin.[57] If this were applied to the analysis of uncorroded alloys containing gold and silver, it would be a simple matter to derive an error factor for the gold content. In fact, when applied to Merovingian, or any other ancient coins, the invariable presence of a small amount of copper, together with the probable presence of some corrosion products of silver just below the surface, mean that the error in the analysis must be determined empirically.

On the basis of comparisons with other methods of analysis on the same coins, Oddy and Blackshaw have estimated that the actual gold content will lie somewhere between the value calculated from the measured specific gravity, assuming that only gold and silver are present in the alloy, and a value which is about 3% higher.[58] For coins with a high gold content the error will, on average, be less than this, while it may be greater for very debased pieces.

The table which follows includes all reported specific gravity readings for Merovingian coins after the middle of the sixth century which can reasonably be considered "datable." First are coins in the name of Byzantine emperors with the signatures of mints within the Frankish kingdom (quasi-imperial coins). Next come coins bearing the names of Merovingian kings in alphabetical order, with the dates and sub-kingdoms of each king of that name during the period 561-679. Last, are coins in the name of an identified bishop and the only identified minter, Eligius. Mints are given with a standardized Latin spelling of their name, the accepted modern place identification, and the Merovingian province within which the mint was usually included. Within each mint listing, coins are arranged by descending weight, so *solidi* precede *tremisses*. An asterisk (*) in the right column indicates that the coin has been used in compiling Figure 1; a Roman numeral in brackets indicates the attribution used in the case of homonymous monarchs.

Coins with numbers preceded by a P are in the collection of the Bibliothèque Nationale, Paris;[59] ANS coins are published in Dickie and Parrot.[60] BM indicates British Museum;[61] BR is the Bibliothèque Royale, Brussels;[62] F is the Fitzwilliam Museum, Cambridge (including the Grierson Collection).[63] Figures for coins from hoards are published in Oddy 1972; CR is Crondall, ES Escharen, NI Nietap, and SH Sutton Hoo. Among unpublished coins,

---

[54]Kent, "Coins and the Date of the Burial."

[55]W. A. Oddy and M. J. Hughes, "The Specific Gravity Method for the Analysis of Gold Coins," in Hall and Metcalf, *Methods*, 75-87.

[56]W. A. Oddy and S. M. Blackshaw, "The Accuracy of the Specific Gravity Method for the Analysis of Gold Alloys," *Archaeometry* 16 (1974), 81-90.

[57]M. J. Hughes and W. A. Oddy, "A Reappraisal of the Specific Gravity Method for the Analysis of Gold Alloys," *Archaeometry* 12 (1970), 1-11.

[58]Oddy and Blackshaw, "Accuracy of Specific Gravity."

[59]Prou, *Catalogue*.

[60]D. P. Dickie and R. D. Parrott, "Merovingian Coins, 91-96.

[61]Oddy, "Four Hoards," 96-107.

[62]Vanhoudt, "Merovingische munten."

[63]Grierson and Blackburn, *Medieval European Coinage*.

A is the Ashmolean Museum, Oxford; BI the Birmingham Museum; and H the Royal Numismatic Collection in the Hague.

QUASI-IMPERIAL			
Justin II (565-578)			
Coin #	**Weight**	**S.G.**	**% Gold**
Arelate (Arles) [Provence]			
P.1359	1.3148	19.00	98.0
Ucecia (Uzès) [Provence]			
ES.8	1.2811	18.89	97.2
Vivaria (Viviers) [Provence]			
H.KPK.17366	1.2909	18.38	93.8
Tiberius II Constantine (578-582)			
Ucecia (Uzès) [Provence]			
A.36	1.3045	17.60	88.3
Maurice Tiberius (582-602)			
Arelate (Arles) [Provence]			
ES.10	3.8600	18.87	97.1
SH.27	1.2975	18.62	95.4
P.1360	1.2471	18.58	95.2
H.KPK.17367	1.0814	18.90	97.3
Massilia (Marseille) [Provence]			
P.1368	3.9431	19.05	98.3
BM.45	3.8910	18.91	97.3
A.27	3.8739	18.83	96.9
BM.46	3.8716	18.88	97.2
P.1374	3.8292	18.80	96.7
A.29	1.2920	18.52	94.7
P.1369	1.2842	18.87	97.2
BR.174	1.2757	18.95	97.7
BM.48	1.2740	18.84	97.4
P.1376	1.2737	18.77	66.4
P.1370	1.2018	18.96	97.7
P.1375	1.1977	18.89	97.2
ES.11	1.1456	18.91	97.4
A.28	1.1369	18.82	96.8
F.404	1.0779	17.65	88.7

Coin#	Weight	S.G.	% Gold
Ucecia (Uzès) [Provence]			
P.2473	1.2752	18.77	96.4
BM.49	1.2547	18.75	96.3
Valentia (Valence) [Provence]			
P.1352	1.2760	18.10	91.9
SH.26	1.2226	17.82	89.9
P.1353	1.0542	17.89	90.4
Vendasca? (Venasque) [Provence]			
SH.11	1.2566	18.55	95.0
Vienna (Vienne) [Provence]			
P.1303	1.3737	18.63	95.5
A.33	1.3488	18.81	96.8
BM.50	1.2203	18.70	96.0
Vivaria (Viviers) [Provence]			
BM.51	3.8219	18.33	93.5
ES.9	3.7974	19.14	98.8
BM.53	1.2993	17.70	89.0
NI.9	1.2778	17.71	89.1
BM.52	1.2700	17.45	87.2
A.31	1.2641	18.07	91.6
Phocas (602-610)			
Massilia (Marseille) [Provence]			
BM.55	3.8753	18.91	97.3
BM.54	3.8071	18.88	97.2
Heraclius (610-641)			
Vivaria (Viviers) [Provence]			
BM.56	1.2479	17.01	83.5
MEROVINGIAN KINGS			
Charibert I (561-567) [Neustria] or Charibert II (629-632) [Aquitaine]			
Atura (Aire) [Aquitaine]			
P.2433	1.2695	14.85	63.6 *[II]
Bannaciaco (Bannasac) [Aquitaine]			
BM.66	1.2906	14.61	61.0

Coin #	Weight	S.G.	% Gold
Charibert, continued			
P.2060	1.2896	14.73	62.3
ANS.11	1.2838	14.77	62.7
P.2057	1.2814	15.24	67.6
P.2059	1.2723	14.44	59.2
A.43	1.2721	14.75	62.5
P.2056	1.2673	14.68	61.8
BM.67	1.2455	14.93	64.5
BR.146	1.2384	11.94	26.0
BM.65	1.2146	14.67	61.7
Childebert II (575-595) [Austrasia] or Childebert, son of Grimoald (656-657) [Austrasia] or Childebert III (695-711) [all]			
Arvernus (Clermont-Ferrand) [Aquitaine]			
ANS.9	1.3562	18.11	91.9 *[II]
BR.142	1.2618	17.14	84.7 *[II]
F.433	1.2185	18.21	92.6 *[II]
Massilia (Marseille) [Provence]			
P.1420	3.6124	12.98	40.9
P.1421	3.4103	12.47	34.0
BM.70	3.2753	12.16	29.3
P.1422	3.1489	12.52	34.5
Turonus (Tours) [Neustria]			
P.304	1.3943	18.32	93.4 *[II]
Childeric II (662-675) [Austrasia]			
Massilia (Marseille) [Provence]			
P.1413a	3.9404	12.35	32.2
P.1415	3.8617	11.75	23.1
P.1417	3.4532	11.30	15.7?
P.1414	3.4188	12.89	39.6
P.1413	3.3140	11.45	18.2?
Chlothar II: (584-592) [Soissons]; (592-613) [Neustria]; (613-622) [all]; (622-629) [Neustria, Burgundy] or Chlothar III (657-673) [Neustria]			
No mint			
BR.217	1.1835	12.11	28.6 *[III]
P.60	1.1408	15.66	71.6 *[II]

Coin #	Weight	S.G.	% Gold
Chlothar, continued			
Arelate (Arles) [Provence]			
P.1363	1.2348	17.83	90.0
P.1362	1.0505	16.77	81.6
Cabilonno (Chalon-sur-Saône) [Burgundy]			
P.166	1.1366	15.36	68.8 *[II]
P.167	0.9955	14.77	62.7 *[II]
Massilia (Marseille) [Provence] with Eligius (c.625-629)			
P.1390	1.1328	17.82	90.0
P.1389	1.0514	17.39	86.6
Massilia (Marseille) [Provence]			
BM.57	3.7495	18.56	95.0
P.1380	3.7367	17.33	86.2
P.1383	3.6477	18.19	92.5
ANS.8	3.4925	17.87	90.4
H.KPK.17402	3.3274	18.42	94.1
P.1382	1.2144	17.70	89.0
P.1381	1.2094	17.75	89.4
P.1388	1.2074	18.10	91.9
BM.58	1.2178	18.47	94.4
BM.59	0.9724	15.37	68.9
Ucecia (Uzès) [Provence]			
P.2474	1.3231	18.21	92.6
Vivaria (Viviers) [Provence]			
P.1347	1.2474	16.39	78.4
A.32	1.2335	17.32	86.1
BR.241	1.2284	16.51	79.5
Clovis II (639-657) [Neustria]			
No mint			
A.30	1.1469	12.56	35.2 *
P.66	0.9966	14.05	54.7 *
Palatio with Eligius (to 641?)			
P.695	1.2308	14.13	55.7 *

Coin #	Weight	S.G.	% Gold
Clovis, continued			
Ambianis (Amiens) [Neustria]			
P.1107	1.2847	13.24	44.2 *
Arelate (Arles) [Provence] with Eligius (to 641?)			
P.1365	1.1156	15.57	70.9
P.1364	1.0527	14.00	54.1
Aurelianis (Orléans) [Neustria]			
P.617	1.2939	13.90	52.9 *
Parisius (Paris) [Neustria] with Eligius (to 641?)			
BM. 69	1.2676	12.98	40.9 *
P.686	1.2508	13.47	47.4 *
P.687	1.2467	13.28	44.4 *
P.688	1.1834	12.66	36.6 *
P.689	1.1414	12.06	27.9 *
P.690	1.0822	10.07	?
Parisius (Paris) [Neustria]			
P.691	1.1707	10.71	?
Dagobert I (622-629) [Austrasia]; (629-638) [all] or Dagobert II (656) [Austrasia] (676-679); [all]			
No mint			
P.63	1.3930	15.81	73.1 *[I]
P.70	1.3262	16.36	78.1 *[I]
P.62	1.2871	12.49	34.3 *[I]
P.69	1.2552	15.15	66.7 *[I]
P.303	1.2231	13.25	44.5 *[I]
P.67	1.2007	14.00	54.1 *[I]
P.68	1.1539	10.52	?
P.64	1.0957	14.57	60.4 *[I]
Palatio with Eligius			
P.694	1.3885	16.58	80.1 *[I]
P.693	1.3121	16.26	77.2 *[I]
Acauno (St. Moritz) [Austrasia]			
P.1296	1.2447	16.05	75.3 *[I]
Arelate (Arles) [Provence]			

Coin #	Weight	S.G.	% Gold
Dagobert, continued			
BM.63	3.6707	17.59	88.3
Massilia (Marseille) [Provence] with Eligius			
P.1394	3.8562	17.88	90.3
P.1393	3.8215	17.02	83.7
BM.60	3.6102	17.16	84.8
BM.61	1.2013	17.57	88.1
P.1395	1.1321	17.17	85.0
BM.62	1.1522	17.07	84.1
Massilia (Marseille) [Provence]			
P.1418	1.1787	12.41	33.0
P.1419	1.0851	12.90	39.8
P.1419a	1.0635	12.35	32.2
Parisius (Paris) [Neustria] with Eligius			
P.685	1.3580	16.56	79.9 *[I]
BM.64	1.3404	15.72	72.3 *[I]
Ucecia (Uzès) [Provence]			
ANS.12	1.2179	17.62	88.4
P.2475	1.2172	17.20	85.2
P.2476	1.0544	17.21	85.3
Vivaria (Viviers) [Provence]			
H.KPK17418	1.1312	15.09	66.1
ANS.13	1.1197	14.60	61.0
P.1348	1.1078	16.24	77.0
Sigebert I (561-575) [Austrasia] or Sigebert II (613) [Austrasia] or Sigebert III (634-656) [Austrasia]			
Bannaciaco (Banassac) [Aquitaine]			
P.2063	1.2518	12.75	37.8
P.2064	1.2431	12.93	40.1
P.2065	1.2328	13.98	53.9
BR.144	1.2158	12.66	36.6
P.2062	1.1616	11.88	25.1
P.2066	1.1099	11.41	17.5?

Coin #	Weight	S.G.	% Gold
Sigebert, continued			
Massilia (Marseille) [Provence]			
P.1412	3.7989	12.87	39.4
P.1396	3.7292	13.50	47.8
F.406	3.6701	12.40	32.9
P.1400	3.6160	12.01	27.0
P.1401	3.4625	13.18	43.5
BM.68	1.0942	13.19	43.7
P.1397	1.0706	16.34	75.9
P.1408	1.0378	12.81	38.6
P.1407	0.9690	13.20	43.8
F.407 (frag.)	0.7812	13.19	43.7
Remus (Rheims) [Austrasia]			
P.1028	1.2715	15.81	73.0 *[I]
Vivaria (Viviers) [Provence]			
P.1350	1.1711	13.96	53.6
P.1349	1.1646	15.14	66.6
Theodebert II (595-612) [Austrasia]			
No mint			
SH.2	1.2675	17.20	85.2 *
Arvernus (Clermont-Ferrand) [Aquitaine]			
P.1713	1.3114	17.29	85.9 *
BISHOP			
Avitus, Bishop of Clermont-Ferrand (c.674-689)			
Arvernus (Clermont-Ferrand) [Aquitaine]			
P. 1716	1.1455	11.53	19.7
MONETARIUS			
Eligius (c. 625-641)			
Palatio, scola			
P.702	1.3007	15.70	72.0 *
P.703	1.2821	16.71	81.1 *
P.700	1.2764	12.28	31.1 *
P.696	1.2687	12.81	38.6 *

Coin #	Weight	S.G.	% Gold
Eligius, continued			
P.701	0.9833	11.45	18.2 *
Parisius (Paris) [Neustria]			
P.708	1.3067	14.27	57.3 *
BI	1.2869	14.65	61.7 *
A.40	1.2869	14.71	62.1 *
CR.10	1.2682	16.64	80.6 *
P.711	1.2568	14.69	61.9
BM.87	1.2493	15.43	69.5 *
P.707	1.2272	13.71	50.5 *
P.709	1.2095	14.92	64.2 *
P.710	1.2004	15.23	67.5 *

Swedish-Anglian Contacts Antedating Sutton Hoo: The Testimony of the Scandinavian Gold Bracteates

NANCY L. HATCH WICKER

INTRODUCTION

The Swedish character of the helmet and shield found in Burial Mound One at Sutton Hoo and of the boat inhumation form of the grave itself have long been noted,[1] but the precise nature of the apparent Swedish-Anglian connection is still debated. For instance, it has often been suggested that parallels between the shield bosses from Sutton Hoo and "Shield One" from Vendel grave XII are so close that the objects might have been made in the same workshop.[2] Were these Sutton Hoo objects made by Swedish crafts workers in Sweden, by Swedish crafts workers at the Anglian court, or perhaps by English crafts workers using or imitating Swedish dies in England? Was the apparent Swedish-Anglian connection, as evidenced by the parallels between Vendel and Sutton Hoo, an isolated phenomenon reflecting a one-time connection, or was there continuing interchange between Anglia and Scandinavia during this period? Insight into the possibilities of ongoing contact may be attained by examining analogous material to see what, if any, connection is demonstrated by other objects and other burials, and thus providing some background to the apparent connection between Vendel and Sutton Hoo.

In this paper I investigate examples of communication between Scandinavia and Anglian England during the century preceding the Sutton Hoo Mound One burial of the first half of the seventh century by focusing on the Scandinavian-type gold bracteates and their silver derivatives found in Anglian England as an example of such cultural interaction. Already in 1926, Nils Åberg used them "to draw direct parallels between English and Northern chronology," and as evidence of trade between the two areas.[3]

The latin term *bractea*, "thin plate," has been used since 1694[4] to refer to these small gold or silver discs, usually three to six centimeters in diameter, which are stamped on one side with various motifs in the central circular field often surrounded by one or more punched border zones. Although found primarily in Scandinavia, these objects have also been found as far away as England, Hungary, and perhaps even Russia. Although only forty-three of the 907 known bracteates have been found in England,[5] the Insular examples are crucial to our interpretation of how they were worn, since many of these have recently been found in grave contexts, whereas most of the Scandinavian specimens have come from hoards and loose finds or were found long ago. Bracteates usually seem to have been worn by women as a pendant on a necklace, suspended by a loop on a cord, as indicated by inhumation burials in which the bracteate was found lying in the chest area of the body in association with other pendants and beads, and by the remains of a braided leather cord through the loop of a bracteate from Sievern (M325).[6]

---

[1] R. L. S. Bruce-Mitford, "Sutton Hoo and Sweden," *The Archaeological News Letter*, No. 2 (May 1948), 5-7; R. L. S. Bruce-Mitford, "The Sutton Hoo Ship Burial: Recent Theories and Some Comments on General Interpretation," *Proc. of the Suffolk Inst. of Archaeol.* 25 (1950), 1-78; S. Lindqvist, "Sutton Hoo och *Beowulf*," *Fornvännen* 43 (1948), 94-110.

[2] R. L. S. Bruce-Mitford, *The Sutton Hoo Ship Burial: A Handbook*, 3rd ed. (London 1979), 116; A. C. Evans, *The Sutton Hoo Ship Burial* (London 1986), 49.

[3] N. Åberg, *The Anglo-Saxons in England During the Early Centuries After the Invasions* (Uppsala 1926), 101-02.

[4] M. Mackeprang, *De Nordiske Guldbrakteater*, Jysk Arkæologisk Selskabs Skrifter 2 (Aarhus 1952), 9.

[5] The numbers I have listed are current to December 1988, reflecting totals circulated by K. Hauck at the "Colloquium in Bad Homburg zum geschichtlichen Horizont der Götterbildamulette in der spätantiken Randkultur des Nordens," Nov. 28 - Dec. 1, 1989, plus one more from Broa recently published by J. P. Lamm and M. Axboe, "Neues zu Brakteaten und Anhängern in Schweden," *FS* 23 (1989), 453-77.

[6] M325 = Mackeprang, *Nordiske Guldbrakteater*, no. 325. Wherever possible, bracteates will be referred to in this paper by Mackeprang's corpus number with plate reference added if there was more than one bracteate in the find. For bracteates not included by Mackeprang, reference will be made to "Ax" for Axboe's 1982 supplement to Mackeprang's work ("The Scandinavian Gold Bracteates: Studies on their Manufacture and Regional Variations," *Acta Archaeologica* 52 [1981], 1-87), or to "IK" for K. Hauck, "Ikonographischer Katalog," in K.

The principal problems associated with the study of the Scandinavian-type bracteates found in England are analogous to the issues at question concerning the objects of Swedish character found at Sutton Hoo; namely, were the bracteates found in Anglia imported or brought from Scandinavia by immigrants? Were they made in England by Scandinavian crafts workers, or were the locally-made imitations of Scandinavian material? John Hines has recently considered such problems in his work, *The Scandinavian Character of Anglian England in the Pre-Viking Period.*[7] His study goes into much more detail than is possible in this short paper in which I consider only one class of objects, the bracteates of the region. Although he includes a lengthy discussion of the bracteates, his argument centers around support for his theory of migration from Norway to Anglia as evidenced by the Scandinavian-type wrist clasps found in Anglian England. I set my sights farther east and concentrate on possible evidence for communication with eastern Scandinavia during this period in order to investigate the background to the Vendel-Sutton Hoo parallels.

TYPES OF BRACTEATES FOUND IN ENGLAND AND THEIR DISTRIBUTION

Although many of the forty-three Migration Period (A.D. fifth to sixth century) bracteates found in England are either indistinguishable from, or closely imitative of, Scandinavian examples, variations were also developed in England that depart significantly from the Scandinavian bracteates in either iconography or techniques (Map 1). However, most of the English bracteates can be referred to according to the system used by Mogens Mackeprang in 1952, which was based on the following types established in 1869 by Oscar Montelius:[8]

A. Imitations of Roman or Byzantine gold-coins from the fourth and fifth century; with (barbarien [*sic*] imitations of) Roman letters.
B. With human figures, except the head over an animal. Often with runes.
C. With a human head over a (quadruped) animal. Often with runes.
D. With drakes. Never with legends.

In a few cases, bracteate motifs are so anomalous (often called "degenerate") or the piece is so fragmentary that types may be indeterminable. Morton Axboe, Karl Hauck, and John Hines have disagreed on the assignment of a few bracteates to particular groups, as will be noted below. The bracteates found in England customarily have been divided into two geographic groupings – twenty-six from Kent and seventeen from areas outside of Kent, loosely referred to as "Anglia" since the bracteates are concentrated in that region.

THE KENTISH BRACTEATES

The Kentish bracteates have been studied more thoroughly than the Anglian examples, perhaps because there are more of them, and many of these have been known for a long time,[9] and because these gold bracteates clearly are akin to Scandinavian examples. All but one of the bracteates from Kent are of Type D,[10] closely related to Jutish bracteates. Connections between Kent and Jutland as evidenced by bracteates have been discussed by E. T. Leeds,

Hauck, *et al.*, *Die Golbrakteaten der Völkerwanderungszeit*, vols. 1-3 (Munich 1985-1989), for the most recent finds.

[7]J. Hines, *The Scandinavian Character of Anglian England in the pre-Viking Period*, BAR Brit. Ser. 124 (Oxford 1984).

[8]O. Montelius, *Från järnåldern*, 2. Häftet (Stockholm 1869). Montelius included this parenthetical list as a note on the last page of text before the plates.

[9]For example, the Sarre finds of seven bracteates from two graves (M309, 310) were published by J. Brent ("Account of the Society's Researches in the Anglo-Saxon Cemetery at Sarr," *AC* 5 [1863], 305-22; "Account of the Society's Researches in the Anglo-Saxon Cemetery at Sarr," *AC* 6 [1866] 157-85), and the Bifrons finds of six bracteates from three graves (M311, 312, 323) by T. G. Godfrey-Fausett ("The Saxon Cemetery at Bifrons," *AC* 10 [1876], 298-315; "The Saxon Cemetery at Bifrons," *AC* 13 [1880], 526-56).

[10]The exception is the type B bracteate from Bifrons grave 29 (M311, Pl. 5.5). I also exclude the silver bucket mount from Broadstairs (Ax314b) that was stamped with a bracteate die.

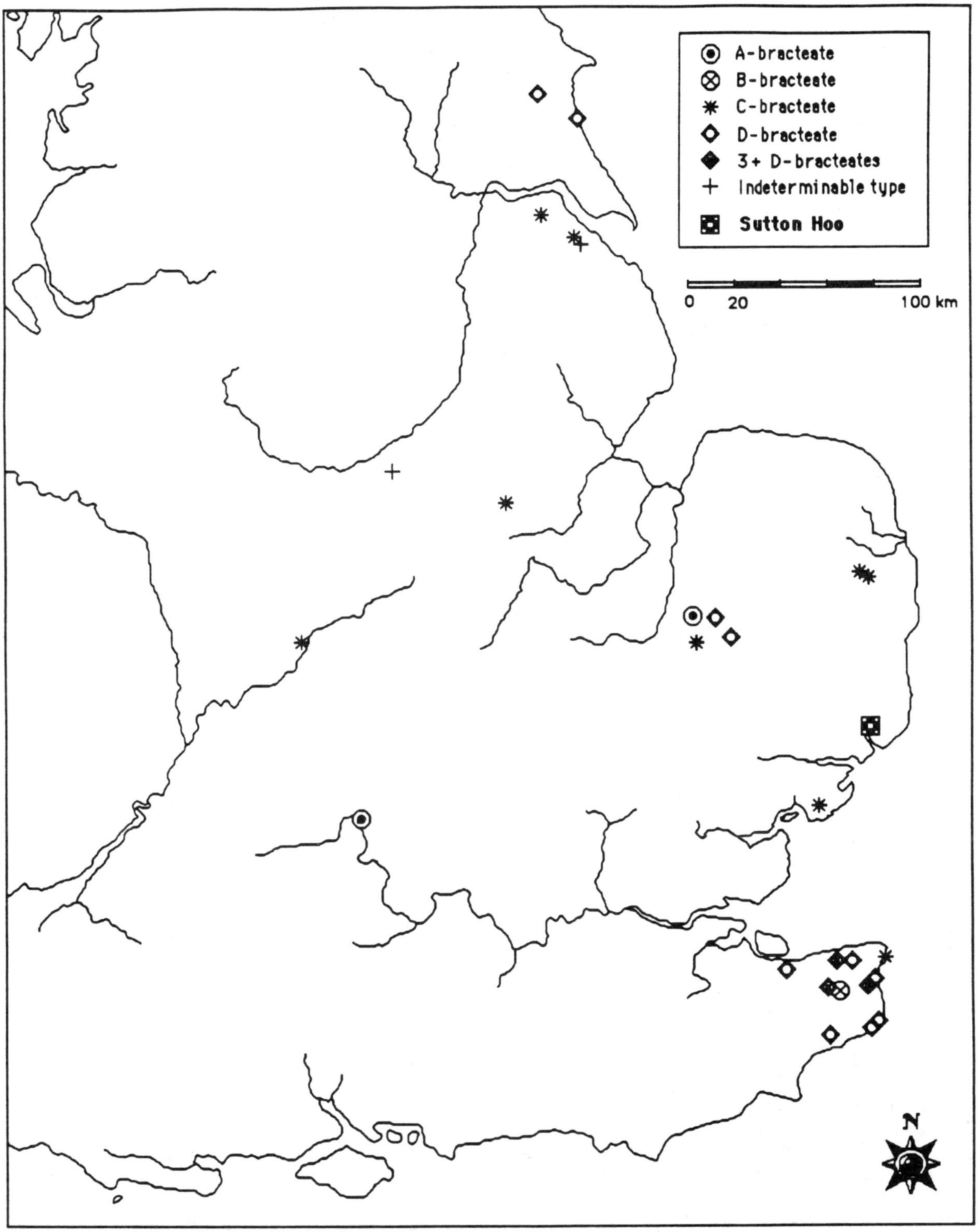

Map 1. Distribution of Scandinavian and Insular gold bracteates and their silver derivatives.

Sonia Hawkes and Egil Bakka.[11] These authors debated whether the Kentish bracteates were made in Denmark and brought to Kent by trade, immigration, or with intermarriage, or whether they were made in England by craft workers from Denmark. Hawkes and Bakka have demonstrated that the Kentish bracteates are too late to have been brought by the original Jutish settlers but may reflect continuing contact with the homeland, whether by trade or intermarriage – as suggested by Hawkes – or as products made in Kent by skilled Danish crafts workers, as favored by Bakka.[12]

BRACTEATES FOUND IN ENGLAND OUTSIDE OF KENT ("ANGLIAN BRACTEATES")

Many of the seventeen Anglian bracteates are recent discoveries, and seven of them are of silver or copper alloys rather than gold (Map 2 and Appendix 1). There have been no spectacular finds of more than two bracteates from one site, as with the Kentish finds from Sarre (M309, 310), Bifrons (M311, 312, 313), and Finglesham (M314, Ax314a). In his catalogue, Mackeprang included the gold bracteates from St. Giles Field, Oxford (M307), Longbridge, Warwickshire (M306), and Market Overton, Leicestershire (M305), which have been known for quite some time,[13] but he disregarded the silver bracteates from West Stow (Ax307b) and Driffield, Humberside (Ax305a), which were published in 1853 and 1905, respectively.[14] The silver bracteates received little or no attention outside of England until they finally were brought to light by Hayo Vierck in 1970[15] and then included by Morten Axboe in his update to Mackeprang's catalogue. Hauck also includes them in his "Ikonographischer Katalog," while John Hines has considered them in by far the greatest detail, and much of the following discussion is indebted to his work.

The Anglian bracteates form a more disparate group than the Kentish examples, including types A, C, and D, as well as examples with anomalous iconography and modifications of the technical qualities of the Scandinavian bracteates. The anomalous examples may reflect the re-interpretation of bracteate iconography for Anglian taste, a cognitive change made in order to make sense of these objects which conveyed cultural-specific information that might have been lost when transported into a new milieu.[16] There are three of type A, six of type C, four of type D, and four others that are of indeterminable type due to anomalous motifs or the fragmentary nature of the remains. Unlike the gold bracteates, the silver and copper bracteates are particularly susceptible to deterioration.

---

[11]See E. T. Leeds, *The Archaeology of the Anglo-Saxon Settlements* (Oxford 1913), 124-26; E. T. Leeds, *Early Anglo-Saxon Art and Archaeology* (Oxford 1936), 41-78; E. T. Leeds, "Denmark and Early England," *AntJ* 26 (1946), 22-37; E. T. Leeds, "Notes on Jutish Art in Kent between 450 and 575," ed. by S. Chadwick, *MA* 1 (1957), 25-26; S. Chadwick, "The Anglo-Saxon Cemetery at Finglesham, Kent: A Reconsideration," *MA* 2 (1958), 42-44; S. C. Hawkes and M. Pollard, "The Gold Bracteates from Sixth-Century Anglo-Saxon Graves in Kent, in the Light of a new Find from Finglesham," *FS* 15 (1981), 316-52; E. Bakka, *On the Beginnings of Salin's Style I in England*, Universitetet i Bergen Årbok 1958, Historisk-Antikvarisk rekke Nr. 3 (Bergen 1958), 65-78; E. Bakka, "Goldbrakteaten in norwegischen Grabfunden: Datierungsfragen," *FS* 7 (1973), 82-84; E. Bakka, "Scandinavian-type Bracteates in Kentish and Continental Grave Finds," in V. I. Evison (ed.) *Angles, Saxons and Jutes: Essays Presented to J. N. L. Myers* (Oxford 1981), 11-28.

[12]Hawkes and Pollard, "Gold Bracteates," 325; Bakka, "Scandinavian-type Gold Bracteates," 12.

[13]The bracteate from St. Giles Field, Oxford, was included by C. J. Thomsen, "Om Guldbracteaterne og Bracteaternes tidligste Brug som Mynt," *Annaler for nordisk Oldkyndighed udgivne af Det Kongelige Nordiske Oldskrift-Selskab* (1855), 265-347; the Longbridge bracteate was published by J. T. Burgess, "Recent Archaeological Discoveries in Warwickshire," *ArchJ* 33 (1876), 368-81; and the Market Overton piece was presented by V. B. Crowther-Beynon, "Notes on an Anglo-Saxon Cemetery at Market Overton, Rutland," *Archaeologia* 62 (1911), 481-96; and E. T. Leeds, "Supplementary Note on the Gold-bracteate and Silver Brooch from Market Overland, Rutland," *Archaeologia* 62 (1911), 491-96.

[14]The bracteate from West Stow was illustrated by S. Tymms, "Anglo-Saxon Relics from West Stow Heath," *Proc. of the Suffolk Inst. of Archaeol.* 1 (1853), 315-28. The Driffield bracteate was published by J. R. Mortimer, *Forty Years' Researches in British and Saxon Burial Mounds of East Yorkshire* (London 1905), 281, fig. 809; it is also discussed by G. B. Brown, *The Arts in Early England*, vol. 4, *Saxon Art and Industry in the Pagan Period* (New York 1915), 806.

[15]H. Vierck, "Der C-Brakteat von Longbridge in der ostenglischen Gruppe," Anhang VIII, in K. Hauck (ed.) *Goldbrakteaten aus Sievern*, Münstersche Mittelalter-Schriften 1 (Munich 1970), 331-39.

[16]C. Renfrew, "Trade as Action at a Distance: Questions of Integration and Communication," in J. A. Sabloff and C. C. Lamberg-Karlovsky (eds.) *Ancient Civilization and Trade* (Albuquerque 1975), 22-23.

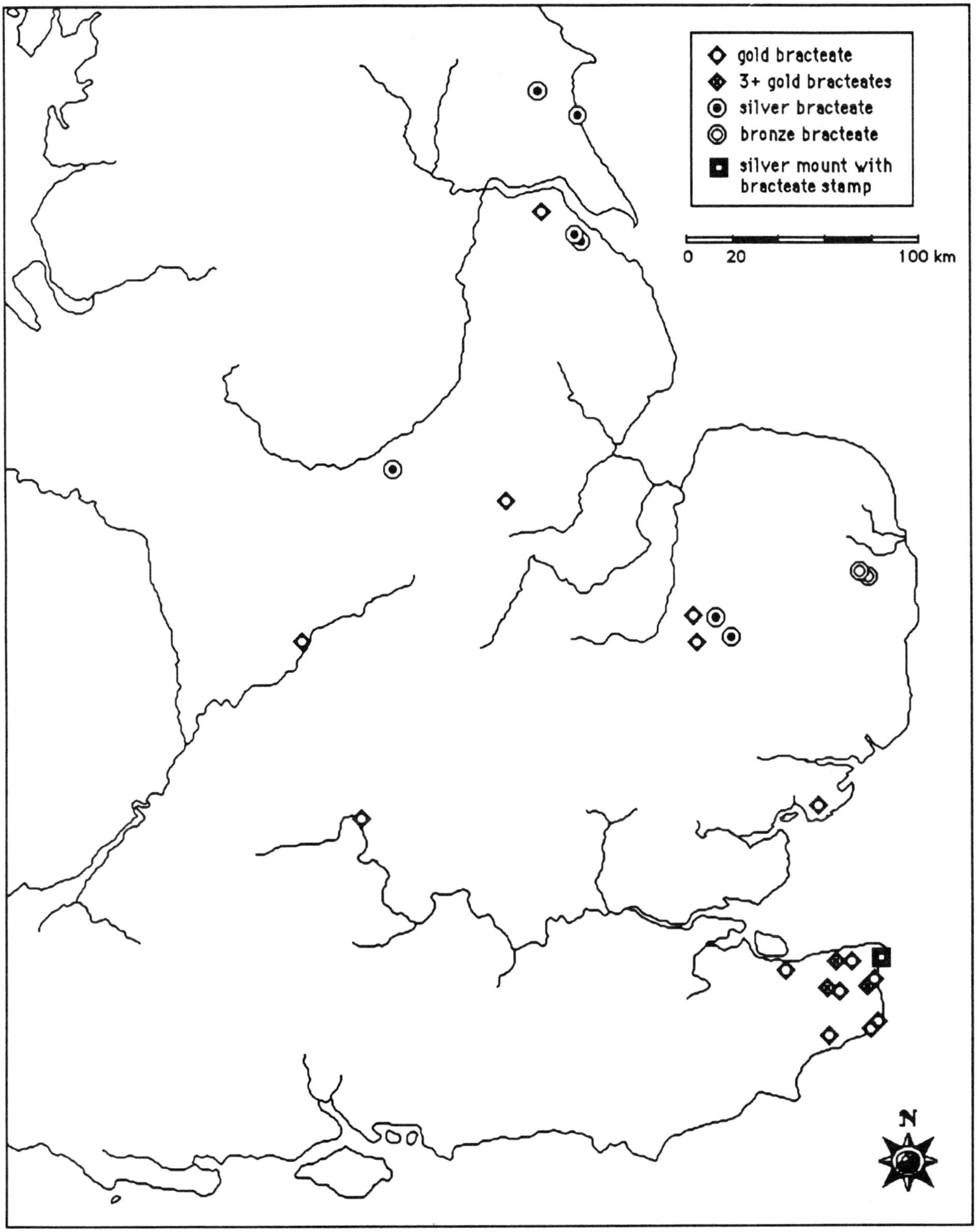

Map 2. Distribution of gold, silver and bronze bracteates and objects with bracteate stamps.

Eight of the Anglian bracteates were made of gold and nine of silver or other alloys. The silver bracteates form a unique group, typical only of the Anglian area, and seem to have been manufactured in England. The only other bracteate of this group found outside of Anglia is the silver-gilt bracteate from Schönebeck, Bezirk Magdeburg, Germany (Ax331a),[17] which Vierck has suggested may have been an export from England.[18] Gold was not as readily available in England as in Scandinavia where abundant *solidi* provided the raw material for bracteates. Apparently bracteates were made with whichever precious metal was most accessible.

TYPE A BRACTEATES OUTSIDE OF KENT

The three type A bracteates under consideration here include those from St. Giles Field, Oxford (M323, Pl. 1a), from Undley, Suffolk (Ax307d, Pl. 1b)[19] and one from an unknown findplace in England which is held in the National Museum in Copenhagen (Ax383). All three can be related to bracteates from southern Denmark and Schleswig-Holstein. The bracteate from St. Giles Field most closely corresponds to one from Terp Hitsum, Friesland (M318), but is also similar to several type A bracteates from Denmark and Schleswig-Holstein,[20] as is the Copenhagen bracteate from an unknown findplace, which will not be discussed further here since so little is known about it. The recently found Undley bracteate also has counterparts from these areas, but its provenance is more problematic because of the runic inscription on the piece.[21] It exhibits an Anglo-Frisian rune, which has led R. I. Page to advocate English manufacture,[22] while John Hines and Bengt Odenstedt consider it a fifth-century import on art historical grounds.[23] The impetus for the Anglian type A bracteates seems to have come from the area from Schleswig-Holstein to Jutland, and not Sweden, so let us now turn to the type C bracteates.

TYPE C BRACTEATES OUTSIDE OF KENT

Although many of the nine possible type C bracteates known from England outside of Kent have idiosyncratic imagery which departs from the Scandinavian types, several emulate the Norwegian and Swedish type C bracteates of Mackeprang's West Scandinavian group.[24] The diagnostic bell-shaped head, spiral hip on the single hind leg, sectioned body, and bird protome extending from the hair above the forehead were among some of the details of the motifs of this type that recently were examined stylistically by Søren Nancke-Krogh.[25] Typical examples of this group from Scandinavia include bracteates from Højbjerg, Lilla Jored, Dalen, Grumpan, Øvre Tøien, Lille-Skjør, Sletner and Høivik (Map 3).

This so-called "West Scandinavian" group includes several bracteates that were not found in western Scandinavia. It seems elementary to point out that bracteates made in one area could be found elsewhere since they are easily transportable objects, but there often is much confusion in the use of distribution maps. Mackeprang assigned geographical names to groupings of bracteates based on similarity of the motifs in the central picture stamp

---

17. Grave 15b, B, Schmidt, "Ein Reihengräberfeld des 6. Jahrhunderts nach Chr. bei Schönebeck (Elbe)," *Jahresschrift für mitteldeutsche Vorgeschichte* 37 (1953), 296-97.

18. H. Vierck, "Der C-Bracteate," 337.

19. Published by S. West, "Gold Bracteate from Undley, Suffolk," *FS* 17 (1983), 459.

20. See J. Hines, *Scandinavian Character of Anglian England*, 209-10 for further parallels.

21. Explored in detail in J. Hines, "The Undley Bracteate and its Runic Inscription, I. The Undley Bracteate in the Context of Other Anglian English Bracteate Finds," *Studien zur Sachsenforschung* 6 (1987), 73-84; and B. Odenstedt, "The Undley Bracteate and its Runic Inscription. II. The Runic Inscription on the Undley Bracteate," *Studien zur Sachsenforschung* 6 (1987), 85-94.

22. R. I. Page, "On the Transliteration of English Runes," *MA* 28 (1984), 37-38; R. I. Page, "Runic Links Across the North Sea in the pre-Viking Age," in H. Bekker-Nielsen and H. F. Nielsen (eds.) *Beretning fra Fjerde Tværfaglige Vikingesymposium* (Moesgård 1985), 186-97; R. I. Page, "New Runic Finds in England," *Runor och Runinskrifter*, KVHAA Konferenser 15 (Stockholm 1987), 194.

23. J. Hines, "The Undley Bracteate"; B. Odenstedt, "The Undley Bracteate."

24. Mackeprang, *Nordiske Guldbrakteater*, 41-42.

25. S. Nancke-Krogh, "De gyldne *ryttere*. En analyse og vurdering af en gruppe C-bracteater," *Hikuin* 10 (1984), 235-46.

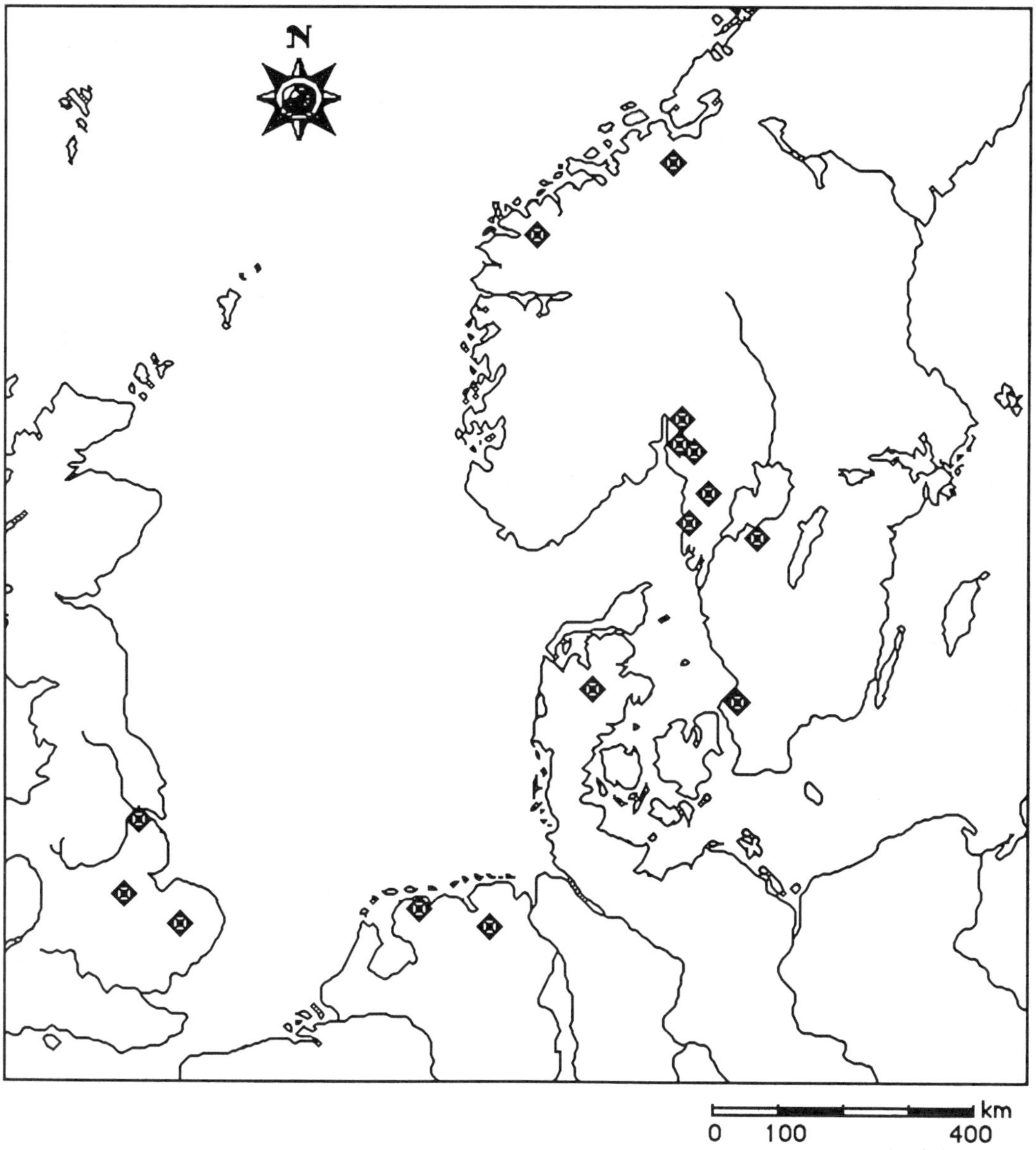

Map 3. Mackeprang's West Scandinavian group, Type C bracteates.

as well as on a subjective, impressionistic interpretation of "style." Underlying his system was the unstated assumption that bracteates that are typologically similar must be related geographically and chronologically.

The English bracteates from Kirmington, Humberside (Ax305e, Pl. 2a), and Market Overton, Leicestershire (M305, Pl. 2b), most closely parallel the designs of the West Scandinavian group, but a pair of bracteates of the same stamp with bell-shaped animal's heads from grave 80 at Morning Thorpe, Norfolk (IK306, Pls. 3 and 4),[26]

[26]B. Green, A. Rogerson and S. G. White, *The Anglo-Saxon Cemetery at Morning Thorpe, Norfolk*, East Anglian Archaeology Report No. 36 (Suffolk 1988), 58 and fig. 320.

and one from Longbridge, Warwickshire (M306, Pl. 5a),[27] are also clearly related to the group. Hines also relates the piece from Chippenham, Cambridgeshire (Ax307e, Pl. 5b) to the same group,[28] but this assignment is not convincing to me. I agree, however, with his conclusion concerning the Market Overton, Kirmington, and Chippenham bracteates: "English manufacture seems more probable than the importation of these objects to England... Some model for that group must have crossed at some stage to England, but none of these examples would appear to be it."[29]

Although I believe that the Chippenham design is too irregular to include with the West Scandinavian group, I would count among this group another object, the silver bucket mount with bracteate stamp design from Broadstairs, Kent (Ax314b, Pl. 6a).[30] The material and motifs of this object have more in common with the non-Kentish bracteates than with the bracteates from that area. It is one of only two examples known of bracteate stamps used on objects other than the pendant bracteates; the other example was stamped on two silver-gilt bucket mounts from Rhenen in the Netherlands (Ax319a).[31] Within Scandinavia the use of a bracteate stamp or bracteate imagery on any other kind of object is unknown. Even though a bracteate stamp had a particular meaning to a Scandinavian crafts worker who would not have considered using it in other contexts, the piece may have had a different significance to the non-Scandinavian crafts worker who appropriated the bracteate imagery, but used it in a different context or even executed it on different materials.

Among the remaining possible type C bracteates is one from Jaywick Sands, Essex (Ax307c, Pl. 6b),[32] which has been counted with the type C bracteates by Hines and, less confidently, by Axboe.[33] Hauck (IK285), on the other hand, finds the attempts at identifying type C imagery in this design unconvincing. The silver fragment from Broughton Lodge (the site referred to by Hines as Willoughby on the Wolds), Nottinghamshire (Ax305f, Pl. 7a), has been identified by Hauck as part of a type B or type C bracteate since a portion of the head of a man with a linear joined eye and nose is visible (IK227). The features probably are too small to be part of a type A bracteate, so Hauck's assignment seems reasonable, though Axboe is more cautious and simply considers it indeterminable. Hines did not recognize the eye and nose motif and includes this silver piece under the rubric "?C?D-bracteates" since it resembles type D bracteates in its material.[34] Finally, the bracteate from Welbeck Hill, Humberside (grave 52, Ax305d, Pl. 7b) one of two bracteates from that site, has been considered as type C by Hauck (IK 387) and Axboe. Hines does not assign it to a group, but he finds parallels to the face and bird combination on type C bracteates of Mackeprang's "East Norway-West Swedish Group" and "South and East Swedish Group,"[35] such as from Hede parish, Järnskogsboda, Böja Parish, Lunnane, Fröslunda, Berg, Stora Ryk, Asmundtorp, Börringe, Ravnstorp, Murum, Norra Torlunda, Silleby, and Viby.

The imagery on the other silver bracteate from Welbeck Hill, from grave 14 (Ax305c, Pl. 8a), has not been satisfactorily explained, though Hauck has attempted.[36] Axboe listed it as a possible type D bracteate, but since it has a runic inscription and none has been found on type D bracteates, this would seem unlikely. Hines compares the bird and face placement on it to bracteates of several Mackeprang types from Scandinavia, including the "East

---

[27]Vierck, "Der C-Brakteat."

[28]Hines, *Scandinavian Character of Anglian England*, 211-12.

[29]Hines, "Undley Bracteate," 80.

[30]K. Hauck, "Zur Ikonologie der Golbrakteaten XXV: Text und Bild in einer oralen Kultur. Antworten auf die zeugniskritische Frage nach der Erreichbarkeit mündlicher Überlieferung im frühen Mittelalter," *FS* 17 (1983), 590.

[31]J. Ypey, "Ein Männergrab mit D-Brakteatenbeschlägen des fränkischen Gräberfeldes bei Rhenen, Provinz Utrecht, Niederland," *FS* 17 (1983), 460-78.

[32]L. Webster, "Medieval Britain in 1976. Pre-Conquest. Essex: Clacton, Jaywick Sands," *MA* 21 (1977), 206.

[33]Hines, *Scandinavian Character of Anglian England*, 220; Axboe, "Scandinavian Gold Bracteates," 75.

[34]Hines, *Scandinavian Character of Anglian England*, 217.

[35]*Ibid.*, 217-18; Mackeprang, *Nordiske Guldbrakteater*, 50-51.

[36]K. Hauck, "Zur Ikonologie der Goldbrakteaten XXXV: Die Wiedergabe von Göttersymbolen und Sinnzeichen der A-, B- und C-Brakteaten auf D- and F-Brakteaten exemplarisch erhellt mit Speer und Kreuz," *FS* 20 (1986), Exkurs 1, 508-11.

Norway-West Sweden Group" and "South and East Swedish Group,"[37] to which he also compared the bracteate from Welbeck Hill grave 52, as above.

In 1973, R. I Page interpreted the inscription as *læw*, perhaps a corruption of the common bracteate inscription *laþu* meaning "invitation," in which the copyist confused "w" (wynn) and "þ" (thorn) (Map 4).[38] He has noted that "it is the sequence of characters which has persuasive Scandinavian parallels, rather than the individual runic forms."[39] The inscription resembles one from Darum (M99 Pl. 4, 7), although *laþu* and variations are found on several bracteates, including ones from Sweden. (See Map 3.) It is the only silver bracteate with an inscription, and since the bracteate is silver, it apparently was locally made. However, as one of only two bracteates with inscriptions from England (the other is from Undley, see above), it evidences continuing contact with Scandinavia by a conservative audience who wanted runic inscriptions.

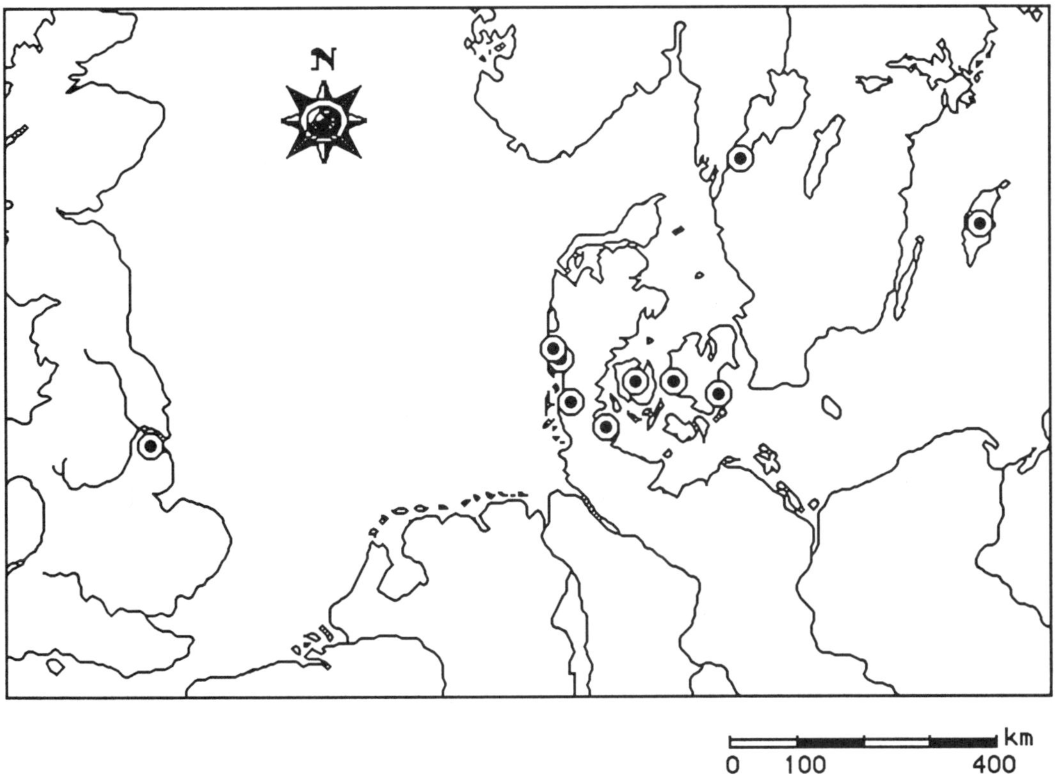

Map 4. Bracteates with possible *laþu* inscriptions.

---

[37]Hines, *Scandinavian Character of Anglian England*, 217; Mackeprang, *Nordiske Guldbrakteater*, 50-51.

[38]R. I. Page, *An Introduction to English Runes* (London 1973), 183-84; Page, "Transliteration," 39.

[39]S. C. Hawkes and R. I. Page, "Swords and Runes in South-East England," *AntJ* 47 (1967), 22.

TYPE D BRACTEATES OUTSIDE OF KENT

Whereas the origin of many of the Anglian bracteates is problematic, the ancestry of the type D Anglian silver bracteates from Driffield (Ax305a, Pl. 8b), Hornsea (Ax305b, Pl. 9a), and West Stow (Ax307b,Pl. 9b),[40] as well as the Schönebeck piece, seems simpler iconographically. These pieces seem to be derivative of Kentish type D bracteates that in turn emulate Jutish types. However, while all of the Kentish bracteates were made of gold, all of these Anglian Type D examples are of silver. In addition, some silver bracteate fragments from grave 27 at Little Eriswell, Suffolk (Ax307a)[41] reputedly belonged to a type D bracteate, according to an inspection by Hayo Vierck, who actually saw the pieces before they disappeared. Sonia Hawkes also confidently endorsed his report.[42]

TECHNICAL DETAILS

The Anglian silver type D bracteates, as well as some of the other Anglian bracteates, also differ from their supposed models in several technical details. Whereas all of the Kentish ones had typically Scandinavian loops and edge rims of attached beaded wire, the Anglian examples lack loops and edge rims, as pointed out by Hines.[43] Of the Anglian bracteates, only type A examples from St. Giles Field and Undley and the irregular type C from Chippenham have applied beaded wire edge rims like Scandinavian bracteates, although the edges of the flan of the Market Overton and Kirmington bracteates are notched, apparently imitating the beaded wire edge rim of the Scandinavian bracteates. The anomalous possible type C bracteate from Jaywick Sands has a smooth wire rim placed on top of the edge of the flan,[44] which is quite unusual in Scandinavia.

PARALLELS BETWEEN ANGLIAN AND GOTLANDIC BRACTEATES

The original impetus for this study was a resemblance between Anglian and Gotlandic bracteates that I had noticed. I was struck by the high percentage of bracteates without rim and/or loop[45] from these two areas. Morten Axboe, in an article co-authored with Jan Peder Lamm introducing new bracteates from Sweden, has also noticed this preponderance of bracteates without loops and/or rims, although he began from the opposite direction with a consideration of the Gotlandic bracteates and mentions the Anglian examples as comparative material.[46] He discovered only a few non-Anglian, non-Gotlandic examples that lack an applied wire edge rim, including the Schönebeck bracteate which, as discussed above, may have been made in Anglia (Map 5). Axboe's nearly comprehensive list seems to overlook only the Longbridge bracteate, which has a notched edge in imitation of beaded wire.[47]

After noticing the technical similarities, I was curious to see if there was any further connection between the two groups. Perhaps it is only a coincidence that the only bracteates from male graves come from these two areas. Axboe discusses the Gotlandic bracteates and medallion imitations from Salands (Ax217a),[48] Kälder (IK286,1), and Gullbacken (M212) that came from burials identified as male by the grave goods which included weapons. Two of these three were also found near the mouth of the interred body, apparently indicating knowledge of the classical

---

[40]West Stow has been newly published by S. West, *West Stow: the Anglo-Saxon Village*, East Anglian Archaeology Report No. 24 (Suffolk 1985), vol. 1, 67, 145; vol. 2, fig. 266.3.

[41]P. Hutchison, "The Anglo-Saxon Cemetery at Little Eriswell, Suffolk," *Proc. of the Cambridge Ant. Soc.* 59 (1966), 1-32.

[42]Hawkes and Pollard, "Gold Bracteates," 363.

[43]Hines, "Undley Bracteate," 81.

[44]*Ibid.*, 80.

[45]Many bracteates have loops damaged or torn away due to wear, but the pieces of concern here seem to never have had a loop.

[46]Lamm and Axboe, "Neues zu Brakteaten," pt. 3, 465-73. I want to express my grateful thanks to Morten Axboe and Jan Peder Lamm for making the manuscripts of this article available to me before it was published.

[47]I have examined this piece myself. Hines ("Undley Bracteate," 80) also notes that it has no rim.

[48]U. Silvén, "Gotländsk vapengrav med Charonsmynt?" *Gotländskt Arkiv* (1956), 97-110.

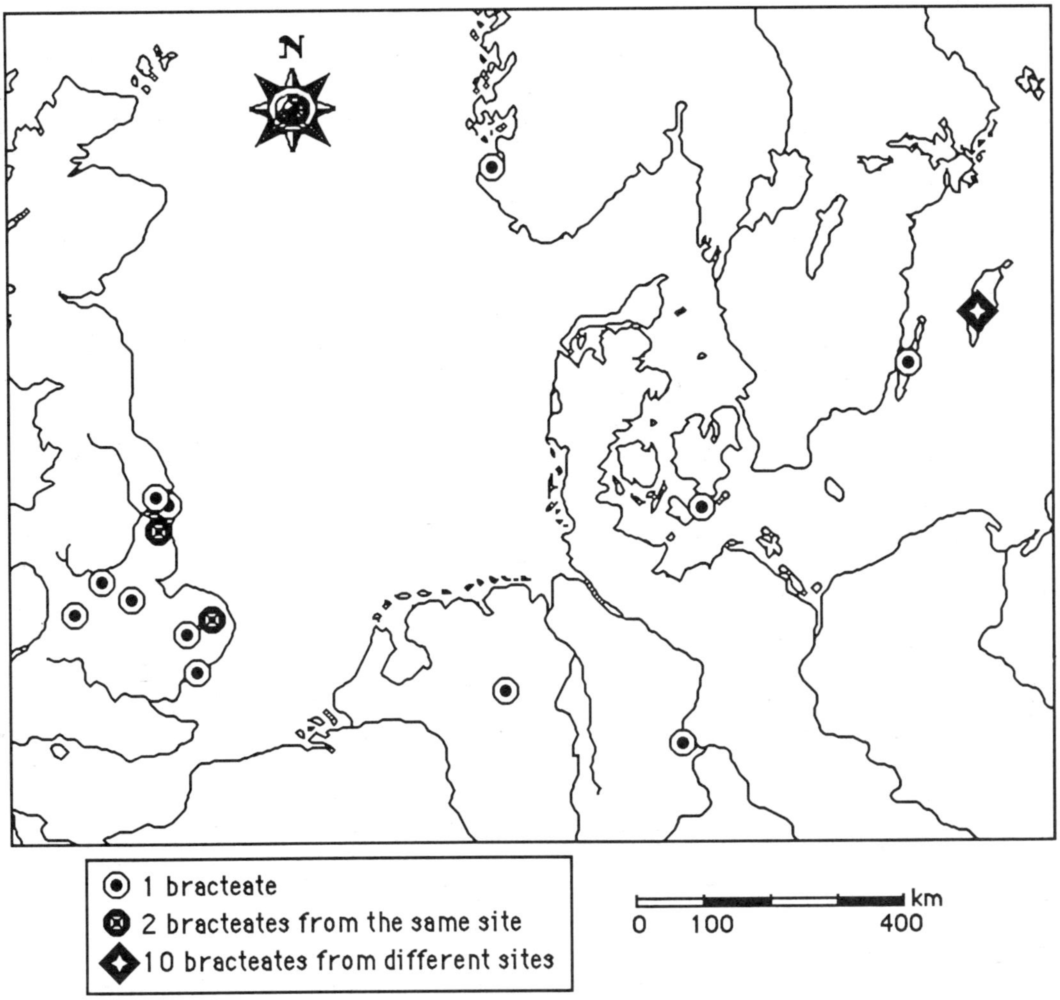

Map 5. Bracteates made without edge rim or suspension loop.

practice of placing a coin known as Charon's obol in the mouth of the deceased to pay the ferryman Charon to take the body across the river Styx to the world of the dead.[49] While no Anglian examples of this practice with bracteates are known, Axboe mentions that the gold type D bracteate from grave 23 at Monkton, Kent (IK467), was found in a male grave in association with the finger bones at the side of the body, which Perkins and Hawkes interpreted as indicating that the bracteate was held in the hand or perhaps in a small bag rather than worn as jewelry.[50] In addition, the bracteate fragment from grave 33 at Broughton Lodge possibly could have come from

---

[49] *Ibid.* See also Lamm and Axboe, "Neues zu Brakteaten," for further Scandinavian examples.

[50] D. R. J. Perkins and S. C, Hawkes, "The Thanet Gas Pipeline Phases I and II (Monkton Parish), 1982," *AC* 101 (1984), 105-06.

a male grave, but the grave was so disturbed that it would be impossible to ascertain sex confidently.[51] Incidentally, the bucket mount with bracteate stamp from Broadstairs, Kent, was also from a male grave.

A final intriguing, yet remote, parallel between the Anglian and Gotlandic bracteates is that the only bronze bracteates come from these two areas. The pair from Morning Thorpe are of bronze, or as Hines specifies, copper-alloy, since he suspects that they may have a high percentage of silver;[52] they are paralleled by several Vendel period bracteates from Gotland. Hines also notes this curious similarity.[53]

During the Vendel Period (seventh and eighth centuries) following the end of the Migration Period, different types of bracteates were developed on Gotland, while they died out elsewhere within Scandinavia.[54] One of these later developments, defined by Oscar Montelius as "group E,"[55] with imagery consisting of three animal heads on curved necks radially arranged around a central point, was made with the same technique of stamped decoration as the Migration Period bracteates. However, these group E bracteates were not limited to gold as were the Swedish Migration Period bracteates, but were made of gold, silver, or bronze. Almost all of the type E pieces are from Gotland, with a few exceptions from Öland and from Birka on the mainland of Sweden.[56] Mackeprang sees no resemblance between the latest Migration Period bracteates and the earliest stage of the characteristically Gotlandic bracteates, with animal heads in Germanic Style II with long upturned jaws and emphasized chin-points.[57] Åberg, however, traces a connection between the Migration Period type C and Vendel Period type E bracteates.[58]

In England, at the same time as the Gotlandic type E bracteates were being produced, bracteates exhibiting ribbon interlace ornamentation characteristic of Salin's Style II[59] were made. The connection between the Kentish style D bracteates and the Style II bracteates has been traced by George Speake.[60] The development into Style II did not take place on the Scandinavian bracteates, although other kinds of object in Scandinavia were decorated with full-fledged Style II interlace. Both the Gotlandic type E and the Anglo-Saxon Style II bracteates represent the alteration and continuation of a type of object in peripheral areas in local styles and materials after it died out elsewhere.

CONCLUSION

Bracteates may be viewed as indicators of exchange between Scandinavia and England in the sixth century A.D., as an example of the broader perspective and background of contacts against which Sutton Hoo should be viewed. Particular examples of correspondences between the two areas have been identified, and even though no single parallel between Anglia and Gotland as evidenced by the bracteates is particularly striking or significant by itself, the combination of the several points of similarity – bracteates without loops and rims, made of silver or bronze, from male graves, and continuing use of the object type after it died out elsewhere – along with the iconographic parallels of type C Anglian bracteates with Swedish bracteates, suggests that contact occurred between the areas.

Most of the Anglian bracteates seem to have been made in England, as indicated by the use of silver and the disintegrated motifs, but under continuing Scandinavian influence as evidenced by the *laþu* runic inscription and West Scandinavian type C imagery. The apparent Gotlandic-Anglian parallels may be attributed in part to similar

[51] Hauck, "Zur Ikonologie der Goldbrakteaten XXXV," IK227.

[52] Hines, *Scandinavian Character of Anglian England*, 210.

[53] Hines, "Undley Bracteate," 79.

[54] Mackeprang, *Nordiske Guldbrakteater*, 102-03.

[55] See Montelius' definition in O. Montelius, *Från järnåldern*, 2. Häftet (Stockholm 1869).

[56] Mackeprang, *Nordiske Guldbrakteater*, 102.

[57] *Ibid.*, 103.

[58] N. Åberg, *Den nordiska folkvandringstidens kronolgi* (Stockholm 1924), 63; N. Åberg, *Den historiska relationen mellan folkvandringstid och vendeltid* (Stockholm 1953), 118-20; M. Stenberger, "Traditionsbundenheti vikingatida gotländsk brakteatkonst," *Tor* 4 (1958), 113-32.

[59] B. Salin, *Die altgermanische Thierornamentik* (Stockholm 1904).

[60] See Åberg, *Anglo-Saxons in England*, 134-35; G. Speake, *Anglo-Saxon Animal Art and its Germanic Background* (Oxford 1980), 65-76.

independent development in areas of the same general sphere of influence from the Baltic to England, as is evidenced in the Sutton Hoo find. However, the similarities may stem from more direct causes, if, when Anglo-Saxon crafts workers made new bracteates based on Scandinavian ones, they copied not only the object type and imagery but also ideas about their usage and certain methods and techniques for their production. Hayo Vierck traced specific examples of trade between eastern England and central Sweden,[61] while John Hines has postulated that itinerant crafts workers could "be responsible for a significant number of earlier correspondences between the two areas in Migration Period metalwork."[62] Similarly, George Speake has proposed that travelling crafts workers could be responsible for the parallels between Sutton Hoo and Uppland.[63]

A case can be made for a Swedish character in certain of the Anglian bracteates, which can be compared to the Vendel and Valsgärde correspondences in the Sutton Hoo material. Although the earlier parallels are overshadowed by the examples from Sutton Hoo and Vendel, they attest to on-going contacts between Scandinavia and England during the century preceding Sutton Hoo. Just as Robert Farrell demonstrated that objects from Sutton Hoo had parallels all over Sweden, not just at Vendel and Valsgärde,[64] so too the Anglian bracteates have parallels in southern Sweden, eastern Sweden, Gotland, Öland, and Uppland. In an essay for the 1980 exhibition of material from Vendel, Valsgärde, and Sutton Hoo, David Wilson essentially concluded that everyone was in contact with everyone else[65] Much the same can be said for the sixth century, and the bracteates testify to such a broad sphere of contacts. Scandinavia was never isolated from the rest of Europe during the Migration Period, but continued close and regular contacts, as is clearly documented in the archaeological record. Sutton Hoo should be seen in the light of this background of continuing contacts and should not be considered in isolation.

[61]H. Vierck, "Zum Fernverkehr über See im 6. Jahrhundert angesichts angelsächsischer Fibelsätze in Thüringen. Eine Problemskizze," Anhang XI, in K. Hauck (ed.) *Goldbrakteaten aus Sievern*, Münstersche Mittelalter-Schriften 1 (Munich 1970), 355-95.

[62]Hines, *Scandinavian Character of Anglian England*, 290.

[63]Speake, *Anglo-Saxon Animal Art*, 94.

[64]See his distribution map of parallels for Sutton Hoo material, in R. T. Farrell, *Beowulf, Swedes and Geats*, *SBVS* 18 (1972), fig. 7.

[65]D. Wilson, "Sverige-England," in A Sandwill (ed.) *Vendeltid* (Stockholm 1980), 218.

APPENDIX

Migration Period Bracteates from Anglian (non-Kentish) England

Findplace	County	Type	Metal
Broughton Lodge (Willoughby on the Wolds)	Nottinghamshire	fragment	silver
Chippenham	Cambridgeshire	C	gold
Driffield	Yorkshire	D	silver
Hornsea	Yorkshire	D	silver
England (unknown findplace)	---	A	gold
Jaywick Sands	Essex	C?	gold
Kirmington	Lincolnshire	C	gold
Little Eriswell	Suffolk	D	silver
Longbridge	Warwickshire	C	gold
Market Overton	Leicestershire	C	gold
Morning Thorpe	Norfolk	C	copper alloy
Morning Thorpe	Norfolk	C	copper alloy
Saint Giles Field	Oxfordshire	A	gold
Undley, Whitby	Suffolk	A	gold
Welbeck Hill, grave 14	Lincolnshire	C or D?	silver
Welbeck Hill, grave 52	Lincolnshire	C?	silver
West Stow	Suffolk	D	silver

Pl. 1. (a) St. Giles Field, Oxfordshire. Diameter 3.28cm. Courtesy of the Ashmolean Museum, Oxford.
(b) Undley, Whitby, Suffolk. Diameter 2.3cm. Courtesy of the British Museum.

Pl. 2. (a) Kirmington, Humberside. Diameter 2.85cm. Courtesy of Scunthorpe Museums (inv. no. KMAA311).
(b) Market Overton, Leicestershire. Diameter 3.27cm. Courtesy of the British Museum.

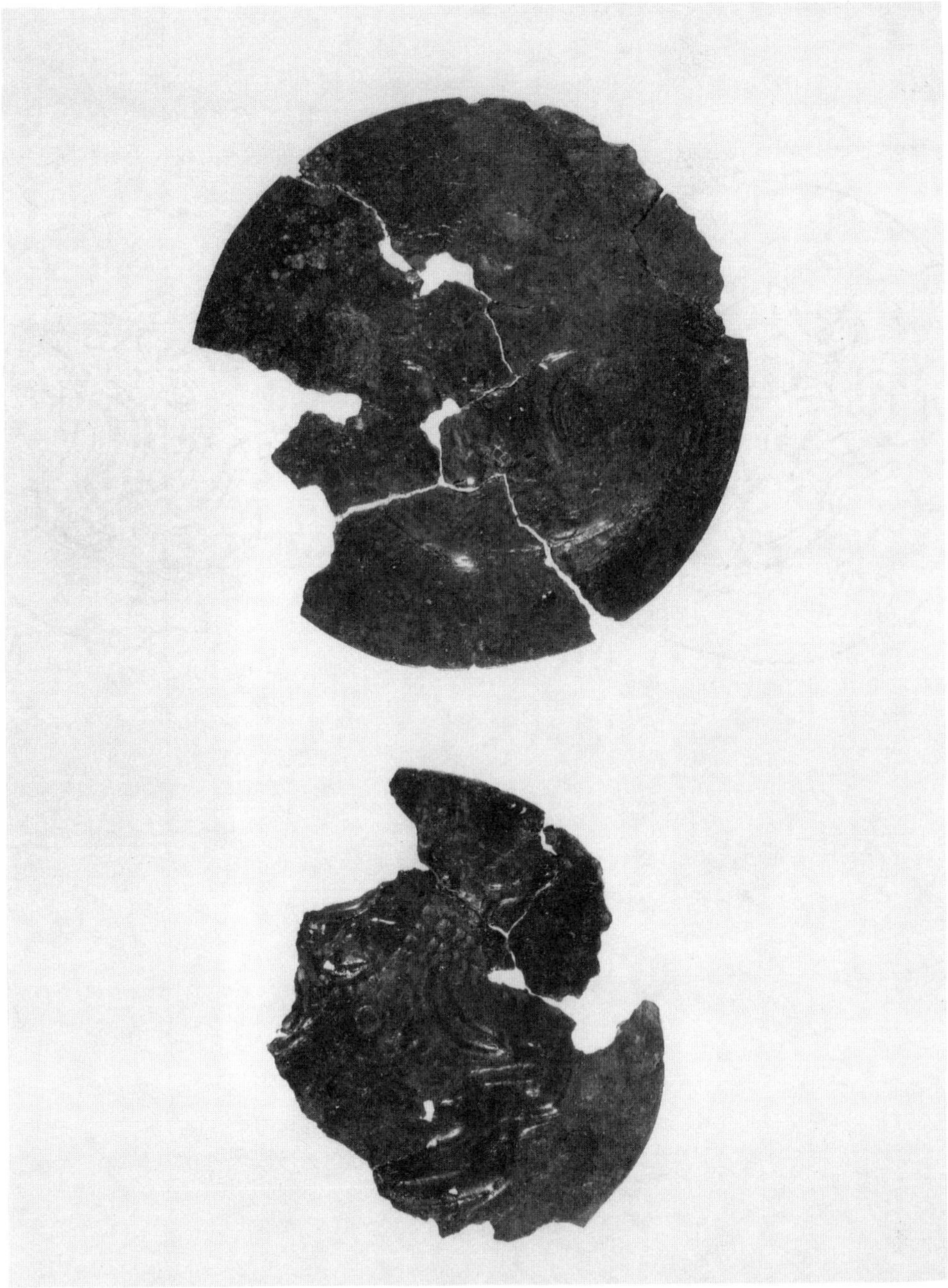

Pl. 3. (a) Morning Thorpe (grave 80 Mi), Norfolk. Estimated diameter 3.2cm. (b) Morning Thorpe (grave 80 Mii), Norfolk. Length 2.7cm. Courtesy Norfolk Museums Service (Norwich Castle Museum).

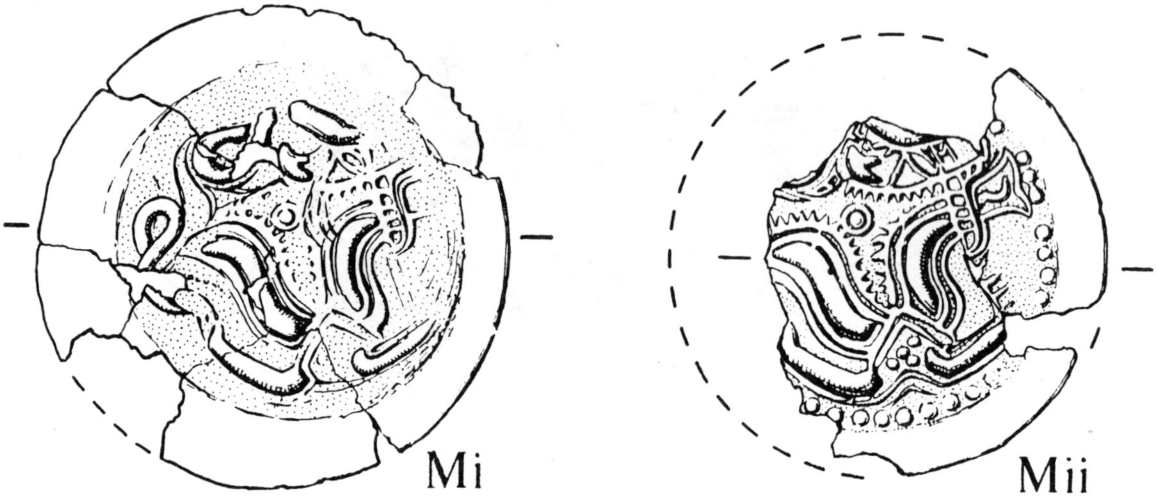

Pl. 4. Composite drawing from the two bracteates from Morning Thorpe (grave 80 Mi and 80 Mii), Norfolk. Diameter 3.2cm. Copyright: Norfolk Archaeological Unit; drawn by Susan G. White.

Pl. 5. (a) Longbridge, Warwickshire. Diameter 5.24cm. Courtesy of the British Museum (inv. no. 76.5-21.1).
(b) Chippenham, Ely, Cambridgeshire. Diameter 1.99cm. Courtesy of Terence A. Volk and the Fitzwilliam Museum, Cambridge.

Pl. 6. (a) Bucket Mount, Broadstairs (grave 71), Kent. 4.46cm x 2.7cm. Courtesy of the British Museum.
(b) Jaywick Sands, Essex. Diameter 2.8cm. Courtesy of the British Museum.

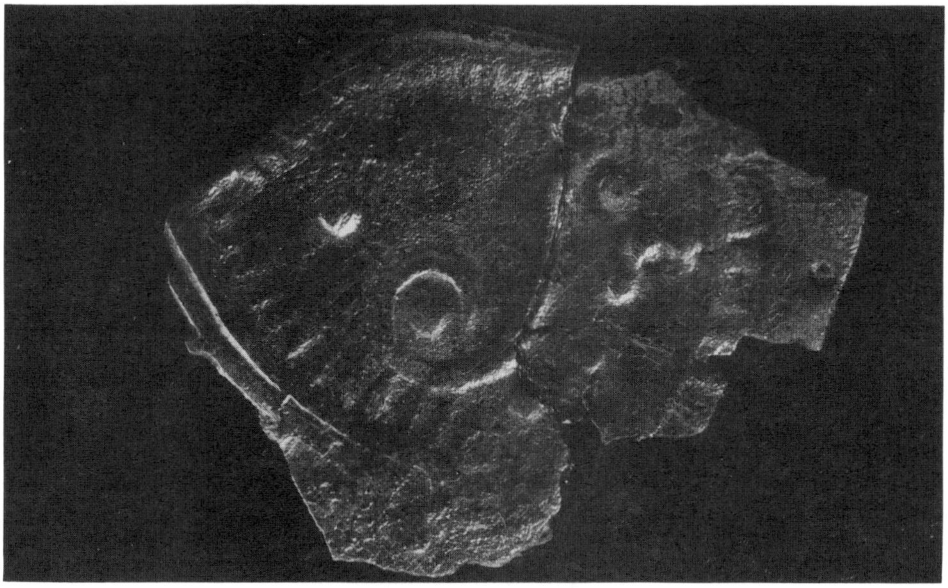

Pl. 7. (a) Broughton Lodge (grave 33), Nottinghamshire. 1.8cm x 1.4cm. Courtesy Brewhouse Yard Museum.
(b) Welbeck Hill (grave 52), Humberside. Diameter 3.1cm. Courtesy of Gordon Taylor and Scunthorpe Museums.

Pl. 8. (a) Welbeck Hill (grave 14), Humberside. Diameter 3.26cm. Courtesy of Gordon Tayler and Scuntorpe Museums
(b) Driffield (grave 26), Humberside. Diameter 2.8cm. Courtesy of Hull City Museums and Art Galleries (inv. no. 1503.1942).

Pl. 9. (a) Hornsea, Humberside. Diameter 2.9cm. Courtesy of Hull City Museums and Art Galleries (inv. no. 1505.1942).
(b) West Stow, Suffolk. Diameter 2.15cm. Courtesy Moyse's Hall Museum, St. Edmundsbury Museum Service.

Ideology and Allegiance in East Anglia

MARTIN CARVER

My people, the Boeremense, are entitled to their land in South Africa. They are entitled to what is theirs – the old Boer Republics: Transvaal, the Free State, and Northern Natal. They are and always have been ours and ours alone. We did not take them away from the black man. It is not even the white man's land – it belongs to the volk... I exist because of what the English and Dutch got up to when they arrived here. They created an entirely new nation, a volk... I will get my land back and return the Boer Republics ... because my volk entered into a contract with my God that this land would be retained for his glory.[1]

This paper is an attempt to explore political changes in the England of the fifth through seventh centuries. That there *were* changes is clear from the documentary record; the hope is that the nature of such changes can be described by using archaeology. The work draws mainly on two earlier papers: "Kingship and Material Culture," which attempted to establish some of the material correlates for stratification in early English society, and "Pre-Viking Traffic in the North Sea," which explored the range of possible types of contact between England and Scandinavia, and why these were, or were not, signalled in the archaeological record.[2] The argument is taken further here by trying to examine the reasons that East Anglia adopted the particular material culture it did, when it did, particularly in burials. It finds these reasons not only to be embedded in economic and political evolution and self-awareness, but also to relate to an imaginative view of North Sea ideologies, a "dreaming out loud" using grave goods as statements which owe as much to poetry as to the realities of life in the seventh century.

When the first Professor of History at Witwatersrand, William MacMillan, broke with South Africa in 1933 over the color bar legislation he undertook a tour of late colonial Africa to collect data for his predictive work on post-colonial political structure entitled *Africa Emergent*.[3] MacMillan found an astonishing variety of political and ideological formations, and, in particular, varieties of economic subsystem – variations which reflected either the local character or the communities of the colonizers' interest in them. Although imperial educators were happy to color the map Imperial pink, direct rule was quite rare. For example, in what was then Tanganyka (a mandated territory taken from the Germans after World War I), the government was looking to white pioneers to increase its revenues by occupying territory; but where the new white settlers encroached on native land the government scarcely had the power to arbitrate and, "such administrative action as was taken aroused the distrust of both sides." Solutions elsewhere (Kenya, Rhodesia) included the creation of native reserves, often on the poorest land, that form of segregation against which MacMillan fought all his life. In northern Nigeria, indirect rule was practiced through Moslem Emirs, while in southern Nigeria there were an amazing number and variety of tribes (offering a happy hunting ground for anthropologists) that remained autonomous and who resisted any form of taxation. There was a similar situation in the Gold Coast where minor chieftains were elected and deposed with alarming frequency by their constituents. The web of land ownership was complex and indeterminate, and here too all forms of direct taxation were absolutely refused. But in Bechuanaland, now Botswana, and "in all the territories from which large drafts of labour had been drawn by the mines," there had been some very considerable changes in the tribal system: and autocratic chiefly dynasty had become established – the Khana family. MacMillan found that "this tendency was all the stronger for having been protected" (i.e. by the British Empire) and recommended that the government's object should be "to make the chief into a sort of constitutional king, with a council."[4]

---

[1]Eugene Terr'Blanche, leader of Afrikaner Weerstandsbeweging, in *The Guardian*, May 24, 1986.

[2]M. O. H. Carver, "Kingship and Material Culture in Early Anglo-Saxon East Anglia," in S. Bassett (ed.) *The Origins of the Anglo-Saxon Kingdoms* (Leicester 1989), 141-58; M. O. H. Carver, "Pre-Viking Traffic in the North Sea," in S. Macgrail (ed.) *Maritime Celts, Frisians and Saxons* (London 1990), 117-25.

[3]M. MacMillan, *Champion of Africa: W. M. MacMillan. The Second Phase* (Long Wittenham 1985).

[4]*Ibid.*, 34ff.

These social and economic configurations have been studies since MacMillan's day by social anthropologists responsible for many nourishing contributions to archaeological theory. Here I simply want to make the point that local economic situations, born of a combination of factors – proximity to the coast, access to slavers, the presence of mineral resources, the attention of imperial and post-imperial agents – created local forms of politics in which ideology and allegiance were differently constructed and expressed. The late imperial African peoples were not intrinsically different from each other, nor were they in different stages of social evolution; they were simply living in different circumstances, defined by the relationships between native government, white settlement and attempts at white government, and by the customs of land-tenure and taxation then current.

Analogies drawn between the late British and late Roman Empires founder in many particulars, but it might be worth emphasizing the possibility of such variations when considering the regions of the former Roman province of Britain in the fifth through seventh centuries A.D. Here the traditionally perceived variations were in rather primary colors: variations in the environment and in race, so that some archaeologists might see a Romanized Celtic people occupying different parts of a province – highland, lowland, maritime – which had different potential yields – cattle, grain, trade – and invaded by groups of Germanic peoples – Angles, Saxons, Jutes – who adapted an imported culture to the new territorial zones. In recent years such variations between peoples, particularly ideological and racial variations, have tended to be over-shadowed by evolutionary models of societies heading eagerly for the goal of statehood, albeit at different speeds.[5] However, both ideology and race can be retained in the argument by supposing that both were being inventively signalled but in reality were just cultural "artefacts" constructed in different ways in different circumstances. This would mean that being an East Angle, being a pagan and being a king were also the artificial constructions of local people. There is, therefore, no reason why these things or their material correlates should look exactly the same in contemporary Kent, Wessex or Northumbria. This is important, since in studies of early medieval peoples it is often assumed that state formation to a common pattern is not only inevitable, but will be signalled by the same archaeology.

This would certainly be convenient, if true, since we could assume that Norway, Sweden, Denmark, Kent, and Frankia were pursuing similar evolutionary itineraries towards what were, and what were known to be, similar forms of kingly government. Determining the social formation and its changing configuration in particular regions then becomes a matter of observing the most visible of its attributes, namely the nucleation of power and the formation of an elite. The onset of the kingly mode can then be chronicled in a number of neighboring polities; and direct or indirect, internal or external, causes evoked to explain it. On the other hand, if there *is* no repeated equation between archaeological remains and societies, such patterns as we have are that much harder to analyze and explain. In other words, social change is sometimes signalled in the material culture and sometimes is not. This is the distinction which this paper attempts to investigate. We shall have to look to ideology, and the allegiance that ideology inspires, to explain why and when the archaeological record is skewed. Communities do not merely proceed at different rates towards a hypothetical state, or a state of social-economic complexity, but they can use different material culture differently to show to other people what progress they believe they are making. To observe this process in action, while fervently hoping to avoid doing too much violence (by compression) to evidence and theses gathered by others, I would like to review briefly some recent models for the North Sea territories.

SOCIAL EVOLUTION IN NORTH SEA TERRITORIES

In southern Scandinavia (Denmark – Schleswig), evidence for increased social stratification has been observed in various territories from at least the second century A.D. Among the correlates are house-sizes and boundaries within settlements which reflect "the extension of private rights and claims in a social system [which are] more

---

[5]See, for example, R. Hodges, *Dark Age Economics* (London 1982); C. J. Arnold, *An Archaeology of the Early Anglo-Saxon Kingdoms* (London 1988).

differentiated and more productive."[6] Votive deposits in bogs, coinciding with periods with few imports, give way to wealthy, high status burials, a process called by M. Parker-Pearson the "privatization of the Gods."[7] V. Näsman draws an analogy between southern Scandinavia and better documented Visigothic peoples where the documents announce, and the material culture endorses, that a tribal confederacy became more stratified in the later fourth century and this hierarchy is consolidated by contact with Romans.[8] The material correlates are an increase in manufacturing activity as well as increase in ranking in cemeteries. Näsman attributes a similar evolution to the peoples of Jutland and reaches documentary home-base with Ongendus, the Danish King visited by Willibrord in the eighth century. He concludes that his analogous Danish society could not have achieved this status of a "kingdom" as a result of internal development alone, but must, like the Visigoths, have drawn on influence and conflict coming from west European kingdoms, especially those of the Merovingian-Carolingian dynasties.

For southern Norway, Bjorn Myhre has used a fine array of material evidence which includes not only ranking in cemeteries but in boat-houses, and the establishment of territories defined by hillforts.[9] He is able to conclude that an elite developed during the fourth and fifth centuries, and he can map chieftain territories and explore their anatomy. "Middlemen" at valley mouths canalize iron and other mountain products and enrich themselves by supplying the major chiefly centers on the coast. The system is articulated in the first place by wealth-creating opportunities provided through the late Roman Empire, and tuned through the urge of emergent chiefs to compete with others, including those overseas. These chiefs were "strong enough to organize regional defence systems and complicated economic structures reaching from the caves in the mountains to the coasts of Europe."[10]

In the Swedish Uppland increased ranking can be observed in cemeteries culminating in rich cremations under large mounds at Uppsala, and, in the seventh century, rich ship burials, for example, at Vendel and Valsgärde. However in the absence of any forceful documentary evidence for "kings," uncertainty pervades the interpretation of these high-status burials, an uncertainty which is reinforced by a dispersed settlement pattern. For Sweden, there are few modern champions of kingship or territorial leadership this early. For Peter Sawyer, any cultural unity observable in Uppland does not imply a unified *Svearike*, and the settlement pattern of dispersed farms is likely "to reflect a stage of social organisation in which relatively small units of lordships was the norm."[11] The debate over Helgõ exemplifies both the contentious issue of territorial control and the difficulty of observing it. Here, the earlier assumption was that Helgõ was proto-urban, the embryonic medieval town, the first of a chain of central places leading to Birka, Sigtuna and Stockholm.[12] This idea has been increasingly challenged. Helgõ is also a settlement which has been shown to be no larger than a pair of contemporary farms, with an agricultural function in addition to its manufacturing and redistribution role.[13] The number and size of the buildings increase during the sixth through eighth centuries, but the increased complexity is not equivalent to "proto-urbanism."[14] The settlement was discovered and the Helgõ project began when a decorated Coptic bronze ladle was unearthed during the erection of a flagpole in 1950. But the ladle's seductive powers, later enhanced by the finds of an Irish crozier and an Indian Buddha, are now, it seems, on the wane. As several contributors to the recent symposium insisted, Helgõ may not be untypical of one of Sawyer's "small units of lordship," a place central only in its neck of Mälaren, having no

[6]For example, Vorbasse. See K. Randsborg, "The Town, the Power and the Land: Denmark and Europe during the First Millennium AD," in T. C. Champion (ed.) *Centre and Periphery*, One World Archaeology 11, (London 1988), 215-16.

[7]M. Parker-Pearson, "Economic and Ideological Change: Cyclical Growth in the pre-State Societies of Jutland," in C. Tilley and D. Miller (eds.) *Ideology, Power and Prehistory* (Cambridge and New York 1984), 70.

[8]V. Näsman, "Analogisutning i Nordisk Jernalder arkeologi," in *Fra Stamme til Stat i Denmark* (Moesgard 1988), 123-40.

[9]B. Myhre, "'Chieftains' graves and chieftain territories in South Norway in the Migration Period," *Studien zur Sachsenforschung* 6 (1987), 169-88.

[10]*Ibid.*, 187.

[11]P. H. Sawyer, "Settlement and Power Among the Svear in the Period," *Vendel Period Studies* (Stockholm 1983), 119.

[12]See A. Lundström, "Short Summary of the Interpretations 1961-1974," in A Lundström (ed.) *Thirteen Studies on Helgö* (Stockholm 1988), 11-13.

[13]O. Kyhlberg, "Chronological and Topographical Analysis of the Cemeteries and Settlements," in K. Lamm *et al.* (eds.) *Excavations at Helgö VIII - The Ancient Monuments*, k VHAA (Stockholm 1982).

[14]O. Kyhlberg, "Spatial Patterns – Social Structures, in A. Lundström (ed.) *Thirteen Studies on Helgö* (1988), 77-88.

"gateway" role and performing no embryonic urban function on behalf of the regional polity.[15] In Sweden there is current reluctance to read ship burial, wealthy graves, or the incidence of exotic finds, as signs that any territorial control has been achieved, other than that of a farm or an estate; and other "Helgős," if not other *Gamla Uppsalas* are therefore awaited.

In France, by contrast, the documentary record should provide some corroboration of how mortuary behavior was used. Edward James's account of the Franks combines, if it does not exactly reconcile, the documentary doings of named persons and peoples with the thousands of graves which have been unearthed.[16] These converge notably in the grave excavated at Tournai in 1653 and thought to represent the obsequies of Childeric, a titled king who gained territorial control in northwest Gaul in the late fifth century. It is possible to look back and forwards from this point in search of the expected changes in ranking, but the situation is obviously complicated by the Frankish peoples' proximity to, and participation in, a continuously articulated imperial structure. The vocabulary of status is the same as that found further north; polychrome jewelry, horses, horsetrappings, the barrow, the chamber grave. High status graves of several ranks can be found, scattered through a cemetery or clustered together.[17] The high status "founder's-grave," in a church or churchyard provides another observable analogue of the small internally-stratified social group.[18] James is rightly skeptical about most equations that have been drawn with ethnicity and religion on the one hand and burial custom on the other.[19] He is marginally more sanguine about burial rite as a signal of status, but it is obviously difficult to see here any simple evolution in time-space. The territory covered is much larger and the social and economic context much more varied than the other examples considered; however, it could be that the status equation can still serve to illuminate some of the diversity. Before Childeric, increased social stratification may have happened and may be observable (eg. at Krefeld-Gellep) in northwest Gaul in the fourth and fifth centuries. The context for this was provided by service in or association with, border garrisons,[20] and increased stratification, as in southwest Norway, is seen as the *result* of this increased contact with the Roman world.[21] After Childeric, the adoption of particular burial rites does not cease to have any social meaning. Nor can it be viewed simply as free ideological choice made within a static social structure. In the sense used in this paper, ideology is not accepted as a "philosophical option," but as a behavioral artefact constructed by a community as a particular moment in history. The choice of burial rite must at least have been controlled by, if not been determined by, the wealth at the disposal of burial parties. How that wealth is used will be socially determined, which in turn is a function of political climate. The adoption of "Frankish" burial rites could, therefore, be equated *not* with Franks but with the social status that goes with exemption from the Roman taxation system, a signal of creeping privatization of the pre-existing and continuing Roman state.[22] In other words, taking three broad hypothetical socio-economic formations – folk, chiefdom or state – the material culture in Frankia can be signalling transition in one of several directions. The net overall change was from a Roman state, via deregulation in folk and chiefdom, to another state. Although the Merovingian state was not the same thing as the Roman state, there is a possibility it was preserved as such, and in that lay its powerful effect on its neighbors to the north. Thus the struggle between localized and centralized allegiance may have had one reification in the burial rites seen in Frankish territory, and another in the burial rites seen among neighboring peoples.

---

[15]*Helgö*, passim.

[16]E. James, *The Franks* (Oxford 1988).

[17]*Ibid.*, 223.

[18]Cf. Arlon, *Ibid.*, 145.

[19]*Ibid.*, 76, 144.

[20]*Ibid.*, 76, 90.

[21]*Ibid.*, 216.

[22]*Ibid*, 191-94.

SOCIAL EVOLUTION IN EAST ANGLIA

The argument for an equation between grave-furnishing and taxable status has been advanced for East Anglia elsewhere,[23] where the theorem was proposed that the transition from furnished to unfurnished burial was a sign of the transition from a "folk" to a taxable community under a "king." In summary, the area considered was Norfolk, Suffolk and Essex, and the attributes examined in pursuit of social change were cemeteries, settlement and the evidence for the environment. Following H. W. Böhme's thesis,[24] East Anglia is seen as the first region of the Roman province of Britannia to be settled by immigrants from north Germany and south Scandinavia, the initial context of this settlement being, as in the Rhineland, that of federated imperial troops. These people show evidence of being stratified from their earliest (non-military) appearance. The type site offered is (and is likely to remain) Spong Hill, where one of the chamber-graves covered by a mound is dated by Böhme to the late fifth century, contemporary with the earliest cremations. Regional or "Anglian" character, however, does not really show in cemeteries until the sixth century. Richards also found evidence for social stratification at a local level from the earliest settlement, in his work on symbolism carried on cremation urns.[25] Exploring the distribution of wealth in Anglo-Saxon cemeteries, Arnold observed a general increase in ranking from a phase showing even distribution of wealth to a phase when the distribution is uneven.[26] Hills would advise against a too eager acceptance of this evolutionary model,[27] but the existence of a final phase which included wealthy barrow-burials, and the general reduction of grave goods in contemporary graves, seems reasonably secure.[28]

These new "princely graves" of the late sixth and early seventh centuries generally feature polychrome jewelry, the round barrow, and, in two cemeteries, boats or ships. These two, Snape and Sutton Hoo, exemplify both the potential of reading social structure from cemeteries, and its problems. The Snape cemetery has been shown to contain cremations, furnished inhumations, and a log-boat burial containing a pair of horns.[29] Formerly there were also several mounds one of which contained a clinker-built vessel excavated with its contents in 1863. Although few grave-furnishings survived, the burial was of high status and probably late sixth-century or later in date. Snape may, therefore, demonstrate both the range and the dynamic of ranking in cemeteries during the fifth and sixth centuries. In contrast, Sutton Hoo now appears to be an example of *Separierung*, a separated cemetery reserved for the elite. In the five mounds examined so far the variation on the theme of high status burial is formidable. Mounds Three, Four and Five contained cremations in or on various receptacles. Mound Five was ringed with pits, some of which were cut through by graves; one of the pits contained bones (of oxen?). Several of the graves here, and others in the periphery of the cemetery, seem to contain examples of ritual killing. A tiny burial-mound near Mound Five contained a child. Beneath Mound Two was a large chamber-grave which had formerly been richly furnished and had contained the body of a male; above the chamber and within the barrow was placed a ship 12-20 meters long, keel down.[30] The parallels to this ritual are later, in the early Viking period.[31] Finally, Mound One contained a ship 27 meters long placed in a trench below ground with a timber chamber amidships; this mound also, of course, anticipates Viking practice. Sutton Hoo Mound One stands out not only because of the great size of the ship, still the longest known from the early Middle Ages, but because the intact grave-group contained items which

---

[23]Carver, "Kingship and Material Culture."

[24]H. W. Böhme, "Das ende der Romer Herrschaft in Britannien und die Angelsächsische Besiedlung Englands im 5 Jahrhundert," *Jahrbuch des Romisch-Germanischen Zentralmuseum* 33 (1986), 466-574.

[25]J. D. Richards, *The Significance of Form and Decoration of Anglo-Saxon Cremation Urns*, BAR Brit. Ser. 166 (Oxford 1987).

[26]Arnold, *Archaeology of the Early Anglo-Saxon Kingdoms*, 157.

[27]C. M. Hills, Review of Arnold, *Archaeology of the Early Anglo-Saxon Kingdoms*, *Archaeol. Rev. from Cambridge* 7.2 (1988), 268-70.

[28]J. F. Shephard, "The Social Identity of the Individual in Isolated Barrows and Barrow Cemeteries in Anglo-Saxon England," in B. C. Burnham and J. Kingsbury (eds.) *Space, Hierarchy and Society*, BAR Int. Ser. 59 (Oxford 1979), 47-80.

[29]Filmer-Sankey, pers. comm.

[30]M. O. H. Carver, *et al.*, *Bulletin of the Sutton Hoo Research Committee* 5, Sutton Hoo Research Institute (1989).

[31]For example, Haithabu. See M. Müller-Wille, "Das bootkammergrab von Haithabu," *Berichte über die Ausgrabungen in Haithabu* 8 (1976), 187-204.

have been claimed as regalia.[32] So, the Sutton Hoo cemetery as a whole can claim both to have regional status and to have no obvious local antecedent. A link between Mound One and the documented Rædwald, King of the East Angles (died 627 A.D.) is possible although other equations can be made between other named rulers, and now, of course, other mounds.

A similar trend toward a hierarchy and an early seventh-century acceleration in ranking can be very dimly observed in the settlement evidence.[33] West Stow, a marginal community in the Lark Valley comprising two or three households endures from the fifth century to the seventh when it acquired a fenced property. At Wicken Bonhunt, a protomanorial settlement of the seventh century, there is evidence for planning, residential enclosure and surplus aggregation – in the form of animal bones and a granary. At North Elmham, the settlement adjacent to the Cathedral shows residential enclosure, and planned properties are suggested by the eighth century.[34] Due to the exiguous scale at which British archaeology works, these trends towards private property and surplus extraction are but obscure shadows of the settlement evolution that is more brightly illuminated elsewhere, for example, in Denmark. But it is not improbable that it is signalling the same thing as the cemeteries. The East Anglian evidence also includes several sites which seem to have trade or re-distributory functions and these all begin in the early to mid-seventh century or thereabouts. Ipswich, the best known, was shown in the summer of 1988 to have had a cemetery, including wealthy sixth- and seventh-century graves, lying just outside the primary nucleus of the port. Ipswich is, therefore, a permanent settlement from its earliest exploitation,[35] although not certainly involved in trade at that time. When evidence for imports shows, the trade is with Frankia and the Rhineland, rather than Scandinavia.

This evidence is held to show in East Anglia the establishment of "small units of lordship" by the late fifth century and the emergence of an aristocracy by the late sixth. It is proposed that the really fundamental change then took place, that associated in the material culture with settlement shift and nucleation and the discontinuation of grave goods, and it is suggested that these reflect the reimposition of a taxation system – i.e. one that referred to *territory* rather than land ownership even if the tribute took the dual form for the subject of rent to a landlord and tax to a king. An important plank in the royal strategy is to capture and canalize any low level exchange that might be going on, so that it can be controlled and taxed. Ports such as Ipswich could be seen on this model to *decrease* the sum of maritime traffic.[36] "Kingship" in this fiscal sense is also obliged to capture the ideological highground to remain legitimate and to legitimate the succession; and it is argued that the newly self-created kings of East Anglia did this, first in a pagan and then in a Christian context.

AGENCIES OF CHANGE

From these vignettes, it can be seen that in each case archaeologists have argued for the emergence of an aristocracy which may or may not then achieve territorial control under a king. The interesting thing about this change is that the North Sea territories take it in turns to show that it has happened to them, and this must have implications for its causes. Taking "princely burial" as the main index of aristocracy and adding a few more examples to those already cited,[37] we have the following table of "demonstrative aristocracies":

---

[32] R. L. S. Bruce-Mitford, *The Sutton Hoo Ship Burial*, vol. I (London 1975).

[33] Carver, "Kingship and Material Culture."

[34] *Ibid.*, 144.

[35] *Pace* H. Clark, "Seasonally Occupied Settlement and Anglo-Saxon Towns," in B. Hardh, *et al.* (eds.) *Trade and Exchange in Prehistory: Studies in Honour of B. Stjernquist*, Acta Archaeologia Lundensis 16 (1988), 247-54.

[36] M. O. H. Carver, "Pre-Viking Traffic."

[37] See V. Näsman, "Vendel Period Glass from Eketorp-II, Öland, Sweden: On Glass and Trade from the late 6th to the late 8th Century A.D." *Acta Archaeologica* 55 (1984), 55-116.

Fourth century	Lolland
Fifth century	Zealand, north Frankia, southwest Norway
Sixth century	Kent
Seventh century	East Anglia, Uppland.

If we want to use archaeology to read social and political change, it might be more useful to examine not just individual territories but the North Sea cultural area as a whole.

The signals of status apparently surface in one place after another, a roster of power, that could be termed the "Buggins Model." If this phenomenon is not an illusion, we could try and explain it using hypothetical agencies, both internal and external.

Among internal agencies the most notable has been stress caused by over-population and/or land-hunger.[38] This has been questioned for East Anglia, at least, where it would appear that the carrying capacity of the land was never approached, and the real increase in both settlement and arable is after the seventh century rather than before it.[39] The alternative model I proposed was based on tenancies – a picture of successful landlords who became independent of their farms through a series of favorable acquisitions, through debt creation, or inheritance.[40] However, the latter explanation also fails to satisfy on its own, since there seems no good reason why such economic inequity should culminate in the sixth century rather than the fifth or eighth century.

Among external agencies, Näsman and Myhre have favored the wealth-creating influence of neighboring predatory empires, first the Roman and then the Merovingian.[41] So in southwest Norway, social stratification is achieved, not through stress, but through prosperity from trade and exchange. In eighth-century Denmark, the same process obtains but works across what Näsman has called the "new limes" the boundary of the expanding Merovingian empire.[42] A less specific description of this process is embodied in the concept of "peer polity interaction" where the agency can be relatively passive, involving not trade or war, but simply the emulation of a neighbor for purposes of advancement or survival.[43] Richard Hodges has applied this model to England, but concentrates on the ninth-century interaction between England and France, where ideological interplay is not, of course, in any doubt; and he is wrong to assume that ninth-century English society was "undoubtedly more complex than that of the previous centuries."[44] As we have seen, it is these previous centuries, the fifth through eighth, which see the arrival of social complexity, and any attempt to examine it must include the Scandinavian lands as well as Frankia – a far more complex forum of peer polities.

A third model for the external agency is that of the itinerant dynasty.[45] Here, members of a successful family (Inglingas, Wuffingas) move through marriage or military action from one territory to another (Westfold, Uppland, East Anglia) and signal their arrival by the erection of princely burial mounds. This scenario has the merit of being reflected in later medieval documentation: aristocratic families owned and/or ruled land on either side of the seas, whether in England, France or Denmark.

All these models beg one very important question; namely what is, or was, the relationship between social change and the cultural-signal? There are good reasons, drawn from analogies with modern traditional communities and their use of material culture, for thinking that the relationship in question is neither direct nor consistent.[46]

---

[38]C. J. Arnold, "Wealth and Social Structure: A Matter of Life and Death," in P. A. Rahtz, T. M. Dickinson and L. Watts (eds.) *Anglo-Saxon Cemeteries 1979*, BAR Brit. Ser. 82 (Oxford 1980), 81-142; Arnold, *Archaeology of the Early Anglo-Saxon Kingdoms*.

[39]Carver, "Kingship and Material Culture."

[40]*Ibid.*

[41]Näsman, "Vendel Period Glass"; Myhre, "Chieftains' Graves."

[42]Näsman, "Vendel Period Glass," 107.

[43]A. C. Renfrew and J. F. Cherry (eds.) *Peer Polity Interaction and Socio-political Change* (Cambridge 1986).

[44]R. Hodges and J. Moreland, "Power and Exchange in Middle Saxon England," in S. T. Driscoll and M. R. Nieke (eds.) *Power and Politics in Early Medieval Britain and Ireland* (Edinburgh 1988), 92.

[45]See Bruce-Mitford, *Sutton-Hoo Ship Burial*, I.

[46]I. Hodder, *Reading the Past* (Cambridge 1986).

Therefore, there are two ways in which the equation between social change and rich burial may be illusory. The first is that social rank may not be permanently signalled in mortuary behavior except at certain conjunctures, and the second is that the signals may be adopted from another culture for political reasons.

This is by no means an abnegation of the historicity of archaeology; on the contrary, the agenda is altered and an inquiry initiated which could be more historically productive. Instead of viewing the incidence of princely burial as the isolated and fortuitous discovery of a submerged custom, it can be viewed as a theatrical statement by real people at a particular moment in history. The information offered to us is not that a society has developed a hierarchy, but that a hierarchy wishes to state that it is one. The "language" in which this statement is made will say more about how that hierarchy sees itself, than how it actually was. This source criticism is assumed to apply mostly, although not exclusively, to the evidence from cemeteries, the archaeological context deemed most sensitive to ideological license.

The "Buggins Model" can therefore be reconsidered in a different light. The archaeological record, like the documentary record, is partial, and in the case of archaeology, we can be certain (in 1989) that such partiality was deliberate. Rich burial does not occur always and everywhere, even in ranked societies. It has its moment, and that moment can be read as a political signal directed internally, or externally, or both at once.

For Näsman the novelty of aristocracy and aristocratic burial are coincident: "a hypothetical emerging regional power might for a few generations need the outer symbols of power in the form of rich funeral customs; however as its position became more secure and its assumption of power no longer contested, this need would diminish and the number of rich graves would consequently decrease."[47] But theoretically, the princely burial could also be the response of a pre-existing aristocracy to imperial encroachment, as the same author has suggested: "to maintain independence and identity it was necessary to attack [the Merovingian Empire] politically and militarily – but paradoxically the leading elements in society strove at the same time to emulate the lifestyle of the continental aristocracy."[48] Such emulation could theoretically of course include the emulation of both foreign regalia and rituals. The emulation could also include the actual formation of an aristocracy itself.[49]

If, therefore, we notice that contemporary rich burials in East Anglia and Uppland have objects or ornaments in common, we cannot assume a causal relationship between them. They are different sentences composed from a common vocabulary and uttered at politically opportune moments.[50] If the purpose and the context of Vendel and Valsgärde in the Swedish Uppland are presently unclear, we can now make some attempt to locate the political context of the East Anglian princely burial ground at Sutton Hoo.

IDEOLOGY AND ALLEGIANCE IN EAST ANGLIA

The most powerful indication of pre-Christian ideological preference in East Anglia is its adoption of ship-burial in the late sixth century or early seventh century A.D. This funerary ritual is formerly (fifth through seventh century) found only on the island of Bornholm, and in southwestern Norway and eastern Sweden (Uppland). It continued there in the seventh and eighth centuries, and by the ninth century spread to Zealand and Schleswig.[51] It is thus out of step with the incidence of princely burial, with which it has no inevitable connection. Certainly princely cemeteries do, however, adopt ship-funeral, and Sutton Hoo is one of them.

Authors who have discussed the significance of ship and boat burial have naturally pointed not only to the status of the ship as a piece of transport but to its symbolic association as a vehicle of the dead as well. In Scandinavia the latter had deep roots and a number of manifestations, including the ship settings, rock carvings and picture stones. But even if the Scandinavian ship had carried a symbolic association with death since the Bronze Age, what was the *context* that required the special emphasis of this symbol in the Vendel and Viking periods? The Swedish

---

[47] Näsman, "Vendel Period Glass," 104.

[48] *Ibid.*, 107.

[49] Renfrew and Cherry, *Peer Polity*.

[50] See D. M. Wilson, "Sweden-England," *Vendel Studies* (1983), 163-66.

[51] M. Müller-Wille, "Boat Graves in Northern Europe," *IJNA* 3 (1974), 187-204.

context has been seen as "the budding Kingdom of the Svear,"[52] but this must be thought less appropriate if the kingdom were not yet in bud.[53] In East Anglia, however, the coincidence of the larger ship burials with their greatly increased expenditure on demonstrative funeral rites implies princely rank, and the separated cemetery at Sutton Hoo implies territorial control. The burial of ships in this context is no cultural attribute but a statement of a particular ideological flavor. So English "kingly roles," in the sense defined here, were created here in a pagan, Scandinavian mode, albeit not without some symbolic contrivance – even invention. The Sutton Hoo ship burial, with its curious assemblage of artefacts, is not a truthful reference to real life at all; it is itself a heroic text. Drawing on a common Germanic ideology as well as the local cultural jargon, a ship burial is a poem, like *Beowulf*, in another medium, and has many of the same problems of interpretation. Note that such a statement of ideological solidarity does not require the presence of Scandinavians, any more that the Merovingian monarch had to be tutored by Romans from Rome.

The archaeological record would suggest that East Anglia was a frontier area, settled in the fifth century by peoples from homelands across the North Sea in North Germany, Denmark and southwest Norway;[54] and that it continued to share ideology and allegiance with these countries throughout the fifth to seventh centuries, unlike its Insular neighbors, Northumbria, Mercia and Kent. This association was not inhibited in any way by the sea[55] and was enhanced still more in the sixth century under a new stimulus, the heavy breathing of the Merovingian Empire. This encouraged the emergence among the East Anglian elite of regional autocrats who could claim an association with a (newly named) folk and demand fiscal support from it. The political tension between the ideology of a taxable kingdom and allegiance to the homelands was a conflict finally resolved only be taking up a political position compatible with Kent and Continental Europe – a Christian kingdom, with a new symbolic apparatus including baptism, and the church.[56] At this point, the ideology of the folk, a supernatural nation, was replaced by the ideology of a kingdom, a real one. Allegiance to Scandinavia was replaced by emulation of Frankia. Open trade was superseded by canalized, controlled trade, free enterprise by state enterprise. Grave goods were superseded by princely burial, princely burial by church burial, barrow by crypt. Settlement shifted to take account of the new tenurial agronomic and social relations. Although many of these changes must have overlapped rather than replaced each other, the current perspective puts most of them in the early seventh century. In seventh-century East Anglia this must have amounted to something of a revolution.

There is no reason why this model should apply in the same form to the other North Sea territories. While the underlying growth of a hierarchy is very probable, the different territories were using material culture eclectically to signal their different ambitions and proposed affiliations. Just as the post-imperial polities of Africa offered a variety of observed structures, from immigrant folk under contract with God to imitations of European "Kingdoms," so the North Sea polities would vary both in reality and in self-advertisement from each other.

The real causes of such adopted status are just as difficult to pin down with confidence as are political changes today. Certainly one can be skeptical about climatic change, or population increase, or the arrival of a member of a successful dynasty as prime movers. Changes in tenurial arrangements and the relations of production, or the emulation of powerful neighbors are also themselves socially determined factors, the effects rather than the causes of change. An important and virtually unknowable factor will be the perception of the communities themselves, induced by their current cultural mixture, by the region in which they live, their travel-distance from the contemporary imperial predator, their natural resources, their visible Roman and prehistoric remains, their current land hunger, how long their families have lived there, how long they imagined their families have lived there, the relatives they have abroad, and whether they still visit them. These variations are sufficient to explain the difference between Northumbria, Mercia, Kent and East Anglia in the early Anglo-Saxon period. The social and economic

---

[52]B. Schönbach, "The Custom of Burial in Boats," *Vendel Studies* (1983), 131.

[53]P. H. Sawyer, "Settlement and Power."

[54]J. Hines, *The Scandinavian Character of Anglian England in the Pre-Viking Period*, BAR Brit. Ser. 124 (1984).

[55]Carver, "Pre-Viking Traffic."

[56]M. O. H. Carver, "Sutton Hoo in Context," *Settimane di studio del Centro italiano di studio sull' alto medioevo* 32 (Spoleto 1986), 77-123.

structure adopted in each at each point in time may itself have no origin beyond a model in the mind, the ideological mood of contemporary society, refurbished and promoted by each successive generation in the light of the cultural landscape which surrounded it.

List of Abbreviations

AC	*Archaeologia Cantiana*
AEMS	American Early Medieval Studies
AntJ	*Antiquaries Journal*
ArchJ	*Archaeological Journal*
ASE	*Anglo-Saxon England*
ASPR	Anglo-Saxon Poetic Records
ASSAH	*Anglo-Saxon Studies in History and Archaeology*
BAR	British Archaeological Reports
BBCS	*Bulletin of the Board of Celtic Studies*
CBA	Council for British Archaeology
CCSL	Corpus Christianorum, Series Latina (Turnhout)
EEMF	Early English Manuscripts in Facsimile (Copenhagen)
ELN	*English Language Notes*
FS	*Frühmittelalterliche Studien*
HE	*Historia Ecclesiastica*
IJNA	*International Journal of Nautical Archaeology*
JBAA	*Journal of the British Archaeological Association*
JEGP	*Journal of English and Germanic Philology*
JRSAI	*Journal of the Royal Society of Antiquaries of Ireland*
MA	*Medieval Archaeology*
NChron	*Numismatic Chronicle*
NM	*Neuphilologische Mitteilungen*
PBA	*Proceedings of the British Academy*
PRIA	*Proceedings of the Royal Irish Academy*
PSAS	*Proceedings of the Society of Antiquaries of Scotland*
SBVC	*Saga-Book of the Viking Society for Northern Research*
SM	*Studi Medievali*
TLS	*Times Literary Supplement*
UJA	*Ulster Journal of Archaeology*

References

Åberg, N. *Den nordiska folkvanderingstidens kronologi*. Stockholm: 1924.

Åberg, N. *The Anglo-Saxons in England during the Early Centuries after the Invasions*. Uppsala: 1926.

Åberg, N. *The Occident and the Orient in the Art of the Seventh Century*. Vol. III, *The Merovingian Empire*. Stockholm: 1947.

Åberg, N. *Den historiska relationen mellan folkvanderingstid och vendeltid*. Stockholm: 1953.

Ackerman, G. "J. M. Kemble and Sir Frederic Madden: 'Conceit and Too Much Germanism?'" In C. T. Berkhout and M. McC. Gatch (eds.) *Anglo-Saxon Scholarship: The First Three Centuries*. Boston: 1982, 167-81.

Ahrens, C. *Sachsen und Angelsachsen*. Ausstellung des Helms-Museums, Hamburgisches Museum für Vor- und Frühgeschichte. Hamburg: 1978.

Alcock, L. "Quantity or Quality: the Anglian Graves of Bernicia." In V. I. Evison (ed.) *Angles, Saxons and Jutes*. Oxford: 1981, 168-83.

Ament, H. "Eschboorn, Main-Taunus-Kreis." *Führer zu archäologischen Denkmälern in Deutschland: Frankfurt am Main und Umgebung*. Nordwestdeutschen und West- und Suddeutschen Verband für Altertumsforschung. Band 19. Stuttgart: 1989, 205-13.

Anon. "Proceedings; Monday 10th December 1923; Donations to the Museum," *PSAS* 58 (1923-24), fig. 5.

Anon. "Medieval Hone from Ireland." *AntJ* 7 (1927), 323-24.

Arnold, C. J. "Wealth and Social Structure: A Matter of Life and Death." In P. H. Rahtz, T. M. Dickinson and L. Watts (eds.) *Anglo-Saxon Cemeteries 1979*. BAR Brit. Ser. 82. Oxford: 1980, 81-142.

Arnold, C. J. *An Archaeology of the Early Anglo-Saxon Settlements*. London: 1988.

Arrhenius, B. *Merovingian Garnet Jewellery*. Stockholm: 1985.

Axboe, M. "The Scandinavian Gold Bracteates. Studies on their Manufacture and Regional Variations." *Acta Archaeologica* 52 (1981), 1-87.

Bailey, R. N. *The Durham Cassiodorus*. Jarrow: 1978.

Bailey, R. N. "Ledsham." *Bulletin of the C.B.A. Churches Committee* 18 (1983), 6-8.

Bakka, E. *On the Beginnings of Salin's Style I in England*. Universitetet i Bergen Årbok 1958. Historisk-Antikvarisk rekke Nr. 3. Bergen: 1958.

Bakka, E. "Scandinavian-type Gold Bracteates in Kentish and Continental Grave Finds." In V. I. Evison (ed.) *Angles, Saxons and Jutes: Essays Presented to J. N. L. Myres*. Oxford: 1981, 11-28.

Baratte, F. and Painter, K. S. *Trésors d'orfèvrerie gallo-romains*. Paris: 1989.

Barrett, J. C. "Fields of Discourse: Reconstituting a Social Archaeology." *Critique of Archaeology* 7.3 (1987-88), 5-16.

Bates, M. L. "The Coinage of Syria under the Umayyads, 692-750 A.D." In M. A. Bakhit and R. Schick (eds.) *The Fourth International Conference on the History of Bilad al-Sham during the Umayyad Period*. Amman: 1989, 195-228.

Bauschatz, P. C. "The Germanic Ritual Feast." In J. Weinstock (ed.) *The Nordic Languages and Modern Linguistics: Proceedings of the Third International Conference of Nordic and General Linguistics*. Vol. III. Austin: 1978, 289-95.

Bauschatz, P. C. *The Well and the Tree: World Time in Early Germanic Culture*. Amherst: 1982.

Berges, W. and Gauert, A. "Die eiserne 'Standarte' und das steinerne 'Szepter' aus dem Grabe eines angelsachischen Konings bei Sutton Hoo." In P. E. Schramm (ed.) *Herrschaftzeichen und Staatsymbolik*. Schriften der Monumenta Germaniae Historica 13. Vol. II. Munich: 1954, 238-80.

Biddle, M. and Kjølbye-Biddle, B. "Repton 1984." Pamphlet distributed at Repton Church, August 1985.

Biel, J. "Die Ausstattung des Toten." In D. Planck, *et al.* (eds.) *Der Keltenfürst von Hochdorf: Methoden und Ergebnisse der Landesarchäologie*. Stuttgart: 1985, 78-105.

Binchy, D. *Crith Gablach*. Dublin: 1941.

Blair, J. "Frithuwold's Kingdom and the Origins of Surrey." In S. Bassett (ed.) *The Origins of the Anglo-Saxon Kingdoms*. Oxford: 1989, 97-107.

Boeles, P. C. J. A. *Friesland tot de Elfde Eeuw*. 's-Gravenhage: 1951.

Böhme, H. W. "Das ende der Romer Herrschaft in Britannien und die Angelsächsische Besiedlung Englands im 5 Jahrhundert." *Jahrbuch des Romisch-Germanischen Zentralmuseum* 33 (1986), 466-574.

Bott, G. (ed.) *Germanen Hunnen und Awaren: Schätze der Volkerwanderungszeit*. Ausstellungs-Kataloge des Germanischen Nationalmuseums. Nüremberg: 1987.

Braudel, F. *On History*. Trans. S. Matthews. Chicago: 1980.

Brent, J. "Account of the Society's Researches in the Anglo-Saxon Cemetery at Sarr." *AC* 5 (1863), 305-22.

Brent, J. "Account of the Society's Researches in the Anglo-Saxon Cemetery at Sarr." *AC* 6 (1864), 157-85.

Brøndsted, J. *Guldhornene, en Oversigt*. Copenhagen: 1954.

Brontë, E. *Wuthering Heights*. New York: 1947.

Brown, D. "The Dating of the Sutton Hoo Coins." In. D. Brown, J. Campbell and S. C. Hawkes (eds.) *ASSAH*. BAR Brit. Ser. 92. Oxford: 1981, 71-86.

Brown, G. B. *The Arts in Early England*. 6 vols. London: 1915.

Bruce-Mitford, R. L. S. *Sutton Hoo Guide*. London: 1947.

Bruce-Mitford, R. L. S. "Sutton Hoo and *Beowulf*." *Antiquity* 12 (1948), 131-40.

Bruce-Mitford, R. L. S. "Sutton Hoo and Sweden." *The Archaeol. News Letter* 2 (May 1948), 5-7.

Bruce-Mitford, R. L. S. "The Sutton Hoo Ship Burial: Recent Theories and Some Comments on General Interpretation." *Proc. of the Suffolk Inst. of Archaeol.* 25 (1950), 1-78.

Bruce-Mitford, R. L. S. "The Snape Boat-grave." *Proc. of the Suffolk Inst. of Archaeol.* 26 (1952), 1-26.

Bruce-Mitford, R. L. S. "Decoration and Miniatures." In T. D. Kendrick, *et al.* (eds.) *Evangeliorum Quattuor Codex Lindisfarnensis*. Vol. II. Olten and Lausanne: 1960, 109-290.

Bruce-Mitford, R. L. S. and Bruce-Mitford, M. "The Sutton Hoo Lyre, *Beowulf*, and the Origins of the Frame Harp." *Antiquity* 44 (1970), 7-13, pls. I-VII.

Bruce-Mitford, R. L. S. *Aspects of Anglo-Saxon Archaeology: Sutton Hoo and Other Discoveries*. London: 1974.

Bruce-Mitford, R. L. S. *The Sutton Hoo Ship Burial*. Vol. I. London: 1975.

Bruce-Mitford, R. L. S. *The Sutton Hoo Ship Burial*. Vol. II. London: 1978.

Bruce-Mitford, R. L. S. *The Sutton Hoo Ship Burial: A Handbook*. 3rd ed. London: 1979.

Bruce-Mitford, R. L. S. *The Sutton Hoo Ship Burial: Reflections After Thirty Years*. University of York Medieval Monograph Series 2. York: 1979.

Bruce-Mitford, R. L. S. *The Sutton Hoo Ship Burial*. Vol. III. London: 1983.

Bruce-Mitford, R. L. S. "The Sutton Hoo Ship Burial: Some Foreign Connections." In *Angli e Sassoni al di qua e al di là del mare. Settimane di studio del Centro italiano di studio sull' alto medioevo* 32. Spoleto: 1986, 143-218.

Bruce-Mitford, R. L. S. "Ireland and the Hanging Bowls - A Review." In M. Ryan (ed.) *Ireland and Insular Art A.D. 500-1200*. Dublin: 1987, 30-39.

Burgess, J. T. "Recent Archaeological Discoveries in Warwickshire." *ArchJ* 33 (1876), 368-81.

Byrne, F. J. *Irish Kings and High Kings*. London: 1973.

Cahen, M. *La Libation: études sur le vocabulaire religieux du vieux-Scandinave*. Paris: 1921.

Caillet, J. P. "La passoire liturgique de Saint-Aubin d'Angers," *Bulletin monumental* 144 (1986), 295-304.

Cameron, A. F. "St. Gildas and Scyld Scefing." *NM* 70.2 (1969), 240-46.

Campbell, J. "Elements in the Background to the Life of St. Cuthbert and his Early Cult." In G. Bonner, *et al.* (eds.) *St. Cuthbert, His Cult and Community to A.D. 1200*. Woodbridge: 1989, 3-19.

Campbell, J. *Essays in Anglo-Saxon History*. London and Ronceverte: 1986.

Campbell, J., *et al.* (eds.) *The Anglo-Saxons*. London: 1982.

Carretta, M. C. *Il catalogo del vasellame bronzeo italiano altomedievale*. Ricerche di archeologia altomedievale e medievale 4. Florence: 1982.

Carver, M. O. H. "Sutton Hoo in Context." *Settimane di studio del Centro italiano di studio sull' alto medioevo* 32. Spoleto: 1986, 77-123.

Carver, M. O. H. "Kingship and Material Culture in Early Anglo-Saxon East Anglia." In S. Bassett (ed.) *The*

Origins of the Anglo-Saxon Kingdoms. Leicester: 1989, 141-58.

Carver, M. O. H. "Pre-Viking Traffic in the North Sea." In S. Macgrail (ed.) *Maritime Celts, Frisians and Saxons*. London: 1990, 117-25.

Carver, M. O. H. *Bulletin of the Sutton Hoo Research Committee* 5 (1989).

Cassiodorus. *Variae*. Ed. J. Fridh. CCSL 96. Turnhout: 1973.

Casson, L. *The Periplus Maris Erythraei*. Princeton: 1989.

Chadwick, H. M. "Who Was He?" *Antiquity* 14.53 (1940), 76-87.

Chadwick, S. "The Anglo-Saxon Cemetery at Finglesham, Kent: A Reconsideration." *MA* 2 (1958), 1-71.

Chambers, R. W. *Beowulf, An Introduction to the Study of the Poem with a Discussion of the Stories of Offa and Finn*. Cambridge: 1959.

Chase, C. (ed.) *The Dating of Beowulf*. Toronto: 1981.

Chifflet, J. *Anastasis Childerici Primi*. Paris: 1655.

Clarke, H. "Seasonally Occupied Settlement and Anglo-Saxon Towns." In B. Hardh, *et al.* (eds.) *Trade and Exchange in Prehistory: Studies in Honour of B. Stjernquist*. Acta Archaeologica Lundensis 16 (1988), 247-54.

Cohen, S. L. "The Sutton Hoo Whetstone." *Speculum* 41 (1966), 466-70.

Colgrave, B. *The Earliest Life of Gregory the Great*. Lawrence, Kansas: 1968.

Colgrave, B. and Mynors, R. (eds.) *Bede's Ecclesiastical History of the English People*. Oxford: 1969.

Coleman, R. F. and Wilson, A. "Activation Analysis of Merovingian Gold Coins." In E. T. Hall and D. M. Metcalf (eds.) *Methods of Chemical and Metallurgical Investigation of Ancient Coinage*. Royal Numismatic Society, Special Publication 8. London: 1972, 88-92.

Cook, A. S. "Some Accounts of the Bewcastle Cross." In R. T. Farrell (ed.) *The Anglo-Saxon Cross*. Hamden: 1977, 127-282.

Cook, E. T. and Wedderburn, A. (eds.) *The Works of John Ruskin*. 39 vols. London: 1904.

Cramp, R. "*Beowulf* and Archaeology." *MA* 1 (1957), 57-77.

Cramp, R. "Monkwearmouth Church." *ArchJ* 133 (1976), 230-37.

Cramp, R. *Corpus of Anglo-Saxon Stone Sculpture*. Vol. I, *County Durham and Northumberland*. Oxford: 1984.

Cramp, R. and Miket, R. *Catalogue of the Anglo-Saxon and Viking Antiquities in the Museum of Antiquities, Newcastle upon Tyne*. Newcastle upon Tyne: 1982.

Crowther-Beynon, V. B. "Notes of an Anglo-Saxon Cemetery at Market Overton, Rutland." *Archaeologia* 62 (1911), 481-96.

D'Amécourt, G. de Ponton. *Recherche des monnaies mérovingiennes du Cenomannicum*. Mamers: 1883.

Davidson, H. R. E. *The Battle God of the Vikings*. York: 1972.

Dickie, D. P. and Parrott, R. D. "Merovingian Coins in the Collection of the American Numismatic Society." *American Numismatic Society Museum Notes* 4 (1950), 91-96.

Dillon, M. *Lebor na Cert: The Book of Rights*. Dublin: 1962.

Dodwell, C. R. *Painting in Europe 800-1200*. Harmondsworth: 1971.

Doht, R. *Der Rauschtrank im Germanischen Mythos. Wiener Arbeiten zur germanischen Altertumskunde und Philologie* 3. Vienna: 1974.

Doppelfeld, O. and Pirling, R. *Fränkischen Fürsten im Rheinland: Die Gräber aus Kölner Dom, von Krefeld-Gellep und Morken*. Bonn: 1966.

Dufrenne, S. *Les illustrations du psautier d'Utrecht: sources et apport carolingien*. Paris: 1978.

Düwel, K. *Das Opferfast von Lade: Quellenkritische Untersuchungen zur germanische Religionsgeschichte. Wiener Arbeiten zur germanischen Altertumskunde und Philologie* 27. Vienna: 1985.

East, K. and Webster, L. *The Anglo-Saxon Burials at Taplow (Bucks.), Broomfield (Essex) and Caenby (Lincs)*. British Museum monograph. Forthcoming.

Edel, D. "The Catalogues in *Culhwch ac Olwen* and Insular Celtic Learning." *BBCS* 30 (1983), 253-67.

Einarsson, S. "Alternate Recital by Twos." *ARV: Tidskrift för Nordisk Folkminnesforskrung* 7 (1951), 59-83.

Enright, M. J. "The Sutton Hoo Whetstone Sceptre: a Study in Iconography and Cultural Milieu." *ASE* 11 (1983), 119-34.

Evans, A. C. *The Sutton Hoo Ship Burial*. London: 1986.
Evison, V. I. "Pagan Saxon Whetstone." *AntJ* 55 (1975), 70-85.
Evison, V. I. "Some Vendel, Viking and Saxon Glass." In B. Hardh, *et al.* (eds.) *Trade and Exchange in Prehistory: Studies in Honour of B. Stjernquist*. Acta Archaeologica Lundensis 16 (1988), 247-54.
Ewig, E. "Die fränkischen Teilungen und Teilreiche (511-613)." *Akademie der Wissenschaften und der Literatur, Mainz, Geistes- und Sozialwissenschaftliche Klasse*. Abhandlungen 9 (1952). Reprinted in E. Ewig, *Spätantikes und fränkisches Gallien, Gesammelte Schriften*. Munich: 1976, 114-71
Farrell, R. T. *Beowulf, Swedes and Geats*. *SBVC* 18. London: 1972.
Farrell, R. T. "Reflections on the Ruthwell and Bewcastle Crosses." In P. Szarmach and V. D. Oggins (eds.) *Sources of Anglo-Saxon Culture*. Kalamazoo: 1986, 357-76.
Farrell, R. T., *et al.* "Reports on the Survey of Artificial Islands in the Irish Midlands." To appear in *IJNA*.
Fell, C. E. "Old English *beor*." In *Leeds Studies in English*, n.s. 8 (1975), 76-95.
Fillon, B. "Tiers de sol mérovingiens inédits." *Revue Numismatique* 10 (1845), 14-25.
Fontaine, J. *L'árt préroman hispanique*. Paris: 1973.
Foster, S. M. "Analysis of Spatial Patterns in Buildings (Access Analysis) as an Insight into Social Structure: Examples from the Scottish Atlantic Iron Age." *Antiquity* 63 (1989), 40-50.
Fowler, E. "Celtic Metalwork of the Fifth and Sixth Centuries A.D." *ArchJ* 120 (1963), 98-160.
Fowler, E. "Hanging Bowls." In J. M. Coles and D. D. A. Simpson (eds.) *Studies in Ancient Europe*. Leicester: 1968, 287-310.
Frank, R. "Snorri and the Mead of Poetry." In U. Dronke, *et al.* (eds.) *Speculum Norroenum: Norse Studies in Memory of Gabriel Turville-Petre*. Odense: 1981, 155-70.
Frank, R. "Skaldic Verse and the Date of *Beowulf*." In C. Chase (ed.) *The Dating of Beowulf*. Toronto: 1981, 123-39.
Frank, R. "'Interdisciplinary': The First Half-Century." In E. G. Stanley and T. F. Hoad (eds.) *Words: For Robert Burchfeld's Sixty-Fifth Birthday*. Cambridge: 1988, 91-101.
Frantzen, A. "Documents and Monuments: Difference and Interdisciplinarity in the Study of Medieval Culture." In A. Frantzen (ed.) *Speaking Two Languages: Tradition and Contemporary Theory in Medieval Studies*. Albany: 1990, 1-33.
Fulford, M. G. "Byzantium and Britain: a Mediterranean Perspective on Post-Roman Mediterranean Imports in Western Britain and Ireland." *MA* 33 (1989), 1-6.
Gaffney, C. F. and Gaffney, V. L. (eds.) *Pragmatic Archaeology: Theory in Crisis*. B.A.R. Brit. Ser. 167. Oxford: 1987.
Gelling, P. and Davidson, H. E. *The Chariot of the Sun*. London: 1969.
Girvan, R. *Beowulf and the Seventh Century: Language and Context*. 2nd ed. London: 1971.
Glosecki, S. O. "*Beowulf* 769: Grendel's Ale-Share." *ELN* 25 (1987), 1-9.
Godfrey-Faussett, T. G. "The Saxon Cemetery at Bifrons." *AC* 10 (1876), 298-315.
Godfrey-Faussett, T. G. "The Saxon Cemetery at Bifrons." *AC* 13 (1880), 526-56.
Gordon, I. L. (ed.) *The Seafarer*. New York: 1960.
Graff, G. *Professing Literature: An Institutional History*. Chicago: 1987.
Graham-Campbell, J. "The High-king's Viaticum." *TLS* (June 1, 1984), 608.
Green, B., Rogerson, A. and White, S. G. *The Anglo-Saxon Cemetery at Morning Thorpe, Norfolk*. East Anglian Archaeology Report No. 36. Suffolk: 1988.
Gregory of Tours. *The History of the Franks*. Trans. L. Thorpe. Harmondsworth: 1974.
Grierson, P. "The Purpose of the Sutton Hoo Coins." *Antiquity* 44 (1970), 14-18.
Grierson, P. "The Sutton Hoo Coins Again." *Antiquity* 48 (1974), 139-40.
Grierson, P. and Blackburn, M. *Medieval European Coinage*. Vol. I, *The Early Middle Ages*. Cambridge: 1986.
Grüss, J. "Zwei altgermanische Trinkhörner mit Bier- und Metresten." *Prähistorische Zeitschrift* 22 (1931), 180-91.
Hachmann, R. *The Germanic Peoples*. Trans. J. Hogarth. Geneva: 1971.

Hahn, W. *Moneta Imperii Byzantini.* Vol. II. Österreichische Akademie der Wissenschaften, Phil.-Hist. Kl Denkschriften 119. Vienna: 1975.

Hall, E. T. and Metcalf, D. M. (eds.) *Methods of Chemical and Metallurgical Investigation of Ancient Coinage.* Royal Numismatic Society Special Publication 8. London: 1972.

Hampel, J. *Der Goldfund von Nagy-Szent Miklós.* Budapest: 1885.

Harden, D. B. "Glass Vessels in Britain and Ireland, A.D. 400-1000." In D. B. Hardin (ed.) *Dark Age Britain.* London: 1956, 132-67.

Hardhe, B., *et al.* (eds.) *Trade and Exchange in Prehistory: Studies in Honour of B. Stjernquist.* Acta Archaeologica Lundensis 16 (1988).

Haseloff, G. "Fragments of a Hanging Bowl from Bekesbourne, Kent, and Some Ornamental Problems." *MA* 2 (1958), 72-103.

Haseloff, G. "Insular Animal Styles with Special Reference to Irish Art in the Early Medieval Period." In M. Ryan (ed.) *Ireland and Insular Art A.D. 500-1200.* Dublin: 1987, 44-55.

Hauck, K. "Herrschaftszeichen eines wodanistischen Königtums." *Jahrbuch für Fränkische Landesforschungen* 14 (1954), 9-59.

Hauck, K. "Halsring und Ahnenstab als herrscherliche Würdezeichen." In P.E. Schramm (ed.) *Herrschaftzeichen und Staatsymbolik.* Schriften der Monumenta Germaniae Historica 13. Vol. 1. Munich: 1954, 145-212.

Hauck, K. *Goldbrakteaten aus Sievern. Spätantike Amulett-bilder der 'Dania Saxonica' und die Sachsen-'Origo' bei Widukind von Corvey.* Münsterische Mittelalter-Schriften 1. Munich: 1970.

Hauck, K. "Zur Ikonologie der Goldbrakteaten XXV: Text und Bild in einer oralen Kultur. Antworden auf die zeugniskritische Frage nach der Erreichbarkeit mündlicher Überlieferung im frühen Mittelalter." *FS* 17 (1983), 510-99.

Hauck, K. "Zur Ikonlogie der Goldbrakteaten XXXV: Die Wiedergabe von Göttersymbolen und Sinnzeichen der A-, B- und C-Brakteaten auf D- und F-Brakteaten exemplarisch erhellt mit Speer und Kreuz." *FS* 20 (1986), 474-512.

Hauck, K., *et al. Die Goldbrakteaten der Völkerwanderungszeit.* Münstersche Mittelalter-Schriften 24/1-3. Munich: 1985-1989.

Hawkes, S. C. "Eastry in Anglo-Saxon Kent: Its Importance and a Newly-Found Grave." *ASSAH* 1. 1979, 81-113.

Hawkes, S. C. and Pollard, M. "The Gold Bracteates from Sixth-Century Anglo-Saxon Graves in Kent, in Light of a new Find from Finglesham." *FS* 15 (1981), 316-70.

Hawkes, S. C. and Page, R. I. "Swords and Runes in South-East England." *AntJ* 47 (1967), 1-26.

Healey, A. diP. and Venezky, R. L. (eds.) *A Microfiche Concordance to Old English.* Toronto: 1980.

Hencken, H. "Ballinderry Crannog No. 2." *PRIA* 47C (1942), 1-76.

Henderson, G. *From Durrow to Kells: The Insular Gospel Books 650-800.* London: 1987.

Henderson, I. *The Picts.* London: 1967.

Henderson, I. "Pictish Art and the Book of Kells." In D. Whitelock, *et al.* (eds.) *Ireland in Early Medieval Europe.* Cambridge: 1982.

Henry, F. "Hanging Bowls." *JRSAI* 66 (1936), 209-46.

Henry, F. "Les débuts de la miniature Irlandaise." *Gazette des Beaux-Arts* 37 (1950), 5-34.

Henry, F. "The Lindisfarne Gospels." *Antiquity* 37 (1963), 100-10.

Henry, F. *Irish Art in the Early Christian Period to 800 A.D.* London: 1965.

Hicks, C. "The Birds on the Sutton Hoo Purse." *ASE* 15 (1986), 14-65.

Higginbottom, R. W. *Anglo-Saxon Contact with the Eastern Mediterranean AD 400-700 and its Context.* Unpublished M.A. thesis, University of Manchester, 1975.

Higgitt, J. "The Dedication Inscription at Jarrow and its Context." *AntJ* 59 (1979), 343-74.

Hills, C. *Spong Hill Part III: Catalogue of Inhumations. East Anglian Archaeology* 21. Norfolk Archaeological Unit, Norfolk Museum Service: 1984.

Hills, C. Review of C. J. Arnold, *An Archaeology of the Early Anglo-Saxon Kingdoms. Archaeological Review from Cambridge* 7.2 (1988), 268-70.

Hines, J. *The Scandinavian Character of Anglian England in the pre-Viking Period*. BAR Brit. Ser. 124. Oxford: 1984.
Hines, J. "The Undley Bracteate and its Runic Inscription. I. The Undley Bracteate in the Context of other Anglian English Bracteate Finds." *Studien zur Sachsenforschung* 6 (1987), 73-84.
Hodder, I. *Reading the Past*. Cambridge: 1986.
Hodder, I. (ed.) *The Archaeology of Contextual Meanings*. Cambridge: 1987.
Hodder, I. (ed.) *Archaeology as Long-Term History*. Cambridge: 1987.
Hodder, I. "The Contextual Analysis of Symbolic Meaning." In I. Hodder (ed.) *The Archaeology of Contextual Meanings*. Cambridge: 1987, 1-10.
Hodges, R. *Dark Age Economics*. London: 1982.
Hodges, R. and Moreland, J. "Power and Exchange in Middle Saxon England." In S. T. Driscoll and M. R. Nieke (eds.) *Power and Politics in Early Medieval Britain and Ireland*. Edinburgh: 1988, 79-95.
Hodgkin, R. H. *History of the Anglo-Saxons*. 3rd ed. Oxford: 1959.
Höfler, O. "Spervogel - Herger -*Harugwari." In U. Hennig and H. Kolb (eds.) *Mediaevalia litteraria: Festschrift für Helmut de Boor zum 80 Geburtstag*. Munich: 1971, 211-27.
Hogarth, A. C. "Structural Features in Anglo-Saxon Graves." *ArchJ* 130 (1973), 104-19.
Hollowell, I. M. "*Scop* and *Wothbora* in OE Poetry." *JEGP* 77 (1978), 317-29.
Hoops, J. *Reallexikon*. 2nd ed. Berlin: 1971
Hope-Taylor, B. Report on Bamburgh Excavations. *University of Durham Gazette*. December 1960, 11-12.
Hope-Taylor, B. Report on Bamburgh Excavations. *University of Durham Gazette*. March 1962, 5-6.
Hope-Taylor, B. *Yeavering: An Anglo-British Centre of Early Northumbria*. London: 1977.
Horedt, K. "Das zweite Fürstengrab von Apahida: neue Völkerwanderungszeit Goldfunde des 5 Jahrhunderts aus Siebenburgen." *Germania* 50 (1972), 174-220.
Hubert, J., *et al.* (eds.) *Europe in the Dark Ages*. London and New York: 1969.
Huggett, J. W. "Imported Grave Goods and the Early Anglo-Saxon Economy." *MA* 32 (1988), 63-96.
Hughes, K. "Evidence for Contacts Between the Churches of the Irish and the English from the Synod of Whitby to the Viking Age." In P. Clemoes and K. Hughes (eds.) *England Before the Conquest*. Cambridge: 1971, 49-67.
Hughes, M. J. and Oddy, W. A. "A Reappraisal of the Specific Gravity Method for the Analysis of Gold Alloys." *Archaeometry* 12 (1970), 1-11.
Hutchinson, P. "The Anglo-Saxon Cemetery at Little Eriswell, Suffolk." *Proc. Cambridge Ant. Soc.* 59 (1966), 1-32.
Jackson, K. *The Gododdin; the Oldest Scottish Poem*. Edinburgh: 1969.
James, E. *The Franks*. Oxford: 1988.
Janssen, W. "Die Sattelbeschläge aus Grab 446 des frankischen Graberfeldes von Wesel-Bislich, Kreis Wesel." *Archäologisches Korrespondenzblatt* 11 (1981), 149-69.
Jones, G. *A History of the Vikings*. Oxford: 1973.
Jourdanes. *History of the Goths*. Trans. C. C. Mierow. Princeton: 1915.
Karkov, C. with R. T. Farrell, "The Gnomic Passages of *Beowulf*." *NM* 3 XCI (1990), 295-310.
Kelly, E. P. Catalogue Entries. In M. Ryan (ed.) *Treasures of Ireland Irish Art 3000 B.C. - 1500 A.D.* Dublin: 1983, 109-11.
Kendall, C. B. and Wells, P. S. *Voyage to the Other World: The Legacy of Sutton Hoo*. Medieval Studies at Minnesota 4. Minneapolis: forthcoming.
Kendrick, T. D. *Anglo-Saxon Art to A.D. 900*. London: 1938.
Kendrick, T. D. "Sutton Hoo and Saxon Archaeology." *British Museum Quarterly* 13 (1939), 131-36.
Kennedy, C. W. *Beowulf; the Oldest English Epic*. Oxford, London and New York: 1950.
Kennett, D. H. "Graves with Swords at Little Wilbraham and Linton Heath." *Proc. of the Cambridge Soc. of Ant.* 63 (1971), 9-26.
Kent, J. P. C. "Gold Standards of the Merovingian Coinage, A.D. 580-700." In E. T. Hall and D. M. Metcalf

(eds.) *Methods of Chemical and Metallurgical Investigation of Ancient Coinage*. Royal Numismatic Society Special Publication 8. London: 1972, 69-74.

Kent, J. P. C. "The Date of the Sutton Hoo Hoard." In R. L. S. Bruce-Mitford, *The Sutton Hoo Ship*. Vol. I. London: 1975, 578-647.

Kiernan, K. *"Beowulf" and the Beowulf Manuscript*. New Brunswick: 1981.

Kilbride- Jones, H. *Zoomorphic Penannular Brooches*. London: 1980.

Knögel, E. "Schriftquellen zur Kunstgeschichte der Merowingerzeit." *Bonner Jahrbücher* 140/1 (1936), 1-258.

Krapp, G. P. and Dobbie, E. V. K. *The Exeter Book*. ASPR, vol. III. Morningside Heights, NY: 1936.

Kyhlberg, O. "Chronological and Topographical Analysis of the Cemeteries and Settlements." In K. Lamm, *et al.* (eds.) *Excavations at Helgö VIII - The Ancient Monument*. Stockholm: 1982.

Kyhlberg, O. "Spatial Patterns - Social Structures." In A. Lundström (ed.) *Thirteen Studies on Helgö*, Stockholm: 1988, 77-88.

Lacerda, A de. *História da Arte em Portugal*. Vol I. Porto: 1942.

Lafaurie, J. "Le trésor d'Escharen (Pays-Bas)." *Revue Numismatique* ser.6, 2 (1959), 153-210.

Lafaurie, J. "Les routes commerciales indiqués par les trésors et trouvailles monétaires mérovingiens." In *Moneta e scambi nell' alto medioevo. Settimane di studio del Centro italiano di studio sull' alto medioevo* 8. Spoleto: 1961, 231-78.

Lafaurie, J. "La monnaie bordelaise du haut moyen âge." In C. Higounet, *Bordeaux pendant le haut moyen âge*. Bordeaux: 1963, 295-325.

Lafaurie, J. "Nouvelles recherches sur le trésor de Chissey-en-Morvan (Saône-et-Loire) I. d. Buis." *Bulletin de la Société Française de Numismatique* 32 (1977), 211-16.

Lafaurie, J. "Eligius Monetarius." *Revue Numismatique* Ser. 6, 19 (1977), 111-51.

Lafaurie, J. "Trouvailles de monnaies des VIe-VIIe siècles de l'Empire d'Orient en Gaule mérovingienne (resumé)." *Bulletin de la Société Française de Numismatique* 97.5 (1972), 206-07.

Lafaurie, J. *et al.* "Le trésor de Wieuwerd," *Oudheidkundige mededelingen uit het Rijksmuseum van Oudheden te Leiden* 42 (1961), 78-107

Laing, L. "The Romanization of Ireland in the Fifth Century." *Peritia* 4 (1985), 261-78.

Lamm, J. P. "On the Cult of Multiple-headed Gods in England and the Baltic Area." *Prezglad Archeologiczny* 34 (1987), 219-31.

Lamm, J. P. and Axboe, M. "Neues zu Brakteaten und Anhängern in Schweden." *FS* 23 (1989), 453-77.

Lamm, J. P. and Nordström, H-A. (eds.) *Vendel Period Studies*. Stockholm: 1983.

László, G. *The Art of the Migration Period*. Coral Gables: 1974.

Lavoix, H. *Catalogue des monnaies musulmanes de la Bibliothèque Nationale, Khalifes orientaux*. Paris: 1887.

Lawson, G. "The Lyre from Grave 22." In. B. Green and A. Rogerson (eds.) The Anglo-Saxon Cemetery at Bergh Apton, Norfolk." East Anglian Archaeology Report 7. Gressenhall: 1978, 87-97.

Layard, N. G. "An Anglo-Saxon Cemetery at Ipswich." *Archaeologia* 60 (1907), 325-52.

Leeds, E. T. "Supplementary Note on the Gold-Bracteate and Silver Brooch from Market Overton, Rutland." *Archaeologia* 62 (1911), 491-96.

Leeds, E. T. *The Archaeology of the Anglo-Saxon Settlements*. Oxford: 1913

Leeds, E. T. "An Anglo-Saxon Cremation Burial of the Seventh Century in Asthall Barrow, Oxfordshire." *AntJ* 4 (1924), 113-26.

Leeds, E. T. *Early Anglo-Saxon Art and Archaeology*. Oxford: 1936. Reprinted Westwood, CN: 1970.

Leeds, E. T. "Denmark and Early England." *AntJ* 26 (1946), 22-37.

Leeds, E. T. "Notes on Jutish Art in Kent between 450 and 575." Ed. by S. Chadwick. *MA* 1 (1957), 5-26.

Le Gentilhomme, P. "Trouvaille de monnaies d'or des Mérovingiens et des Wisigoths faite à Bordeaux en 1803." *Revue Numismatique* Ser. 4, 39 (1936), 87-133. Reprinted in P. Le Gentilhomme, *Mélanges de numismatique mérovingienne*. Paris: 1940, 5-51.

Le Gentilhomme, P. "Les monnaies mérovingiennes de la trouvaille de Buis." *Revue Numismatique* Ser. 5, 2 (1938), 133-68. Reprinted in P. Le Gentilhomme, *Mélanges de numismatique mérovingienne*. Paris: 1940, 95-

130.
Le Gentilhomme, P. "Aperçu sur quelques aspects du monnayage des peuples barbares." *Revue Numismatique* Ser. 4, 4 (1940), 21-37.
Lelewel, J. "Vingt-trois peièces des monétaires mérovingiennes, et une du roi wisigoth Swintilla." *Revue Numismatique* 1 (1836), 321-30.
Lentricchia, F. *After the New Criticism*. Chicago: 1980.
Levine, P. *The Amateur and the Professional: Antiquarians, Historians and Archaeologists in Victorian England, 1838-1886*. Cambridge: 1986.
Levison, W. *England and the Continent in the Eighth Century*. Oxford: 1946.
Lindqvist, S. "Sutton Hoo och *Beowulf*." *Fornvännen* 43 (1948), 94-110.
Lindqvist, S. "Sutton Hoo and *Beowulf*." Trans. by R. L. S. Bruce-Mitford. *Antiquity* 12 (1948), 131-40.
Longley, D. *The Anglo-Saxon Connection*. BAR Brit. Ser. 22. Oxford: 1975.
Lundström, A. *Thirteen Studies on Helgö*. Stockholm: 1988
Lundström, A. "Short Summary of the Interpretations 1961-1974." In A. Lundström (ed.) *Thirteen Studies on Helgö*. Stockholm: 1988, 11-13.
Macalister, R. A. S., *et al*. "The Excavation of Loughpairc Crannog near Tuam." *PRIA* 32C (1914-16), 147-51.
Mackeprang, M. *De Nordiske Guldbracteater*. Jysk Arkæologisk Selskabs Skrifter 2. Aarhus: 1952.
Mackeprang, M. "Menschendarstellungen aus der Eisenzeit Danemarks." *Acta Archaeologica* 6 (1983), 103-126.
MacMillan, M. *Champion of Africa: W. M. MacMillan. The Second Phase*. Long Wittenham: 1985.
Mango, M. M., *et al*. "A Sixth-Century Mediterranean Bucket from Bromeswell Parish, Suffolk." *Antiquity* 63 (1989), 295-311.
Markey, T. L. "Germanic *lib/laib and Funerary Ritual." *FS* 8 (1974), 60-70.
Mattingly, H. (ed.) *Tacitus: Germania*. Harmondsworth: 1970.
Maxe-Werly, L. "Trouvaille de Saint-Aubin (Meuse)." *Revue Numismatique* Ser. 3, 8 (1890), 12-53.
Meany, A. *Anglo-Saxon Amulets and Curing Stones*. BAR Brit Ser. Oxford: 1981.
Meaney, A. and Hawkes, S. C. *Two Anglo-Saxon Cemeteries at Winnall, Winchester, Hampshire*. Medieval Archaeology Monographs IV. London: 1970.
Medieval Archaeology. "Archaeology and the Middle Ages, Recommendation by the Society for Medieval Archaeology to the Historic Buildings and Monuments Concern for England." *MA* 31 (1987), 1-12.
Mellucco Vaccaro, A. *I Longobardi in Italia*. Rome: 1982.
Miket, R. "A Restatement of Evidence for Bernician Anglo-Saxon Burials." In P. Rahtz, *et al*. (eds.) *Anglo-Saxon Cemeteries, 1979*. Oxford: 1980, 289-305.
Miles, G. C. *The Coinage of the Visigoths of Spain: Leovigild to Achila II*. Hispanic Numismatic Series 2. New York: 1952.
Mitchell, B. *Old English Syntax*. 2 vols. Oxford: 1985.
Mitchell, S. A. "The Whetstone as Symbol of Authority in Old English and Old Norse." *Scandinavian Studies* 57 (1985), 1-31.
Moisl, H. "The Bernician Royal Dynasty and the Irish in the Seventh Century." *Peritia* 2 (1983), 103-26.
Monks, G. "The Church of Alexandria and Economic Life." *Speculum* 38 (1953), 349-62.
Montelius, O. *Från järnåldern* 2. Häftet. Stockholm: 1869.
Mortimer, J. R. *Forty Years Researches in British and Saxon Burial Mound of East Yorkshire*. London: 1905.
Müller-Wille, M. "Boat Graves in Northern Europe." *IJNA* 3 (1974), 187-204.
Müller-Wille, M. "Das bootkammergrab von Haithabu." *Berichte über die Ausgrabungen in Haithabu* 8 (1976), 187-204.
Murray, A. C. "Beowulf, the Danish Invasions, and Royal Genealogy." In C. Chase (ed.) *The Dating of Beowulf*. Toronto: 1981, 101-11.
Myhre, B. "Chieftains' Graves and Chieftain Territories in South Norway in the Migration Period." *Studien zur Sachsenforschung* 6 (1987), 169-88.
Nancke-Krogh, S. "De gyldne *ryttere*. En analyse og vurdering af en gruppe C-bracteater." *Hikuin* 10 (1984), 235-

46.
Näsman, V. "Vendel Period Glass from Eketorp-II, Öland, Sweden: on Glass and Trade from the Late 6th to the Late 8th Century A.D." *Acta Archaeologica* 55 (1984), 55-116.
Näsman, V. "Analogisutning i Nordisk Jernalder arkeologi." In *Fra Stamme til stat i Denmark*. Moesgard: 1988, 123-140.
Neckel, G. (ed.) *Edda*. Heidelberg: 1962.
Neff, M. S. *Germanic Sacrifice: An Analytical Study Using Linguistic, Archaeological and Literary Data*. Ph.D. thesis University of Texas at Austin, 1980.
Nerman, B. "Sutton Hoo, en svensk kung-eller hövdinggrav." *Fornvännen* 43 (1948), 65-93.
Neuman de Vegvar, C. "The Iconography of Kingship in Anglo-Saxon Archaeological Finds." In J. Rosenthal (ed.) *Kings and Kingship*. *Acta* 11. Binghamton: 1984, 1-15.
Newman, J. "Barham, Suffolk - Middle Saxon Market or Meeting Place." In D. M. Metcalf (ed.) *Productive Sites (Proceedings of the Twelfth Oxford Symposium on Coinage and Monetary History)*. Forthcoming.
Nicholson, L. E. "*Beowulf* and the Pagan Cult of the Stag." *SM* 27 (1986), 637-69.
Nordenfalk, C. "Before the Book of Durrow." *Acta Archaeologica* 18 (1947), 141-74.
Ó Carragáin, É. "The Ruthwell Cross and Irish High Crosses: Some Points of Comparison and Contrast." In M. Ryan (ed.) *Ireland and Insular Art A.D. 500-1200*. Dublin: 1987, 118-28.
Ó Cróinín, D. "Pride and Prejudice." *Peritia* 1 (1982), 352-62.
Ó Cróinín, D. "Rath Melsigi, Willibrord and the Earliest Echternach Manuscripts." *Peritia* 3 (1984), 17-49.
Ó Cróinín, D. "Is the Augsburg Gospel Codex a Northumbrian Manuscript?" In G. Bonner, *et al.* (eds.) *St. Cuthbert, His Cult and Community to A.D. 1200*. Woodbridge: 1989, 189-201.
Oddy, W. A. "The Analyses of Four Hoards of Merovingian Gold Coins." In E. T. Hall and D. M. Metcalf (eds.) *Methods of Chemical and Metallurgical Investigation of Ancient Coinage*. Royal Numismatic Society Special Publication 8. London: 1972, 112-125.
Oddy, W. A. "Analyses of the Sutton Hoo Gold Coins," and "Analyses of Merovingian Coins in the British Museum." In E. T. Hall and D. M. Metcalf (eds.) *Methods of Chemical and Metallurgical Investigation of Ancient Coinage*. Royal Numismatic Society Special Publication 8. London: 1972, 96-107.
Oddy, W. A. and Blackshaw, S. M. "The Accuracy of the Specific Gravity Method for the Analysis of Gold Alloys." *Archaeometry* 17 (1974), 81-90.
Oddy, W. A. and Hughes, M. J. "The Specific Gravity Method for the Analysis of Gold Coins." In E. T. Hall and D. M. Metcalf (eds.) *Methods of Chemical and Metallurgical Investigation of Ancient Coins*. Royal Numismatic Society Special Publication 8. London: 1972, 75-87.
Odenstedt, B. "The Undley Bracteate and its Runic Inscription. II. The Runic Inscription on the Undley Bracteate." *Studien zur Sachsenforschung* 6 (1987), 85-94.
Ó Floinn, R. "The Kavanaugh 'Charter' Horn." In D. Ó Corráin (ed.) *Irish Antiquity: Essays and Studies Presented to Professor M. J. O'Kelly*. Cork: 1981, 268-78.
O'Kelly, M. J. "Two Ringforts at Garryduff, Co. Cork." *PRIA* 63 (1962-64), 17-126.
O'Laughlin, J. L. N. "Sutton Hoo – the Evidence of the Documents," *MA* 8 (1964), 1-19.
O'Meadhra, U. *Motif Pieces from Ireland*. Theses and Papers in North-European Archaeology 7. Stockholm: 1979.
Ó Ríordáin, A. B. and Rynne, E. "A Settlement in the Sandhills at Dooey, Co. Donegal." *JRSAI* 91 (1961), 58-64.
Ó Ríordáin, S. P. "The Excavation of a Large Earthen Fort at Garranes, Co. Cork." *PRIA* 47C (1942), 77-150.
Ozanne, A. "The Peak Dwellers." *MA* 6-7 (1963), 15-52.
Page, R. I. *An Introduction to English Runes*. London: 1973.
Page, R. I. "On the Transliteration of English Runes." *MA* 28 (1984), 22-45.
Page, R. I. "Runic Links across the North Sea in the pre-Viking Age." In H. Bekker-Nielsen and H. F. Nielsen (eds.) *Beretning fra Fjerde Tværfaglige Vikingesymposium*. Moesgård: 1985, 186-97.
Page, R. I. "New Runic Finds in England." In *Runor och Runinskrifter*. KVHAA Konferenser 15. Stockholm: 1987, 187-97.
Palol, P. de. *Arte hispanico de la época visigoda*. Barcelona: 1968.

Pálsson, E. "Hypothesis as a Tool in Mythology." In. G. Steinsland (ed.) *Words and Objects: Towards a Dialogue Between Archaeology and History of Religion.* Institute for Comparative Research in Human Culture Series 70. Oslo: 1986, 150-67.

Panozza, G. and Tagliaferri, A. *Corpus della scultura altomedievale, III: La Diocesi di Brescia.* Spoleto: 1966.

Parker-Pearson, M. "Economic and Ideological Change: Cyclical Growth in the pre-State Societies of Jutland." In C. Tilley and D. Miller (eds.) *Ideology, Power and Prehistory.* Cambridge and New York: 1984, 69-92.

Patterson, L. *Negotiating the Past: The Historical Understanding of Medieval Literature.* Madison: 1987.

Paulsen, P. *Alemannische Adelsgräber von Niederstotzingen (Kreis Heidenheim).* Veröffentlichungen des Staatlichen Amtes für Denkmalpflege, Stuttgart. Reihe A, Vor- und Frühgeschichte Heft 12/1. Stuttgart: 1967.

Peacock, D. P. S. and Williams, D. F. *Amphorae and the Roman Economy.* London: 1986.

Perin, P. "The Undiscovered Grave of King Clovis." In M. O. H. Carver (ed.) *Sutton Hoo Studies.* Forthcoming 1992.

Perkins, D. R. J. and Hawkes, S. C. "The Thanet Gas Pipeline Phases I and II (Monkton Parish)." *AC* 101 (1984), 83-114.

Phillips, C. W., Kendrick, T. D., *et al.* (eds.) *Antiquity* 14.53 (1940), 6-87.

Pol, A. "De 7e-eeuwse muntvondst Nietap." *Jaarboek voor Munt- en Penningkunde* 62-64 (1975-1977), 23-62.

Poulsen, G. S. "The Complementarity of Magic in Nordic Mythology and in Archaeological Sources." In G. Steinsland (ed.) *Words and Objects: Towards a Dialogue Between Archaeology and History of Religion.* Institute for Comparative Research in Human Culture Series 70. Oslo: 1986, 168-79.

Prou, M. *Catalogue des monnaies françaises de la Bibliothèque Nationale: Les monnaies mérovingiennes.* Paris: 1892.

Radford, C. A. R. "Imported Pottery from Tintagel, Cornwall." In D. B. Harden (ed.) *Dark Age Britain.* London: 1956, 59-70.

Raftery, B. *A Catalogue of Irish Iron Age Antiquities.* Marburg/Lahn: 1983.

Rahtz, P. A., Dickinson, T. M. and Watts, L. (eds.) *Anglo-Saxon Cemeteries 1979.* BAR Brit. Ser. 82. Oxford: 1988.

Randsborg, K. "The Town, the Power and the Land: Denmark and Europe During the First Millenium A.D." In T. C. Champion (ed.) *Centre and Periphery.* One World Archaeology 11. London: 1988, 207-26.

Reinhart, W. "Die früheste Münzprägung im Reiche der Merowinger." *Deutsches Jahrbuch für Numismatik* 2 (1939), 37-56.

Renfrew, C. "Trade as Action at a Distance: Questions of Integration and Communication." In J. A. Sabloff and C. C. Lamberg-Karlovsky (eds.) *Ancient Civilization and Trade.* Albuquerque: 1975, 3-59.

Renfrew, C. and Cherry, J. F. (eds.) *Peer Polity and Socio-Political Change.* Cambridge: 1986.

Reynolds, N. "The King's Whetstone: A Footnote." *Antiquity* 54 (1980), 232-37.

Richards, J. D. *The Significance of Form and Decoration of Anglo-Saxon Cremation Urns.* BAR Brit. Ser. 166. Oxford: 1987.

Richards, P. M. *Byzantine Bronze Vessels in England and Europe: the Origins of Anglo-Saxon Trade.* Unpublished Ph.D. thesis, Cambridge University, 1980.

Rieck, F. and Crumlin-Pedersen, O. *Bade fra Danmarks Oldtid.* Roskilde: 1988.

Rigold, S. E. "An Imperial Coinage in Southern Gaul in the Sixth and Seventh Centuries." *NChron* Ser. 6, 14 (1954), 93-133.

Rigold, S. E. "The Sutton Hoo Coins in the Light of the Contemporary Background of Coinage in England." In R. L. S. Bruce-Mitford, *The Sutton Hoo Ship Burial.* Vol. I. London: 1975.

Ross, A. *Pagan Celtic Britain.* London: 1967.

Roth, H. "Urcei alexandrini: zur Herkunft gegossenen 'koptischen' Buntmetallgerätes auf grund von Schriftquellen." *Germania* 58 (1980), 156-61.

Roth, U. "Early Insular Manuscripts: Ornament and Archaeology with Special Reference to the Dating of the Book of Durrow." In M. Ryan (ed.) *Ireland and Insular Art A.D. 500-1200.* Dublin: 1987, 23-29.

Rouche, M. *L'Aquitaine des Wisigoths aux Arabes, 418-781.* Paris: 1979.

Ruskin, J. *The Stones of Venice*. Vol 2 in E. T. Cook and A. Wedderburn (eds.) *The Works of John Ruskin*. 39 vols. London: 1904.

Ryan, M. Catalogue Entries. In M. Ryan (ed.) *Treasures of Ireland: Irish Art 3000 B.C. - 1500 A.D.* Dublin: 1983.

Ryan, M. *Early Irish Communion Vessels*. Dublin 1985.

Ryan, M. (ed.) *Ireland and Insular Art A.D. 500-1200*. Dublin: 1987.

Ryan, M. and Cahill, M. *Irish Gold 4000 Years of Personal Ornaments*. Melbourne: 1988.

Salin, B. *Die altgermanische Thierornamentik*. Stockholm: 1904.

Sawyer, P. H. "Settlement and Power among the Svear in the Period." In J. P. Lamm and H. A. Nordström (eds.) *Vendel Period Studies*. Stockholm: 1983, 117-22.

Schjødt, J. P. "The 'Meaning' of the Rock Carvings and the Scope for Religio-Historical Interpretation: Some Thoughts on the Limits of the Phenomenology of Religion." In G. Steinsland (ed.) *Words and Objects: Towards a Dialogue Between Archaeology and History of Religion*. Institute for Comparative Research in Human Culture Series 70. Oslo: 1986, 180-96.

Schmidt, B. "Ein Reinhengräberfeld des 6. Jahrhunderts nach Chr. bei Schönebeck (Elbe)." *Jahresschrift für mitteldeutsche Vorgeschichte* 37 (1953), 281-311.

Schönbach, B. "The Custom of Burial in Boats." In J. P. Lamm and H. J. Nordström (eds.) *Vendel Period Studies*. Stockholm: 1983, 123-32.

Scott, B. G. "Iron 'Slave Collars' from Lagore Crannog, Co. Meath." *PRIA* 78C (1978), 213-30.

Scudder, V. D. *Social Ideals in English Letters*. New York: 1898.

Scudder, V. D. *On Journey*. New York: 1937.

Shanks, M. and Tilley, C. *Re-Constructing Archaeology: Theory and Practice* Cambridge: 1987.

Shanks, M. and Tilley, C. *Social Theory and Archaeology*. Albuquerque: 1988.

Shephard, J. F. "The Social Identity of the Individual in Isolated Barrows and Barrow Cemeteries in Anglo-Saxon England." In B. C. Burnham and J. Kingsbury (eds.) *Space, Hierarchy and Society*. BAR Int. Ser. 59. Oxford: 1979, 163-66.

Sherman, S. "Professor Kittredge and the Teaching of English." *The Nation* 1913. Reprinted in G. Graff and M. Warner (eds.) The *Origins of Literary Studies in America: A Documentary Anthology*. New York: 1989, 147-55.

Shetelig, H. *Kunst*. *Nordisk Kultur* 27. Stockholm: 1931.

Silvén, U. "Gotländsk vapengrav med Charonsmynt?" *Gotländskt Arkiv* (1956), 97-110.

Simpson, J. "The King's Whetstone." *Antiquity* 53 (1979), 96-101.

Sippel, K. *Neue Grabfunde des frühen Mittelalters aus Eschwege, Werra-Meissner Kreis*. Archäologische Denkmäler in Hessen 53, 1986.

Slomann, W. and Christensen, A.-E. "The Åker Find. Facts, Theories and Speculations." *Festskrift til Thorlief Sjøvold på 70-årsdagen*. Universitetets Oldsaksamlings Skrifter. Ny rekke. Nr.5. Oslo: 1984, 173-90.

Smith, R. *A Guide to the Anglo-Saxon and Foreign Teutonic Antiquities in the Department of British and Medieval Antiquities*. London: 1923.

Speake, G. *Anglo-Saxon Animal Art and its Germanic Background*. Oxford: 1980.

Stahl, A. M. *The Merovingian Coinage of the Region of Metz*. Publications d'histoire de l'art et d'archéologie de l'Université Catholique de Louvain 30. Louvain-la-Neuve: 1982.

Stanley, E. "The Date of *Beowulf*: Some Doubts and No Conclusions." In C. Chase (ed.) *The Dating of Beowulf*. Toronto: 1981, 197-211.

Steger, H. *David Rex et Propheta*. Nürnberg: 1961.

Steinsland, G. (ed.) *Words and Objects: Towards a Dialogue Between Archaeology and History of Religion*. Institute for Comparative Research in Human Culture Series 70. Oslo: 1986.

Stenberger, M. "Traditionsbundenhet i vikingtida gotläändsk brakteatkonst." *Tor* 4 (1958), 113-32.

Stenton, F. "The Historical Bearing of Place-Name Studies: Anglo-Saxon Heathenism." Reprint of 1941 paper. In D. M. Stenton (ed.) *Preparatory to Anglo-Saxon England*. Oxford: 1971, 281-97.

Stevens, J. "On the Remains Found in an Anglo-Saxon Tumulus at Taplow, Bucks." *JBAA* 40 (1884), 61-71.

Stevenson, R. B. K. "The Hunterston Brooch and its Significance." *MA* 18 (1974), 16-42.
Stevenson, R. B. K. "The Earlier Metalwork of Pictland." In J. V. S. Megaw (ed.) *To Illustrate the Monuments: Essays on Archaeology Presented to Stuart Piggott.* London: 1976, 246-51.
Stevenson, R. B. K. "Aspects of Ambiguity in Crosses and Interlace." *UJA* 44-45 (1981-82), 1-27.
Stevenson, R. B. K. "Further Notes on the Hunterston and 'Tara' Brooches, Monymusk Reliquary and the Blackness Bracelet." *PSAS* 113 (1983), 469-77.
Stjerna, K. *Essays on Questions Connected with the Old English Poem of Beowulf.* Coventry: 1912.
Sutherland, C. H. V. *Anglo-Saxon Gold Coinage in the Light of the Crondall Hoard.* Oxford: 1948.
Szarmach, P. and Oggins, V. D. (eds.) *Sources of Anglo-Saxon Culture.* Kalamazoo: 1986.
Taylor, H. M. and Taylor, J. *Anglo-Saxon Architecture.* 3 vols. Cambridge: 1965-78.
Thomas, C. "The Interpretation of the Pictish Symbols." *ArchJ* 120 (1963), 31-97.
Thomas, C. *A Provisional List of Imported Pottery in Post-Roman Western Britain and Ireland.* Redruth: 1981.
Thomsen, C. J. "Om Guldbracteaterne og Bracteaternes tidligste Brug som Mynt." *Annaler for nordisk Oldkyndighed udgivne af Det Kongelige Nordiske Oldskrift-Selskab* (1855), 265-347.
Titchenell, E-B. *The Masks of Odin: Wisdom of the Ancient Norse.* Pasadena: 1985.
Tolkien, J. R. R. "*Beowulf*: the Monsters and the Critics." *PBA* 22 (1936), 245-95. Reprinted in L. E. Nicholson (ed.) *An Anthology of Beowulf Criticism.* Notre Dame: 1963, 51-103.
Toynbee, J. M. C. and Painter, K. S. "Silver Picture Plates of Late Antiquity: A.D. 300-700." *Archaeologia* 108 (1986), 17-65.
Twohig, D. C. "Pendant Whetstone." *Jnl. of the Kerry Archaeol. and Hist. Soc.* (1977), 143-44.
Turville-Petre, E. O. G. *Myth and Religion of the North.* New York: 1964.
Tymms, S. "Anglo-Saxon Relics from West Stow Heath." *Proc. of the Suffolk Inst. of Archaeol.* 1 (1853), 315-28.
Ulbert, T. "Skulptor in Spanien." In V. H. Elbern and V. Milojčic (eds.) *Kolloquium über spätantike und frühmittelalterliche Skulptur.* Mainz: 1971, 25-34.
Van der Chijs, P. O. *De munten der Frankische- en Duitsch-Nederlandsche Vorsten.* Harlem: 1866.
Vanhoudt, H. "De merovingische munten in het Penningkabinet van de Koninklijke Bibliotheek te Brussel." *Revue Belge de Numismatique* 128 (1982), 95-194.
Verey, C. D., *et al.* (eds.) *The Durham Gospels (Durham, Cathedral Library MS A.II.17).* EEMF XX. Copenhagen: 1980.
Vezin, J. "L'inscription du 'Missorium' d'Agnéric." *Bulletin de la Société Nationale des Antiquaires de France* (1972), 147-54.
Vierck, H. "Der C-Brakteat von Longbridge in der ostenglischen Gruppe." Anhang VIII. In K. Hauck (ed.) *Goldbrakteaten aus Sievern.* Münsterische Mittelalter-Schriften 1. Munich: 1970, 331-39.
Vierck, H. "Zum Fernverkehr über See im 6. Jahrhundert angesichts angelsächsischer Fibelsätze in Thüringen. Eine Problemskizze." Anhang XI. In K. Hauck (ed.) *Goldbrakteaten aus Sievern.* Münsterische Mittelalter-Schriften 1. Munich: 1970, 355-95.
Vierck, H. "La 'Chemise de Sainte-Bathilde' à Chelles et l'influence Byzantine sur l'art de cour mérovingien au VIIe siècle." *Centenaire de l'Abbé Cochet, 1975. Actes du colloque international d'archéologie.* Rouen: 1978, 521-64.
Vries, J. de. "Das Königtum bei de Germanen." *Speculum* 7 (1956), 289-309.
Wallace-Hadrill, J. M. *Bede's Ecclesiastical History of the English People, A Historical Commentary.* Oxford: 1988.
Wallace-Hadrill, J. M. *Early Germanic Kingship in England and on the Continent.* Oxford: 1971.
Wallace-Hadrill, J. M. "The Graves of Kings: an Historical Note on Some Archaeological Evidence." *SM* 3rd ser. 1. (1960), 177-94.
Wander, S. H. "The Cyprus Plates and the *Chronicle* of Fredegar." *Dumbarton Oaks Papers* 29 (1973), 345-46.
Ward-Perkins, B. *From Classical Antiquity to the Middle Ages: Urban Public Building in Northern and Central Italy, AD 300-850.* Oxford: 1984.
Ward Perkins, J. B. and Goodchild, R. G. "The Christian Antiquities of Tripolitania." *Archaeolgia* 95 (1953), 1-

83.
Warner, R. "The Clogher Yellow Layer." *Medieval Ceramics: Bulletin of the Medieval Pottery Research Group* 3 (1979), 37-40.
Warner, R. "A Case Study: Clochar Macc Daimini." *Bulletin of the Ulster Placename Society* 4 (1981-82), 27-31.
Warner, R. "Ireland and the Origins of Escutcheon Art." In M. Ryan (ed.) *Ireland and Insular Art A.D. 500-1200*. Dublin: 1987, 19-22.
Webster, L. "Medieval Britain in 1976. Pre-Conquest Essex: Clacton, Jaywick Sands." *MA* 21 (1977), 206.
Webster, L. "Anglo-Saxon England AD 400-1100." In I. Longworth and J. Cherry (eds.) *Archaeology in Britain Since 1945*. London: 1986, 119-59.
Werlich, E. "Der Westgermanische Skop: der Ursprung des Sängerstandes in semasiologischer und etymologischer Sicht." *Zeitschrift für Deutsche Philologie* 86 (1967), 352-75.
Werner, J. "Italienisches und koptisches Bronzgeschirr des 6. und 7. Jahrhunderts." In *Mnemosyne Th. Wiegand*. Munich: 1938, 74-86.
Werner, J. "Fernhandel und Naturalwirtschaft im östlichen Merowingerreich nach archäologischen und numismatischen Zeugnissen." *Bericht der Römisch-Germanisch Kommission* 42 (1961), 307-46.
Werner, J. "The Frankish Royal Tombs in the Cathedrals of Cologne and Saint-Denis." *Antiquity* 38 (1964), 201-16.
Werner, J. "Arbaldo (Haribaldus). Ein merowingischer Vir Inluster aus der Provence." In *Mélanges de numismatique, d'archéologie et d'histoire offerts à Jean Lafaurie*. Paris: 1980, 257-63.
Werner, J. "Der Grabfund von Malaja Pereščepina und Kuvrat, Kagan des Bulgaren." *Bayerische Akademie der Wissenschaften*. Phil. -hist. Klasse Abandlungen. Neue Folge 91 (1984).
West, S. "Gold Bracteate from Undley, Suffolk." *FS* 17 (1983), 459.
West, S. *West Stow: the Anglo-Saxon Village*. East Anglian Archaeology Report No. 24. Suffolk: 1985.
Wickham, C. *Early Medieval Italy*. London and Basingstoke: 1981.
Wilde, W. R. *A Descriptive Catalogue of the Antiquities of Animal Materials and Bronze in the Museum of the Royal Irish Academy*. Dublin: 1861.
Wiley, R. A. (ed.) *John Mitchell Kemple and Jakob Grimm: A Correspondence*. Leiden: 1971.
Wilke, G. "Der Weltenbaum und die beiden kosmischen Vögel in der vorgeschichtlichen Kunst." *Mannus* 14 (1922), 73-99.
Wilson. D. M. *Anglo-Saxon Ornamental Metalwork 700-1100 in the British Museum*. London: 1964.
Wilson, D. M. "Sverige-England." In A. Sandwall (ed.) *Vendeltid*. Stockholm: 1980, 212-18.
Wilson, D. M. "Sweden-England." In J. P. Lamm and H. A. Nordström (eds.) *Vendel Period Studies*. Stockholm: 1983, 163-66.
Wilson, D. M. *Anglo-Saxon Art from the Seventh Century to the Norman Conquest*. London: 1984.
Wilson, D. M. *The Bayeaux Tapestry*. London: 1985.
Wilson, D. M. *The Vikings and Their Origins*. New York: 1989.
Wormald, P. "Bede, 'Beowulf' and the Conversion of the Anglo-Saxon Aristocracy." In R. T. Farrell (ed.) *Bede and Anglo-Saxon England*. Oxford: 1978, 32-95.
Wormald, P. "Bede, *Bretwaldas* and the Origin of the *Gens Anglorum*." In P. Wormald, D. Bullough and R. Collins (eds.) *Ideal and Reality in Frankish and Anglo-Saxon Society: Studies Presented to J. M. Wallace-Hadrill*. Oxford: 1983, 99-121.
Wrenn, C. L. "Supplement," to *Beowulf: an Introduction to the Study of the Poem with a Discussion of the Stories of Offa and Finn*. Ed. by R. W. Chambers. 3rd ed. Cambridge: 1959.
Wrenn, C. L. "Sutton Hoo and *Beowulf*." *Mélanges de linguistique et de philologie*, (Fernand Mossé in Memorium). Paris: 1959, 495-507. Reprinted in L. E. Nicholson (ed.) *An Anthology of Beowulf Criticism*. Notre Dame: 1963, 311-30.
Yorston, R., with Gaffney, C. F. and Gaffney, V. L. "A Manifesto for Pragmatic Archaeology." In C. F. Gaffney and V. L. Gaffney (eds.) *Pragmatic Archaeology: Theory in Crisis?* BAR Brit. Ser. 167. Oxford: 1987, 107-13.
Ypey, J. "Ein Männergrab mit D-Brakteatenbeschlägen des fränkischen Gräberfeldes bei Rhenen, Provinz Utrecht,

Niederland." *FS* 17 (1983), 460-78.

Yvon, J. "Note sur deux groupes de monnaies mérovingiennes du Nord-Est de la Gaule." *Revue Numismatique* Ser. 5, 15 (1953), 67-77.

Zumthor, P. *Speaking of the Middle Ages*. Trans. S. White. Lincoln and London: 1986.

List of Contributors

Richard Bailey
School of English, University of Newcastle upon Tyne

Martin Carver
Department of Archaeology, University of York

Robert Farrell
Department of English, Cornell University

Allen J. Frantzen
Department of English, Loyola University

W. A. Oddy
British Museum

Michael Ryan
National Museum of Ireland

Alan M. Stahl
American Numismatic Society

Carol Neuman de Vegvar
Department of Fine Arts, Ohio Wesleyan University

Leslie Webster
British Museum

David Whitehouse
Corning Museum of Glass

Nancy L. Hatch Wicker
Mankato State University

Kelley Wickham-Crowley
Department of English, Georgetown University

Sir David Wilson
British Museum